HOW THE
Special Needs
Brain Learns

*Treat people as if they were
what they ought to be and
you help them to become
what they are capable of being.*

— Johann von Goethe

David A. Sousa

HOW THE
Special Needs
Brain Learns

CORWIN PRESS, INC.
A Sage Publications Company
Thousand Oaks, California

For information:

Corwin Press, Inc.
A Sage Publications Company
2455 Teller Road
Thousand Oaks, California 91320
E-mail: order@corwinpress.com

Sage Publications Ltd.
6 Bonhill Street
London EC2A 4PU
United Kingdom

Sage Publications India Pvt. Ltd.
M-32 Market
Greater Kailash I
New Delhi 110 048 India

Printed in the United States of America

Library of Congress Cataloging-in-Publication Data

Sousa, David A.
    How the special needs brain learns / David A. Sousa.
        p.   cm.
    Includes bibliographical references and index.
    ISBN 0-7619-7850-X (cloth) — ISBN 0-7619-7851-8 (pbk.)
    1. Learning disabled children—Education.   2. Learning.
3. Cognition in children.   I. Title.
    LC4704.5.S68   2001
    370.15'23—dc21   2001001280

This book is printed on acid-free paper.

01   02   03   04   05   06   07   7   6   5   4   3   2   1

Acquiring Editor: Robb Clouse
Editorial Assistant: Kylee Liegl
Cover Designer: Tracy E. Miller

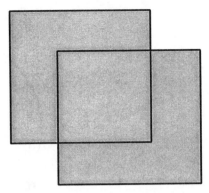

CONTENTS

LIST OF STRATEGIES TO CONSIDER

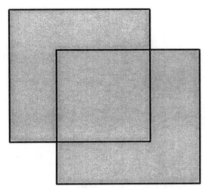

ABOUT THE AUTHOR

David A. Sousa, Ed.D., is an international educational consultant. He has made presentations at national conventions of educational organizations and has conducted workshops on brain research and science education in hundreds of school districts and at several colleges and universities across the United States, Canada, and Europe.

Dr. Sousa has a bachelor's degree in chemistry from Massachusetts State College at Bridgewater, a master of arts in teaching degree in science from Harvard University, and a doctorate from Rutgers University. His teaching experience covers all levels. He has taught junior and senior high school science, served as a K–12 director of science, and was Supervisor of Instruction for the West Orange, New Jersey, schools. He then became superintendent of the New Providence, New Jersey, public schools. He has been an adjunct professor of education at Seton Hall University, and a visiting lecturer at Rutgers University. He was president of the National Staff Development Council in 1992.

Dr. Sousa has edited science books and published numerous articles in leading educational journals on staff development, science education, and brain research. He is listed in *Who's Who in the East* and *Who's Who in American Education* and has received awards from professional associations and school districts for his commitment to research, staff development, and science education.

He has been interviewed on the NBC *Today* show and on National Public Radio about his work with schools using brain research. He makes his home in Florida.

CORWIN
PRESS

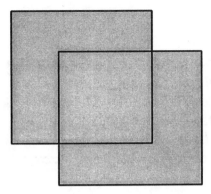

INTRODUCTION

Teachers and students get up every school-day morning hoping to succeed. That hope is not always realized because many factors exist that affect the degree of success or failure in a teaching and learning situation. Some of these factors are well beyond the control of the teacher and the school staff. What teachers *do* control, of course, are the decisions they make about what to teach and about how to present the lesson so that student learning is most likely to occur. In making these decisions, teachers draw on their knowledge base and experience to design activities, ask questions, and respond to the efforts of their students.

Educators are finding themselves searching for new strategies and techniques to meet the needs of an ethnically, culturally, and socially diverse student population. Some tried-and-true strategies do not seem to be as successful as they were in the past, and more students seem to be having difficulty acquiring just the basic skills of reading, writing, and computation. The number of public school students being diagnosed with specific learning disabilities is growing. The total public school population classified as having specific learning disabilities between the 1988-89 and 1997-98 school years rose from 4.90 to 5.91 percent, a 20.6 percent increase (USDE, 1999).

This situation is generating frustration in different parts of the educational community. As a result, educators are searching for new approaches, parents are seeking alternative schooling formats (charter schools and vouchers), and legislators are demanding more standards and testing. It remains to be seen whether any of these efforts will result in more effective services to students with special needs.

Meanwhile, more students diagnosed with learning disabilities are being mainstreamed into regular classrooms and teachers continue to search for new ways to help these struggling students achieve. The percentage of students classified with specific learning disabilities who receive instruction in regular classrooms between the 1988-89 and 1995-96 school years rose from 17.6 percent to 42.4 percent, a dramatic 141 percent increase. As more students with learning

1

difficulties are mainstreamed into regular classes, general education teachers are finding that they need help adjusting to the added responsibility of meeting the varied needs of these students. Consequently, special education teachers will need to collaborate more than ever with their general education colleagues on ways to differentiate instruction in the mainstreamed classroom.

> *General and special education teachers will need to collaborate more than ever on ways to differentiate instruction.*

Who Are Special Needs Students?

For the purposes of this book, the term "special needs" refers to students

- ▶ diagnosed and classified as having specific learning problems, including speech, reading, writing, and mathematics disorders
- ▶ enrolled in Title I programs
- ▶ not classified for special education nor assigned to Title I, but still struggling with problems affecting their learning, such as those with sleep deprivation

The term does not refer to students with learning problems resulting primarily from hearing, visual, or physical handicaps, or from economic or environmental disadvantage.

Can Brain Research Help?

Teachers may face significant challenges when meeting the needs of children who have learning problems. Trying to figure out what is happening in the brains of these children can be frustrating and exhausting. Until recently, science could tell us little about the causes of learning disorders and even less about ways to address them successfully.

The nature of the difficulties facing students with learning problems vary from maintaining focus, acquiring language, learning to read and write, solving mathematical problems, and remembering important information, to just plain staying awake. Thanks to the development of imaging and other technologies, neuroscientists can now look inside the live brain and, as a result, are gaining new knowledge about its structure and functions. Some of this research may reveal enough clues to help guide the decisions and practices of educators working with students who have special needs.

Because of the efforts of scientists over the years to cure brain disorders, we know more about troubled brains than we do about healthy ones. Early ventures into the brain involved extensive risks which were justified by the potential for curing or improving the patient's condition. But now, essentially risk-free imaging technologies (such as functional magnetic resonance imaging) are giving us greater knowledge about how the normal brain works. For instance, a program created in 1999, called the Interagency Education Research Initiative (IERI), has been established to fund scientific research to study the brain activity of children with and without learning disabilities. IERI is a joint project of the National Science Foundation, the U.S. Department of Education, and the National Institute of Child Health and Human Development. The initiative supports a variety of programs. One study, based at the University of Texas at Houston, uses brain imaging technology to detect the activity patterns in the brains of kindergartners as they learn to read. Researchers meet periodically to discuss their progress and results. IERI's goal is to establish a new research community that uses the results of hard science to influence educational decisions and practice (Viadero, 2001).

Another promising approach to working with diverse learners is being directed by the National Center for Accessing the Curriculum (NCAC). Funded by the Office of Special Education and Programs in the U.S. Department of Education, the NCAC focuses on Universal Design for Learning (UDL), an evolving approach that combines brain research and a digitized curriculum to provide individualized and differentiated instruction in the classroom. Teachers can use the technology to ease the burden of selecting multiple UDL teaching strategies that address different learning styles, abilities, and disabilities in a variety of learning contexts. Although no universally designed curriculum is currently available, NCAC is encouraging publishers to develop digital companions for all printed curriculum materials that they publish.

Because all students with learning problems comprise such a heterogeneous group, no one strategy, technique, or intervention can address all their needs. Today, more than ever, neuroscientists, psychologists, computer experts, and educators are working together in a common crusade to improve our understanding of the learning process. Comparing the functions of brains without deficits to the functions of brains with deficits is revealing some remarkable new insights about learning and behavioral disorders. Some of the findings are challenging long-held beliefs about the cause, progress, and treatment of specific learning disorders. Educators in both general and special education should be aware of this research so that they can decide what implications the findings have for their practice.

> *Comparing the functions of brains without deficits to the functions of brains with deficits is revealing some remarkable new insights about learning and behavioral disorders.*

What Is in This Book?

This book provides research information about common learning disabilities to prospective and current teachers and administrators so that they may consider alternative instructional approaches. Basic brain structures and their functions, as well as a brief description of learning and retention are the subjects of the first chapter. The second chapter provides an overview of factors that can affect brain development and a general discussion of learning disabilities. Subsequent chapters focus on specific learning difficulties, ranging from attention disorders to autism. Putting it all together is the purpose of the final chapter, which summarizes the types of interventions that can address the learning difficulties found in today's classrooms.

Practical applications of the research can be found in the chapter sections called *Strategies to Consider*, which suggest how educators might translate the research into school and classroom practice so that students with learning difficulties can be more successful. Obviously, some of the strategies would be appropriate for all learners. However, the suggestions have been written specifically to address the special needs of students with learning difficulties.

The book will help answer such questions as:

- ◆ How different are the brains of today's students?
- ◆ What kinds of strategies are particularly effective for students with learning disabilities?
- ◆ What progress is brain research making in discovering the causes of different learning disorders?
- ◆ Will brain research help us make more accurate diagnoses of learning problems?
- ◆ Can schools inadvertently exacerbate ADHD-like behavior in students?
- ◆ Can students with native language problems learn a second language?
- ◆ How does the brain learn to read?
- ◆ How much does lack of sleep affect student performance in schools?
- ◆ How can we address the emotional needs of students in the classroom?
- ◆ What more do we know about autism?

Some of the information and suggestions found here came from advocacy organizations, including the National Institute of Mental Health, the National Information Center for Children and Youth With Disabilities, and the Learning Disability Association of America (see the resources section). Where possible, I have sought out original medical research reports, and these are included in the references section of the book. A few of the strategies are derived or adapted from the second edition of my previous book, *How the Brain Learns*, also published by Corwin Press.

This book is not intended to be a compre- hensive text describing all the types of barriers that can affect learning. Rather, it focuses on the common difficulties and disorders that any teacher is likely to encounter in the general or special education classroom. On a broader scale, the updates on research and some of the suggested strategies may benefit all who work to educate children.

> *As we gain a greater understanding of the human brain, we may discover that some students designated as "learning disabled" may be merely "schooling disabled."*

As we gain a greater understanding of the human brain, we may discover that some students designated as "learning disabled" may be merely "schooling disabled." Sometimes, these students are struggling to learn in an environment that is designed inadvertently to frustrate their efforts. Just changing our instructional approach may be enough to move these students to the ranks of successful learners. My hope is that this book will encourage all school professionals to learn more about how the brain learns so that they can work together for the benefit of all students.

A Word of Caution

Several chapters contain lists of symptoms that are used to help identify specific disorders. The symptoms are included only for informational purposes and they should not be used as a basis for diagnosis. Any individual who exhibits persistent learning problems should be referred to qualified clinical personnel for assessment.

HOW THE BRAIN LEARNS

The human brain is an amazing structure. At birth, it is equipped with over 100 billion nerve cells designed to collect information and learn the skills necessary to keep its owner alive. Although comparatively slow in its growth and development compared to the brains of other mammals, it can learn complex skills, master any of over 6,000 languages, store memories for a lifetime, and marvel at the glory of a radiant sunset. Early in life, the brain's cells grow and connect with each other—at the rate of thousands per second—to store information and skills. Most of the connections result in the development of neural networks that will help the individual successfully face life's challenges. But sometimes, certain connections go awry, setting the stage instead for problems.

To understand the complexity of human brain growth and development, let's review some basic information about its structure. For our purposes, we will first look at major parts of the outside of the brain (Figure 1.1): the frontal, temporal, occipital, and parietal lobes; the motor cortex; and the cerebellum. Although the minor wrinkles are unique in each brain, several major wrinkles and folds are common to all brains. These folds form a set of four lobes in the largest part of the brain, called the *cerebrum* (Latin for brain). Each lobe specializes in performing certain functions.

The frontal lobe contains almost 50 percent of the volume of each cerebral hemisphere and is often referred to as the executive control center. The temporal lobe is the speech center. Visual processing is the main function of the occipital lobe, while the parietal lobe is responsible for sensory integration and orientation. Table 1.1 lists the functions of the four lobes as well as of the motor cortex.

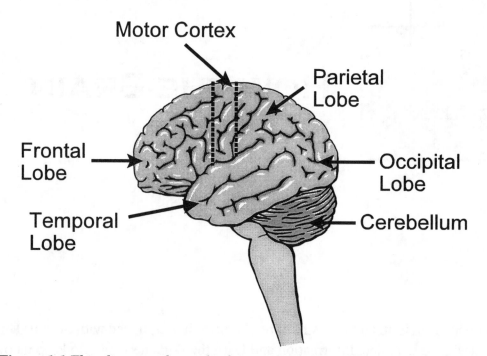

Figure 1.1 *This diagram shows the four major lobes of the brain (cerebrum) as well as the motor cortex and the cerebellum.*

Table 1.1 Some Exterior Parts of the Brain		
	Structure	**Function**
Cerebrum	Frontal Lobe (often referred to as the *executive control center*)	Personality, curiosity, planning, problem solving, higher-order thinking, and emotional restraint
	Temporal Lobe	Interpretation of sound, speech (usually on the left side only), and some aspects of long-term memory
	Occipital Lobe	Visual processing
	Parietal Lobe	Orientation, calculation, and certain types of recognition
	Motor Cortex	Control of body movements

Next, we will look at the inside of the brain and at some of its major structures (see Figure 1.2). Table 1.2 lists the functions of some of the interior parts of the brain: the brain stem, limbic area, cerebrum, and cerebellum.

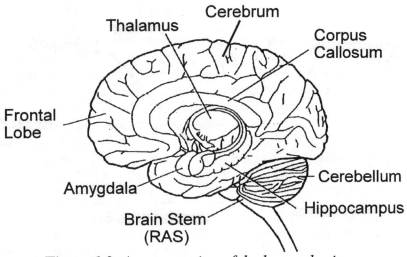

Figure 1.2 *A cross section of the human brain.*

Table 1.2 Some Interior Parts of the Brain	
Structure	**Function**
Brain Stem	The oldest and deepest area of the brain, this is often referred to as the reptilian brain because it resembles the entire brain of a reptile. Here is where vital body functions (such as respiration, body temperature, blood pressure, and digestion) are monitored and controlled. The brain stem also houses the reticular activating system (RAS), responsible for the brain's alertness.
Limbic Area	Above the brain stem lies the limbic area, whose structures are duplicated in each hemisphere of the brain. Three parts of the limbic area are important to learning and memory: *Thalamus.* All incoming sensory information (except smell) goes first to the thalamus. From here it is directed to other parts of the brain for additional processing. *Hippocampus.* Named for the Greek word for a sea monster resembling a seahorse, because of its shape, it plays a major role in consolidating learning and in converting information from working memory via electronic signals to the long-term storage regions, a process that may take from days to months. This brain area constantly checks information relayed to working memory and compares it to stored experiences. This process is essential for the creation of meaning. *Amygdala.* Attached to the end of the hippocampus, the amygdala (Greek for almond) plays an important role in emotions, especially fear. Because of its proximity to the hippocampus and its activity on PET scans, researchers believe that the amygdala encodes an emotional message, if one is present, whenever a memory is tagged for long-term storage.

Table 1.2 Some Interior Parts of the Brain — Continued	
Cerebrum	The cerebrum represents over 80 percent of the brain by weight. For some still unexplained reason, the nerves from the left side of the body cross over to the right hemisphere, and those from the right side of the body cross over to the left hemisphere. The two hemispheres are connected by a thick cable, called the *corpus callosum,* composed of over 250 million nerve fibers. The hemispheres use this bridge to communicate with each other and to coordinate activities. The hemispheres are covered by a thin but tough laminated *cortex* (Latin for tree bark). The cortex is composed of six layers of cells meshed in approximately 10,000 miles of connecting fibers per cubic inch! Here is where thinking, memory, speech, and muscular movement are controlled.
Cerebellum	The cerebellum (Latin for little brain) coordinates every movement. Because the cerebellum monitors impulses from nerve endings in the muscles, it is important in the learning, performance, and timing of complex motor tasks, including speaking. The cerebellum may also store the memory of rote movements, such as touch-typing and tying a shoelace. A person whose cerebellum is damaged cannot coordinate movement, has difficulty with speech, and may display the symptoms of autism.

The Control Functions of the Brain

The Frontal Lobe

The frontal lobe is the executive control center of the brain, monitoring higher-order thinking, directing problem solving, and regulating the excesses of the emotional system. Because emotions drive attention, the efficiency of this area is linked to the limbic centers. The frontal lobe also contains our self-will area—what some might call our personality. Trauma to the frontal lobe can cause dramatic—and sometimes permanent—behavior and personality changes. (One wonders why we allow 10-year-olds to play football and soccer where the risk of trauma to the frontal lobe is so high.)

Because most of the working memory is located in the frontal lobe, it is the area where focus occurs. The frontal lobe, however, matures slowly. MRI studies of postadolescents reveal that the frontal lobe continues to mature into early adulthood. Thus, the emotional regulation capability of the frontal lobe is not fully operational during adolescence (Sowell, Thompson, Holmes, Jernigan, and

> *The brain's executive system matures slower than the emotional system, so adolescents may resort to high-risk behavior.*

10

Toga, 1999). This is one reason why adolescents are more likely than adults to submit to their emotions and may resort to high-risk behavior.

Brain Cells

The control functions and other activities of the brain are carried out by signals traveling along brain cells. The brain is composed of a trillion cells of at least two known types: nerve cells and their support cells. Nerve cells are called *neurons* and represent about one-tenth of the total number of cells—roughly 100 billion. Most of the cells are support cells, called *glial* (Greek for glue) cells, that hold the neurons together and act as filters to keep harmful substances out of the neurons.

Neurons are the functioning core for the brain and the entire nervous system. They come in different sizes, but it takes about 30,000 brain neurons to fit on the head of a pin. Unlike other cells, the neuron (Figure 1.3) has tens of thousands of branches or *dendrites* (from the Greek word for tree) emerging from its center. The dendrites receive electrical impulses from other neurons and transmit them along a long fiber, called the *axon* (Greek for axis). Each neuron has only one axon. A layer called the *myelin* (related to the Greek word for marrow) *sheath* surrounds each axon. The sheath insulates the axon from the other cells and increases the speed of impulse transmission. The impulse travels along the neurons through an electrochemical process and can move the entire length of a 6-foot adult in 2/10ths of a second. A neuron can transmit between 250 and 2,500 impulses per second.

Neurons have no direct contact with each other. Between each dendrite and axon is a small gap of about a millionth of an inch called a *synapse* (from the Greek meaning to join together). A typical neuron collects signals from others through the dendrites. The neuron sends out spikes of electrical activity (impulses) through the axon to the synapse where the activity releases chemicals stored in sacs (called *synaptic vesicles*) at the end of the axon.

The chemicals, called *neurotransmitters*, either excite or inhibit the neighboring neuron. Nearly 100 different neurotransmitters have been discovered so far. Some of the common neurotransmitters are acetylcholine, epinephrine, serotonin, and dopamine.

Learning and Retention

Learning occurs when the synapses make physical and chemical changes so that the influence of one neuron on another also changes. For instance, a set of neurons "learns" to fire together. Repeated firings make successive firings easier and, eventually, automatic under certain conditions. Thus, a memory is formed.

11

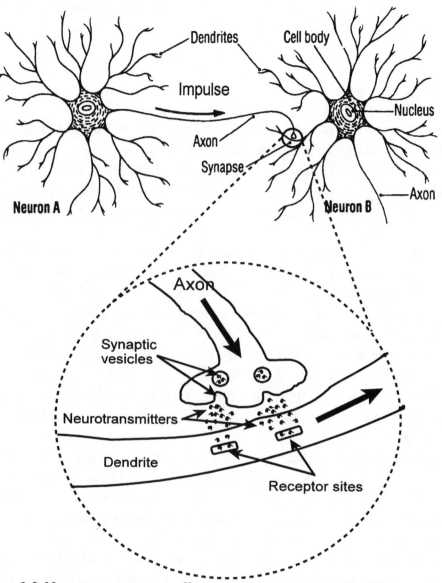

Figure 1.3 Neurons, or nerve cells, transmit impulses along an axon and across the synapse to the dendrites of the neighboring cell. The impulse is carried across the synapse to receptor sites by chemicals called neurotransmitters that lie within synaptic vesicles (Sousa, 2001, p. 21).

For all practical purposes, the capacity of the brain to store information is unlimited. That is, with about 100 billion neurons, each with thousands of dendrites, the number of potential neural pathways is incomprehensible. The brain will hardly run out of space to store all that an individual learns in a lifetime. Learning is the process by which we *acquire* new knowledge and skills; memory is the process by which we *retain* knowledge and skills for the future.

Investigations into the neural mechanisms required for different types of learning are revealing more about the interactions between learning new information, memory, and changes in brain structure. Just as muscles improve with exercise, the brain seems to improve with use. Although learning does not increase the number of brain cells, it does increase their size, their branches, and their ability to form more complex networks.

> *Learning is the process by which we acquire knowledge; memory is the process by which we retain it.*

The brain goes through physical and chemical changes when it stores new information as the result of learning. Storing gives rise to new neural pathways and strengthens existing pathways. Hence, every time we learn something, our long-term storage areas undergo anatomical changes that, together with our unique genetic makeup, constitute the expression of our individuality (Beatty, 2001).

Learning and retention also occur in different ways. Learning involves the brain, the nervous system, and the environment, and the process by which their interplay acquires information and skills. Sometimes, we need information for just a short period of time, like the telephone number for a pizza delivery, and then the information decays after just a few seconds. Thus, learning does not always involve long-term retention.

A good portion of the teaching done in schools centers on delivering facts and information to build concepts that explain a body of knowledge. We teach numbers, arithmetic operations, ratios, and theorems to explain mathematics. We teach about atoms, momentum, gravity, and cells to explain science. We talk about countries and famous leaders and discuss their trials and battles to explain history, and so on. Students may hold on to this information in working memory just long enough to take a test, after which the knowledge readily decays and is lost. Retention, however, requires that the learner not only give conscious attention but also build conceptual frameworks that have sense and meaning for eventual consolidation into long-term storage networks.

Implications for Students With Learning Disabilities. Because students with learning disabilities can have difficulty focusing for very long, they are even more likely to perceive learning facts as a temporary effort just to please the teacher or to pass a test. It becomes increasingly important, then, for teachers of these students to emphasize *why* they need to learn certain material. Meaning (or relevancy) becomes the key to focus, learning, and retention.

Retention is the process whereby long-term memory preserves a learning in such a way that the memory can be located, identified, and retrieved accurately in the future. This is an inexact process influenced by many factors including the degree of student focus, the length and type of rehearsal that occurred, the critical attributes that may have been identified, the student's learning style, any learning disabilities, and, of course, the inescapable influence of prior learning.

Rehearsal

The brain's decision to retain a learning seems to be based primarily on two criteria: *sense* and *meaning*. Sense refers to whether the student understands the learning, "Does this fit my perception of how the world works?" Meaning, on the other hand, refers to relevancy. Although the student may understand the learning, the more important question may be, "So what? What's this got to do with me?" Attaching sense and meaning to new learning can occur only if the learner has adequate time to process and reprocess it. This continuing reprocessing is called *rehearsal* and is a critical component in the transference of information from working memory to long-term storage.

> Learning is likely to be remembered if it makes sense and has meaning to the learner.

Two major factors should be considered in evaluating rehearsal: the amount of time devoted to it, which determines whether there is both initial and secondary rehearsal, and the type of rehearsal carried out, which can be rote or elaborative.

Time for Initial and Secondary Rehearsal

Time is a critical component of rehearsal. Initial rehearsal occurs when the information first enters working memory. If the learner cannot attach sense or meaning, and if there is no time

for further processing, the new information is likely to be lost. Providing sufficient time to go beyond initial processing to secondary rehearsal allows the learner to review the information, to make sense of it, to elaborate on the details, and to assign value and relevance, thus increasing significantly the chance of long-term storage.

Scanning studies of the brain indicate that the frontal lobe is very much involved during the rehearsal process and, ultimately, in long-term memory formation. This makes sense because working memory is also located in the frontal lobe. Several studies using fMRI scans of humans showed that, during longer rehearsals, the amount of activity in the frontal lobe determined whether items were stored or forgotten (Buckner, Kelley, and Petersen, 1999; Wagner, Schacter, Rotte, Koutstaal, Maril, Dale, Rosen, and Buckner, 1998).

Students carry out initial and secondary rehearsal at different rates of speed and in different ways, depending on the type of information in the new learning and on their learning styles, including any learning disabilities. As the learning task changes, learners automatically shift to different patterns of rehearsal.

Rote and Elaborative Rehearsal

Rote Rehearsal. This type of rehearsal is used when learners need to remember and store information exactly as it is entered into working memory. This involves a simple strategy necessary to learn information or a skill in a specific form or sequence. We employ rote rehearsal to remember a poem, the lyrics and melody of a song, multiplication tables, telephone numbers, and steps in a procedure. This rehearsal usually involves direct instruction. However, students with learning disabilities often perceive rote rehearsal as intensely boring, forcing the teacher to find creative and interesting ways to accomplish the rehearsal while keeping students on task.

Elaborative Rehearsal. This type of rehearsal is used when it is unnecessary to store information exactly as learned, and when it is important to associate new learnings with prior learnings to detect relationships. This is a complex thinking process, in which the learners reprocess the information several times to make connections to previous learnings and assign meaning. Students use rote rehearsal to memorize a poem, but elaborative rehearsal to interpret its message, for example. When students get very little time for, or training in, elaborative rehearsal, they resort more frequently to rote rehearsal. Consequently, they fail to make the associations or discover the relationships that only elaborative rehearsal can provide. Also, they continue to believe that the value of learning is merely the recalling of information as learned rather than the generating of new ideas, concepts, and solutions.

> Students with learning disabilities need more time and guidance than others to rehearse the new learning in order to determine sense and recognize meaning.

Students with learning disabilities need more time and guidance than others to rehearse the new learning in order to determine sense and recognize meaning. They need help with both types of rehearsal, including a rationale for each. When deciding how to use rehearsal in a lesson, teachers need to consider the time available as well as the type of rehearsal appropriate for the specific learning objective. Keep in mind that rehearsal only contributes to, but does not guarantee, information transfer into long-term storage. However, there is almost no long-term retention *without* rehearsal.

How Different Are the Brains of Today's Students?

We often hear teachers remark that students of today are more different in the way they learn. They seem to have shorter attention spans and become bored more easily than ever before. Why is that? Is something happening in the environment of learners that alters the way they approach the learning process? Does this mean that more students will have learning problems?

Students *are* different today and so are their brains. They have grown up in an environment different from their parents'. Beginning at birth (some say earlier), the brain is collecting information and learning from its environment. The home environment of a child several decades ago was usually quiet—some might say boring compared to today. Parents and children did a lot of talking and reading, often together. The occasional radio program was an exciting event. For these children, school was an interesting place because it had television, films, field trips, and guest speakers—experiences not usually found at home. With few cultural distractions, school was an important influence in a child's life and the primary source of new information.

> The brains of today's students are attracted more than ever to the unique and different—what is called novelty.

Today, children have become accustomed to rapid sensory and emotional changes in their environment and respond by engaging in all types of activities of short duration at home and in the malls. By acclimating itself to these changes, the brain is attracted more than ever to the unique and different—what is called *novelty*. This attraction to novelty is not the result of any changes in the physical structures of the brain, but the result of neural associations and networks responding to the multiplicity of today's input.

Adult skeptics need but watch MTV for just a few minutes to discover that the images change every few seconds and play heavily on emotions. Better yet, compare the toys of the millennium with the toys of the 1950s and 1960s. The major difference is advancing technology. School children can now play an inexpensive yet mentally challenging electronic game while riding on the school bus only to be met with a paper-and-pencil, fill-in-the-blank worksheet in the classroom.

Furthermore, school is but one of *many* factors influencing our children. Even the younger students are wrestling with the need to be unique while under pressure to conform. As preteens enter puberty, they have to develop and deal with relationships, identify peer groups, and respond to religious influences without adequate maturity. Add to this mix the changes in family patterns and lifestyles, as well as the sometimes drastic effects of modern diets, drugs, and sleep deprivation (see Chapter 8), and we can realize how very different the environment of today's child is from that of just a few years ago.

Changing Sensory Preferences of Students

Our five senses collect enormous amounts of information from the environment. This information is filtered by the brain so that important data (e.g., your favorite television show) is processed while unimportant stimuli (e.g., background noise) is ignored. For most of us, the five primary senses do not all contribute equally to our learning. We have preferences. Just as most of us are either left-handed or right-handed, most of us also have sensory preferences, that is, we tend to favor one or two senses over the others when gathering information to deal with a complex learning situation. The preferences tend to be among the senses of sight, hearing, and kinesthetic-tactile (the expanded concept of touch).

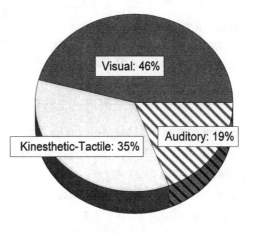

Although no one knows for sure *exactly* what causes sensory preferences, the current explanation is that it is a mix of both mild genetic and strong environmental influences, especially in an individual's early years. Preferences, of course, are just that: *preferences*. They do not mean that the individual is not able to process with other senses. Just as a right-handed person can certainly use the left hand with competence, a visually preferred person is able to use all the other senses when needed. But when faced with

Figure 1.4 *The sensory preferences of the U.S. student population in grades 3-12 for the mid- 1990s. (Swanson, 1995; Sousa, 1997)*

a complex task, most of us will rely more on our preferences to accomplish that task.

Studies of sensory preferences in school children over the past 40 years have shown shifts among the percentage of students with particular preferences. Figure 1.4 shows the best estimates for the sensory preferences of the student population in grades 3 to 12 in the mid-1990s (Sousa, 1997). Other studies have found similar results (Swanson, 1995). Note that nearly one-half of this population has a visual preference and just under one-fifth has an auditory preference. Yet, in too many secondary school classrooms, talk is the main mode of instruction, often accompanied by minimal overheads or charts. Over one-third of students have a kinesthetic-tactile preference, indicating that movement helps their learning. But think of how much kids in secondary schools just sit at their desks, moving only to change classrooms.

Have Schools Changed to Deal With This Different Brain?

Schools and teaching really haven't changed that much. The computers used in many schools provide few of the options that students get with their more powerful computers at home. In high schools, lecturing continues to be the main method of instruction, and the overhead projector is often the most advanced technology used. Many students remark that school is a dull, nonengaging environment that is much less interesting than what is available outside of school.

They have a difficult time focusing for extended periods and are easily distracted. Because they see little novelty and relevancy in what they are learning, they keep asking the eternal question, "Why do we need to know this?" Some teachers interpret this attitude as alienation from school while other teachers see it as a sign of a learning disability. In both instances, they are likely to refer the student for counseling and diagnosis. Consequently, it is possible that more children are being referred for special education evaluation not because they have true learning difficulties but because an inflexible (though well-meaning) school environment has not adapted to their changing brains.

> *By rethinking what we do in schools and classrooms, perhaps more children will get the education they need and deserve.*

Rather than disparaging the changing brain and culture, perhaps we should recognize that we must adjust schools to accommodate these changes. As we gain a more scientifically based understanding about today's novel brain and how it learns, we must rethink what we do in classrooms and schools. Maybe then more children will stay in the educational mainstream rather than be sidelined for labeling.

Some students, of course, do develop learning disabilities that need to be accurately diagnosed and addressed. The following chapters will discuss several types of learning disabilities, review recent research about them, and suggest ways of helping students who demonstrate them.

WHEN BRAINS DIFFER

Neuron development starts in the embryo shortly after conception and proceeds at an astonishing rate. Between 50,000 and 100,000 new brain cells are generated *each second* from the fifth to the twentieth week of life. Genetic instructions govern the rate of growth and direct the migration of neurons to different levels, forming the six layers of the fetus's cerebral cortex. In the first four months of gestation, about 200 billion neurons are formed, but about half will die off during the fifth month because they fail to connect with any areas of the growing embryo. This purposeful destruction of neurons (called *apoptosis*) is genetically programmed to ensure that only those neurons that have made connections are preserved, and to prevent the brain from being overcrowded with unconnected cells. Sometimes apoptosis gets out of control and connections that might otherwise have imparted certain intuitive skills—such as photographic memory—may be pruned as well. Defective apoptosis may also explain both the amazing abilities and deficits of autistic savants, and the impaired intelligence associated with Down syndrome. Any drugs or alcohol that the mother takes during this time can interfere with the growing brain cells, increasing the risk of fetal addiction and mental defects. Neuron growth in the fetus can also be damaged if the mother is under continual stress.

The neurons in a child's brain make many more connections than do those in an adult's brain. A newborn's brain makes connections at an incredible pace as the child absorbs its environment. The richer the environment, the greater the number of interconnections that are made; consequently, learning can take place faster and with greater meaning.

As the child approaches puberty, the pace slackens and two other processes begin: Connections the brain finds useful become permanent; those not useful are eliminated (apoptosis) as the brain selectively strengthens and prunes connections based on experience. This process continues throughout our lives, but it appears to be most intense between the ages of 3 and 12.

Thus at an early age experiences are already shaping the brain and designing the unique neural architecture that will influence how it handles future experiences in school, work, and other places.

Research Examines Learning Disabilities

Possible Causes of Learning Disabilities

Neuroscientists once believed that all learning disabilities were caused by a single neurological problem. By contrast, recent research has shown that learning disabilities do not stem from a single cause but from difficulties in bringing together information from different regions of the brain. These difficulties can arise during the fetal development of the child.

During pregnancy, the development of the brain is vulnerable to all kinds of disruptions. If the disruption occurs later in the pregnancy, errors may occur in the makeup of brain cells, their location, or the connections they make with neighboring cells. Some researchers believe that these errors may show up later as learning disorders.

> *Some children may exhibit behavior that looks like a learning disability but may simply be a delay in maturation.*

Experiments with animals have shown that other factors can disrupt brain development as well. Table 2.1 shows some of the factors currently under investigation and their potential impact on the development of the young brain. Problems in brain development that occur before, during, or after the birth of a child may eventually lead to learning difficulties. But not all learning difficulties are technically disabilities. For example, many children are just slower in developing certain skills. Therefore, some children may exhibit behavior that *looks like* a learning disability but may simply be a delay in maturation.

Learning disabilities are characterized by a significant difference between a child's achievement and that individual's overall intelligence. Students with learning disabilities often exhibit a wide variety of traits including problems with spoken and written language, reading, arithmetic, reasoning ability, and organization skills. These may be accompanied by inattention, hyperactivity, impulsivity, motor disorders, perceptual impairment, and a low tolerance for frustration. Because each of these traits can run the gamut from mild to severe, it is necessary to assess each student's disabilities carefully to determine the best approach for effective teaching.

Table 2.1 Some Factors That Affect Brain Development
(Adapted from NIMH, 1995)

Genetic Links	Because learning disabilities tend to run in families, there may be a genetic link. However, the parent's learning disability often takes a slightly different form in the child. This may indicate that directly inheriting a specific learning disability is unlikely. It is possible that the child inherits a subtle brain dysfunction that can lead to a learning disability. It is also possible that some learning difficulties may stem from the family environment. Parents with an expressive language disorder, for example, may talk less to their children, or their language may be atypical. Hence, the child lacks a good model for acquiring language and, consequently, may seem learning disabled.
Tobacco, Alcohol, and Other Drug Use	The mother's use of cigarettes, alcohol, or other drugs may damage the unborn child. Mothers who smoke during pregnancy often bear smaller babies who tend to be at risk for problems including learning disorders. Alcohol can distort neural growth and result in fetal alcohol syndrome, which often leads to hyperactivity and intellectual impairment. Even small amounts of alcohol during pregnancy can affect the frontal lobe and lead later to problems with attention, learning, and memory. Drugs like cocaine (especially crack) seem to affect the development of the receptor cells that transmit incoming information from our senses. This receptor damage may cause children to have difficulty understanding speech sounds or letters, a common problem found in the offspring of crack-addicted mothers.
Problems During Pregnancy or Delivery	Sometimes the mother's immune system attacks the fetus causing newly formed brain cells to settle in the wrong part of the brain. This migration may disturb the formation of neural networks needed for language and cognitive thought. During delivery, the umbilical cord may become twisted and temporarily cut off oxygen to the brain, which can damage or kill neurons and lead to learning disorders.
Toxins in the Child's Environment	Environmental toxins may disrupt brain cell growth and development in the early years. Lead and cadmium are getting particular research attention. Lead was once common in gasoline and paint and is still found in some homes and water pipes. Exposure to lead can cause learning difficulties. Cadmium is used for making some steel products and can get into the soil. Moreover, evidence exists showing that children with cancer can develop learning difficulties if treated with radiation or chemotherapy at an early age.
Stress in the Child's Environment	Prolonged and inappropriate stress in the environment can harm the brain at any age. Corticosteroids released into the bloodstream during stress can damage the hippocampus and thus interfere with the coding of new information into memory. These chemicals also damage neurons in other brain areas, thereby increasing the risk of stroke, seizure, and infections (Restak, 2000).

Gender Differences

Of increasing concern is the observation that more than twice as many boys as girls are diagnosed with learning difficulties; over four times as many boys are diagnosed with dyslexia and autism. What accounts for these gender differences? No one knows for sure. Some neuroscientists believe that male fetuses are more likely than female fetuses to invoke a foreign-body response by the mother's immune system. The response may induce a hostile environment that leads to fetal brain damage and eventual brain disorders.

Other researchers contend that an unknown factor present during the last trimester of pregnancy slows the formation of the brain's cortex, especially in the left hemisphere. Because girls are not influenced by this mysterious factor, their brains mature normally and are therefore better able to handle the stresses of pregnancy and birth. This may explain why females recover better than males from fetal brain damage (Restak, 2000). The research continues.

A third possibility is that certain brain deficits affecting learning result from genetic mutations on the X chromosome. Females have two X chromosomes, so they are protected if the healthy chromosome can prevent the effects of the mutated one. Males, on the other hand, possess only one X chromosome, so they suffer the full consequences of any mutations on that chromosome.

What Forms of Instruction Are Most Effective?

An analysis of almost 30 years of research indicates that the following interventions are most effective with learning disabled students:

- The most effective form of teaching was one that combined direct instruction (e.g., teacher-directed lecture, discussion, and learning from textbooks) with teaching students the strategies of learning (e.g., memorization techniques, study skills).

- The component that had the greatest effect on student achievement was *control of task difficulty*, in which, for example, the teacher provided the necessary assistance or sequenced tasks from easy to difficult. Working in small groups (five or less) and using structured questioning were also highly effective.

- When groups of students with learning disabilities were exposed to strategy instruction (i.e., how to learn), their achievement was greater than that of groups exposed solely to direct instruction.

Misconceptions About Learning Disabilities

Table 2.2 deals with some common misconceptions about the causes and implications of learning disabilities.

Table 2.2 Misconceptions About Learning Disabilities	
MISCONCEPTION	**EXPLANATION**
Learning disabilities are common and therefore easy to diagnose.	Although common, learning disabilities are often hidden and thus difficult to diagnose. Brain imaging shows promise in the diagnosis of some learning disabilities, but no X-ray-type imaging at this time can definitively reveal a brain defect that causes a specific learning problem. Thus, diagnosis needs to result from extensive observation and testing by a clinical team.
Children outgrow their learning disabilities.	Most learning disabilities last throughout life. However, many adults have devised strategies to cope successfully with their disabilities and lead productive lives.
Learning disabilities are caused by poor parenting.	No definitive association exists between the child rearing skills of parents and the presence or absence of permanent learning disabilities in their children. However, home discipline, the degree of parental interaction, and other factors may affect a child's self-image and enthusiasm for success in school. Physical abuse *can* cause permanent changes in the brain.
All students with learning disabilities will attend special education classes.	Many students with learning disabilities can have their problems addressed in the regular classroom. However, students who are classified typically have an individualized education plan that specifies how certain interventions will be implemented.
Medication, diet, or other treatments can cure learning disabilities.	No quick fix exists to cure learning disabilities. Even medication given to ADHD children acts by mediating the symptoms and does not cure the disorder. Because most learning disabilities are considered lifelong, the support and understanding of, and attention to the child's needs are basic to long-term treatment.
Students with learning disabilities don't try hard enough in school.	Ironically, brain scans show that many students with learning disabilities are working harder at certain tasks than other students, but the result is less successful. Students with learning disabilities often give up trying at school because of their fear of failure.
Learning disabilities affect everything the child does at school.	Some learning disabilities are very specific. Thus, a student's weakness may affect performance in one classroom setting but not in another, or only at a particular grade level.
Children with learning disabilities are just "slow."	Most learning disabilities are independent of cognitive ability. Children at all intellectual levels—including the gifted—can have learning problems.

Helping Students Become Strategic Learners

What actually makes learning difficult for students with learning disabilities has been the subject of research for many years. Examining the challenges of these students yields clues about the way they interact with their environment and possible interventions that may help them be more successful. Neil Sturomski has proposed that learners will benefit from strategies to help them learn. This section presents some of the findings and suggestions he included in an article for the National Information Center for Children and Youth with Disabilities (Sturomski, 1997).

What Is Learning?

Learning is an active process of acquiring and retaining knowledge so it can be applied in future situations. The ability to recall and apply new learning involves a complex interaction between the learner and the material being learned. Learning is likely to occur when a student has opportunities to practice the new information, receive feedback from the teacher, and apply the knowledge or skill in familiar and unfamiliar situations with less and less assistance from others.

Students bring to each new learning task a varied background of their own ideas, beliefs, opinions, attitudes, motivation, skills, and prior knowledge. They also bring the strategies and techniques they have learned in order to make learning more efficient. All these aspects contribute directly to students' ability to learn, and to remember and use what has been learned.

Teachers can facilitate a lifetime of successful learning by equipping students with a repertoire of strategies and tools for learning. These might include ways to organize oneself and new material; techniques to use while reading, writing, and studying mathematics or other subjects; and systematic steps to follow when working through a learning task or reflecting upon one's own learning.

Learning Difficulties of Students With Learning Disabilities

Sturomski (1997) stresses that students who have learning disabilities may have problems because they

- Are often overwhelmed, disorganized, and frustrated in new learning situations.
- Have difficulty following directions.
- Have trouble with the visual or auditory perception of information.
- Have problems performing school tasks, such as writing compositions, taking notes, doing written homework, or taking paper-and-pencil tests.
- Have a history of academic problems. Such students may believe that they

cannot learn, that school tasks are just too difficult and not worth the effort, or that, if they do succeed at a task, it must have been due to luck.

• Do not readily believe that there is a connection between what they do, the effort they make, and the likelihood of academic success. These negative beliefs about their ability to learn, and the nature of learning itself, can lower self-esteem and have far-reaching academic consequences.

Coping With the Difficulties

Acquiring the necessary knowledge, skills, and strategies for functioning independently in our society is as important to students with learning disabilities as it is to their peers without disabilities. Perhaps one of the most fundamental skills for everyone to learn is *how to learn*. Students can become effective, lifelong learners when they master certain techniques and strategies to assist learning and know which techniques are useful in different kinds of learning situations.

> *Students with learning disabilities need to know what strategies are useful in a learning situation and be able to use them effectively.*

We all use various methods and strategies to help us remember new information or skills. Yet, some of us are more conscious of our own learning processes than others. For instance, many students know little about the learning process, their own strengths and weaknesses in a learning situation, and what strategies and techniques they naturally tend to use when learning something new.

Hence, students with learning disabilities need to become strategic learners, and not haphazardly use whatever strategies or techniques they have developed on their own. To be able to decide which strategies to use, for example, students need to observe how others think or act when using various strategies. Learning skills develop when students receive opportunities to discuss, reflect upon, and practice personal strategies with classroom materials and appropriate skills. Through feedback, teachers help students refine new strategies and monitor their choices. Over time, teachers can diminish active guidance as students assume more responsibility for their own strategic learning.

What Are Learning Strategies?

Learning strategies are efficient, effective, and organized steps or procedures used when learning, remembering, or performing. These tools and techniques help us to understand and to retain new material or skills, to integrate this new information with what we already know in a way that makes sense, and to recall the information or skill later. When we are trying to learn new information or perform a task, our strategies include both cognitive and behavioral aspects.

Strategies can be simple or complex. Simple learning strategies are cognitive activities usually associated with less challenging learning tasks. Some examples of simple strategies are the following:

- Taking notes
- Making a chart or outline
- Asking the teacher questions
- Asking ourselves questions
- Using resource books or the Internet
- Re-reading what we don't understand
- Asking someone to check our work
- Developing a mnemonic device

Complex strategies help us accomplish more complex tasks involving multiple steps or higher-order thinking, such as analysis or answering "What if...?" questions. The following are examples of complex strategies:

- Planning, writing, and revising an essay
- Identifying sources of information
- Stating main ideas and supporting our position
- Distinguishing fact from opinion
- Searching for and correcting errors in our work
- Keeping track of our progress
- Being aware of our thought processes
- Evaluating the validity of sources

The research literature is full of suggestions for strategy interventions designed to make learners more aware of what they are doing. Some of these suggestions are found at the end of this chapter.

Types of Learning Strategies

Sturomski (1997) also notes the different ways learning strategies can be categorized. One way, for example, is to classify strategies as either cognitive or metacognitive.

Cognitive Strategies. These help a person process and manipulate information to perform tasks such as taking notes, asking questions, or filling out a chart. They tend to be task specific, that is, certain cognitive strategies are useful when learning or performing certain tasks.

Metacognitive Strategies. These are more executive in nature and are used when planning, monitoring, and evaluating learning or strategy performance. They are often referred to as self-regulatory strategies, helping students become aware of learning as a process and of what actions will facilitate that process. For example, taking the time to plan before writing assists students in writing a good composition. The ability to evaluate one's work, the effectiveness of learning, or even the use of a strategy is also metacognitive, demonstrating that a learner is aware of and thinking about how learning occurs.

Students who use metacognitive strategies frequently tend to become self-regulated learners. They set goals for learning, coach themselves in positive ways, and use self-instruction to guide themselves through learning problems. Further, they monitor their comprehension or progress and reward themselves for success. Just as students can be taught cognitive, task-specific strategies, so can they be taught self-regulatory, metacognitive ones. In fact, the most effective interventions combine the use of cognitive and metacognitive strategies.

Strategies have also been categorized by their purpose or function for the learner. Lenz, Ellis, and Scanlon (1996) suggest three types of functional strategies:

1. Acquisition strategy: Used initially to learn new information or skills
2. Storage strategy: Used to manipulate or transform information so that it can effectively be placed in memory
3. Knowledge strategy: Used to recall or to show what has been learned

Research About the Effectiveness of Learning Strategies

Research into strategies of learning has been going on for over 30 years, long before the availability of brain scanning technologies. Since the 1970s, researchers at the University of Kansas have investigated the benefits of strategy instruction, especially for individuals with learning disabilities. Their work

> *Learning and retention are more likely to occur when students can observe, engage in, discuss, reflect upon, and practice the new learning.*

produced one of the most well researched and well articulated models for teaching students to use learning strategies. Known as the Strategies Integration Model, or SIM, this method outlines a series of steps so that educators can effectively teach any number of strategies or strategic approaches. See the model at the end of this chapter in Strategies to Consider.

Recent cognitive research supports the notion that learning and retention are more likely to occur when students can observe, engage in, discuss, reflect upon, and practice the new learning. When teachers help students to use learning strategies and to generalize their strategic knowledge to other academic and nonacademic situations, they are promoting student independence in the process of learning.

For students who have learning disabilities, learning strategy instruction holds great educational promise for the following reasons:

- Instruction helps students learn how to learn and become more effective in the successful performance of academic, social, or job-related tasks. Students can better deal with immediate academic demands as well as cope with similar tasks in different settings under different conditions throughout life. The strategies are particularly powerful in the face of new learning situations.

- Instruction makes students aware of how strategies work, why they work, when they work, and where they can be used. To assist students, teachers will need to
  - ▶ talk about strategies explicitly,
  - ▶ name and describe each strategy,
  - ▶ model how each strategy is used by thinking aloud while performing tasks relevant to students,
  - ▶ provide students with multiple opportunities to use the strategies with a variety of materials, and
  - ▶ provide feedback and guidance while students refine and internalize the use of each strategy.

Ultimately, responsibility for strategy use needs to shift from teachers to students. This promotes independent learners with the cognitive flexibility necessary to address the many learning challenges they will encounter in their lives.

Learning strategies help students become better equipped to face current and future learning tasks.

Although no single technique or intervention can address all the varied needs of students with learning disabilities, teaching the strategies of learning will help these students become better equipped to face current and future learning tasks. By learning how to learn, they can become independent, lifelong learners—one of the primary goals of education.

The Importance of Positive Self-Statements

Students with learning disabilities often have negative feelings about learning and about themselves. Because of past experiences, these students believe they cannot learn or that the work is simply too difficult. As a result, they may believe they cannot achieve success in learning through their own efforts. Teachers need to address this issue when presenting information on the strategies of learning. By modeling positive self-statements, teachers can convince students to attribute success in learning to their own efforts and to the use of appropriate learning strategies. For learning strategies to be successful, students need to have a positive self-image and recognize the connection between effort and success. See the Strategies to Consider for suggestions on how to build student self-esteem.

Gifted Children With Learning Disabilities

Albert Einstein is considered one of the greatest scientists of the twentieth century. His great mind was able to discuss the quantum nature of light, provide a description of molecular motion, and introduce the special theory of relativity. Einstein was famous for continually reexamining traditional scientific assumptions and coming to straightforward, elegant conclusions no one else had reached. Yet for all his brilliance, he was considered a slow student in school because he could not sit still, would go off on abstract tangents during discussion, and rarely obeyed the rules. Given all the accounts of his early school behavior, in modern times we would most likely have diagnosed him as having attention-deficit hyperactivity disorder.

> *It is only in recent years that educators have accepted that high ability and learning problems can exist in the same person.*

The notion that a gifted child can have learning disabilities strikes some people as bizarre, something like an oxymoron. Consequently, many children who are gifted in some ways and deficient in others go undetected and unserved by their schools. They tend to fall through the cracks because the system is not designed to deal with such widely different conditions occurring in the same student. In fact, it is only in recent years that educators have even begun to accept that high abilities and learning problems can exist together in the same person.

Variations Within These Students

Researchers in this area have identified three subgroups of children with this dual exceptionality (Baum, 1994):

1. The first group includes students identified as gifted but who exhibit learning difficulties in school. Through poor motivation, laziness, or low self-esteem, they perform poorly and are often labeled as underachievers. As a result, their learning disabilities remain unrecognized until they fall far behind their peers.

2. The second group includes students who have already been diagnosed with learning disabilities but whose high abilities have never been recognized. This may be a larger group than one might believe at first. If their high ability remains unrecognized, then it never becomes part of their educational program and these children never benefit from services to gifted children.

3. The third—and perhaps largest—group represents those children whose abilities and disabilities mask each other. They often function at grade level, are considered average students, and do not seem to have problems or any special needs. Although they may be seem to be performing well, they are in fact functioning well below their potential. In later high school years, as course work becomes more difficult, learning difficulties may become apparent, but their true potential will not be realized.

Children in all three groups are at risk for social and emotional problems when either their potential or learning disabilities go unrecognized. The problem is further compounded by the identification process because the activities used to select students for either learning disability or gifted services tend to be mutually exclusive. Consequently, these students fail to meet the criteria for either type of services.

The Difficulties of Identification

Researchers have not been successful to date in finding measurement activities that will accurately identify children with both talents and learning disabilities. Further, the number of possible combinations of intellectual giftedness and learning disabilities is so great that any attempt to devise a single set of reliable measures is probably futile. Nonetheless, researchers agree that a battery of measurements should be developed to assess these students. The battery should include an achievement battery, an intelligence test, indicators of cognitive processing, and behavioral observations (Brody and Mills, 1997). The goal is early identification and intervention for gifted students with learning disabilities so that their needs and talents are recognized and appropriately addressed by the school staff.

Strategies to Consider

Guidelines for Working With Special Needs Students

Teachers should consider these guidelines to help students with special needs succeed. The following general strategies are appropriate for all grade levels and subject areas (NICHCY, 1997).

- **Capitalize on the student's strengths.** This is more likely to give the student a feeling of success and lessen any feelings of inadequacy that flow from the disability.

- **Provide high structure and clear expectations.** These students do better in an organized environment and need to know what is expected of them. Take nothing for granted and make sure the student is aware of acceptable and unacceptable types of behavior.

- **Use short sentences and simple vocabulary.** These students often have difficulty processing complex sentence structures and usually have a limited vocabulary. Behavior problems can arise when the student is unclear about what the teacher said.

- **Provide opportunities for success in a supportive atmosphere to help build self-esteem.** Students with learning problems often have low self-esteem. Any opportunity the teacher provides to improve self-esteem may convince the student to pay more attention to learning and to be more persistent.

- **Allow flexibility in classroom procedures.** For example, permit students with written language difficulties to use tape recorders for note taking and test taking.

Guidelines for Working With Special Needs Students—Continued

- **Make use of self-correcting materials that provide immediate feedback without embarrassment.** Because many of these students have a short attention span, activities that give immediate feedback are desirable. Students can assess their own progress quickly and without knowing each other's results.

- **Use computers for drill and practice and for teaching word processing.** Computers are patient devices for drill and practice. Many programs provide varied opportunities to practice and usually give a running score of the student's progress. Word processing programs can often convince students to try creative writing despite any problems with written language.

- **Provide positive reinforcement of appropriate social skills.** Appropriate social behavior at school is likely to be repeated if it is positively reinforced. Look for opportunities to "catch the student being good."

- **Recognize that students with learning disabilities can greatly benefit from the gift of time to grow and mature.** These students often progress slowly, but many progress nonetheless. Patience with them can be rewarding for both teachers and students.

Strategies to Consider

Strategies for Involvement and Retention

Students with attention difficulties need help to maximize their engagement and to improve their retention of learning. The following strategies are appropriate for all students, and especially those who have learning problems (Fulk, 2000).

- ▶ **Get Their Attention.** Use humor, unexpected introductions, and various other "attention grabbers" to stimulate student interest in the lesson.

- ▶ **Make It Relevant.** Relevancy (or meaning) is one of the major factors affecting retention. Students are not likely to retain what they perceive as irrelevant. Keep in mind that it is *their* perception of relevancy that matters, not *yours*.

- ▶ **Model, Model, Model.** Show students how to do it. Use models, simulations, and examples for simple as well as complex concepts. Ask them to develop original models.

- ▶ **Use Teams.** The research indicates that these students are particularly successful when working in teams. The opportunity to discuss what they are learning keeps them actively engaged and helps them to practice interpersonal skills.

- ▶ **Set Goals.** Success is a key factor in maintaining involvement. Set realistic goals with the students (e.g., "Let's try to solve three problems this time.").

- ▶ **Find Out What They Already Know.** Take the time to assess what students already know about the topic being taught. Building on this prior knowledge is an effective way of helping students establish relevancy.

Strategies for Involvement and Retention—Continued

▸ **Use Visuals.** We live in a visually oriented culture and students are acclimated to visual stimuli. Graphs, pictures, diagrams, and visual organizers are very effective learning and retention devices.

▸ **Go for the Big Picture.** The brain is a pattern seeker. Use graphics to put together the big picture, showing how concepts are connected. Discuss the patterns that emerge and link them to what students have already learned.

▸ **Think and Talk Aloud.** When teachers think aloud, they model the steps in cognitive processing and reveal what information or skills can be used to approach and solve a problem. Talking aloud is an excellent memory enhancer, especially when students discuss open-ended questions, such as "What might have happened if...?" or "What would you have done instead?"

▸ **Suggest Mnemonic Devices.** All memory tricks are valuable. Teach mnemonic devices, such as acronyms (ROY G BIV for colors of the spectrum, HOMES for the Great Lakes), keywords, and imaging to help students remember factual information or steps in a procedure.

▸ **Use a Variety of Practice Formats.** Practice is the key to retention but can be perceived as boring when the teacher uses only one practice format. Try small dry-erase boards, computer programs, or simulations to keep practice interesting and varied. And, if students can correctly solve five problems, do we need to give them 20?

▸ **Explain the Value of Note-Taking.** Writing is not only a good memory tool, but it also helps students organize their thoughts and focus on what is important. Gradually decrease the amount of information you give in an outline so that students need to provide more input.

▸ **Use Closure Strategies Regularly.** Closure strategies, such as journal writing and group processing ("Tell your partner two things you learned today."), enhance retention of learning.

Strategies to Consider

Teaching Students to Use Learning Strategies

Much has been learned through research regarding effective learning-strategy instruction. As mentioned earlier, a well-articulated instructional approach known as the Strategies Integration Model (SIM) has emerged from research conducted at the University of Kansas (Ellis, Deshler, Lenz, Schumaker, and Clark, 1991). Based on cognitive behavior modification, the SIM is one of the field's most comprehensive tools for providing strategy instruction. It can be used to teach virtually any strategic intervention (Sturomski, 1997).

Selecting the Strategy. First, the teacher selects a strategy that is clearly linked to the tasks students need to perform at the place they need to perform them. When the strategy is matched to student needs, they perceive relevancy and tend to be motivated to learn and use the strategy. After selecting the strategy or approach to teach, the six steps of the SIM guide the actual instruction.

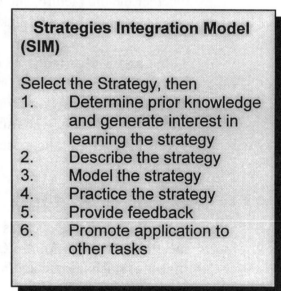

Strategies Integration Model (SIM)

Select the Strategy, then
1. Determine prior knowledge and generate interest in learning the strategy
2. Describe the strategy
3. Model the strategy
4. Practice the strategy
5. Provide feedback
6. Promote application to other tasks

Step 1. Determine Prior Knowledge and Generate Interest in Learning the Strategy. It is important to use a type of pretest to determine how much students already know about using the strategy. This information provides a starting point for instruction. Younger students, for example, may have no understanding of how they learn; older students may have already encountered their learning weaknesses. Motivate students by letting them know that gains in learning can occur when the strategy is used effectively. Studies have shown that it is important to tell students directly that learning this strategy using effort and persistence will help them achieve whatever skill is being addressed.

Teaching Students to Use Learning Strategies—Continued

Use a pretest that centers on the materials and tasks that students actually encounter in class. Following the pretest, the class should discuss the results by asking questions such as:

- ▶ How did we do?
- ▶ Were we able to perform the task successfully?
- ▶ What types of errors did we make? Why?
- ▶ What did we do, or think about, to help ourselves while taking the pretest?
- ▶ What difficulties did we have? How did we address those difficulties?

If students did not perform particularly well, then discuss a strategy or technique that will help them perform that task more successfully in the future.

According to the SIM model, it is important to obtain a commitment from students to learn the strategy. To accomplish this, teachers can discuss the value of the strategy and the fact that they are committed to helping the students. Teachers should point out the likelihood that success may not be immediate, but that success will come if the student perseveres and practices the strategy.

Student-teacher collaboration in use of the strategy is especially important with elementary school students. Teachers need to discuss and practice strategies with these young students frequently. The commitments can be verbal or in writing, but the idea here is to get the students involved and to make them aware that their participation in learning and in using the strategy is vital to their eventual success.

Step 2. Describe the Strategy. In this step, teachers clearly define the strategy, give examples, discuss the benefits of learning the strategy, and ask students to determine various ways the strategy can be used. The teacher should also identify real-life assignments in specific classes in which students can apply the strategy and ask students if they can think of other work for which the strategy might be useful. Students should also be told the various stages involved in learning the strategy, so they know what to expect.

After this overview, the students are ready to delve more deeply into hearing about and using the strategy. Instruction becomes more specific so that

– Continued –

Teaching Students to Use Learning Strategies—Continued

each step of the strategy is described in detail and presented in such a way that students can easily remember it. Acronyms can help students remember the various steps involved. An example is the COPS strategy, which helps students detect common writing errors (Shannon & Polloway, 1993).

Displaying a poster or chart about the strategy and its steps will also help memory and retention. During this phase, the class also discusses how this new approach to a specific task differs from what students are currently using. For closure, conclude with a review of what has been learned.

> **Acronyms Help Students Remember the Steps in Using a Strategy**
>
> **COPS** is the acronym for a strategic approach that helps students detect and correct common writing errors. Each letter stands for an aspect of writing that students need to check for accuracy.
>
> C — Capitalization of appropriate letters
> O — Overall appearance of paper
> P — Punctuation used correctly
> S — Spelling accuracy

Step 3. Model the Strategy. Modeling the strategy is an essential component of strategy instruction. In this step, teachers overtly use the strategy to help students perform a relevant classroom or authentic task, talking aloud as they work so that students can observe how a person thinks and what a person does while using the strategy. For example, you could model

▸ deciding which strategy to use to perform the task at hand;
▸ working through the task using that strategy;
▸ monitoring performance (i.e., is the strategy being applied correctly, and is it helping the learner effectively complete the work?);
▸ revising one's strategic approach; and,
▸ making positive self-statements.

The self-talk that the teacher provides as a model can become a powerful guide for students as responsibility for using the strategy transfers to them.

Step 4. Practice the Strategy. Practice leads to retention. The more students and teachers collaborate to use the strategy, the more likely the strategy will become part of the students' strategic repertoire. Initial guided practice is designed to check for understanding and first applications.

Teaching Students to Use Learning Strategies—Continued

Students should be encouraged to think aloud as they work through their practice tasks, explaining the problems they are having, the decisions they are making, or the physical actions they are taking. These student "think alouds" should increasingly reveal the specific strategy being used to help them complete the task successfully. Initially, the "think alouds" should be part of teacher-directed instruction. Later, the students benefit greatly from practicing in small groups, where they listen and help each other understand the task, why the strategy might be useful in completing the task, and how to apply the strategy to the task. Eventually, the practice sessions become self-mediated as students work independently to complete tasks while using the strategy.

As practice continues, the level of difficulty of the materials being used should gradually increase. In the beginning, students practice using the strategy with materials that are at or slightly below their comfort level, so they do not become frustrated by overly difficult content. The materials must be well matched to the strategy so that students can readily understand the strategy's value. As students become more proficient in using the strategy, introduce materials that are more difficult.

Step 5. Provide Feedback. The feedback that teachers give students on their use of the strategy is a critical component of the SIM model. It helps students learn how to use a strategy effectively and how to change what they are doing when a particular approach is unsuccessful. It is also important for students to reflect upon their approach to and completion of the task and to self-correct when necessary. What aspects of the task did they complete well? What aspects were hard? Did any problems arise, and what did they do to solve the problems? What might they do differently the next time they have to complete a similar task?

Step 6. Promote Application to Other Tasks (Generalization). The value of using learning strategies increases greatly when students are able to apply the strategy in new situations. It may not become obvious to many students that the strategy they have been learning and practicing may be ideal for helping them to complete a learning task in a different classroom or learning situation; this is particularly true of students with learning disabilities (Borkowski, Estrada, Milstead, and Hale, 1989). Thus, merely exposing the students to strategy training

– Continued –

Teaching Students to Use Learning Strategies—Continued

is not sufficient for both strategy learning and strategy utilization to occur (Wood, Rosenburg, and Carran, 1993). Guided and consistent practice in generalizing how the strategies can transfer to various settings and tasks is vital for students with learning disabilities (Pressley, Symons, Snyder, and Cariglia-Bull, 1989), as are repeated reminders that strategies of learning can be used in new situations (Borkowski et al., 1989).

Therefore, teachers need to discuss with students what transfer is all about (Sousa, 2001, pp. 136-165) and how and when students might use the strategy in other settings. An important part of this discussion will be getting students to review the actual work that they have in other classes and discussing with students how the strategy might be useful in completing that work. Actually going through the steps of the strategy with specific work assignments can be very effective.

Students can generate their own examples of contexts in which to apply the strategy. For example, they could use the COPS strategy discussed in Step 2 for homework assignments, job applications, friendly letters, English papers, written problems in mathematics, and spelling practice. Additionally, teachers within a school may wish to coordinate among themselves to promote student use of strategies across settings, so that the strategies being taught in one classroom are mentioned and supported by other teachers as well. All of these approaches will promote student generalization of the strategy.

Strategies to Consider

Building Self-Esteem

The following strategies can be used to help students build their self-esteem:

☺ Use students' names when addressing them.

☺ Have conversations with *every* student.

☺ Have student work occasionally assessed by other audiences (students, other teachers, parents).

☺ Avoid making assumptions about student behavior, and separate the behavior from the person.

☺ Point out positive aspects of your students' work.

☺ Shake hands with students, especially when you greet them.

☺ Allow students to explore different learning options (Internet, resource works, interviews, etc.).

☺ Display student work (with the student's permission).

☺ Give each student a responsibility in the classroom.

☺ Avoid criticizing a student's question.

☺ Provide multiple opportunities for students to be successful in your classroom (especially when giving tests).

– Continued –

Building Self-Esteem—Continued

☺   Help students turn failure into a positive learning experience.

☺   Celebrate your students' achievements, no matter how small.

☺   Allow students to make decisions about some aspects of class work (what kind of report to do, what color something can be, etc.).

☺   Try to get to know about the student's life outside of school (without prying).

☺   Provide opportunities for students to work in productive groups.

☺   Spend extra time with struggling students.

☺   Ask students about their other activities (sports, music and drama groups, etc.).

☺   Encourage students to take *appropriate* risks.

☺   Allow students to suffer the consequences of their behavior and avoid being overprotective.

Strategies to Consider

Working With Special Needs Students in Groups

Chapter 1 discusses the value of rehearsal. Group activities are effective means for students to rehearse by talking to each other about their learning. However, teachers are often concerned that special needs students may remain passive, drift off-task, or disrupt the group process.

Wood and Jones (1998) report that group activities, especially if they include cooperative learning strategies, are particularly effective in getting struggling students to participate in the regular classroom setting. Group work is often a more effective alternative to the more traditional assignment of having a student read the text and answer questions at the end of the chapter—a practice that special needs students find frustrating. For example, speaking in front of a small group is less intimidating than speaking in front of the entire class. These students also find that their own experiences can be triggered when others in the group remember an event.

The following suggest some of the many ways to implement this strategy. Remember to make appropriate adjustments for the age of the students.

■ **Assign Students to Heterogeneous Groups**
  ▸ Divide the class into three sections—high, middle, and low—based on their mastery of the subject matter. Assign one student from each section to a group.
  ▸ If necessary, switch students so that each group is made up of students who can benefit from each other, but not so different that they are intimidated by other members of the group.
  ▸ Give the group assignment and stress the importance of working together. Students can read to each other, answer questions, discuss what they already know, or show a partner how to do something. The object is for all members of the group to accomplish the learning objective successfully.

– Continued –

Working With Special Needs Students in Groups—Continued

■ **Use the Retelling Strategy in Each Group**

▶ Ask the students to read a portion of their text, either silently or whispering to their partners. When finished, allow some think time and ask them to tell their partners what they learned and what they remembered about the text.

▶ If necessary, model this retelling strategy by telling aloud something you have read. Include analogies, personal anecdotes, and other imagery to embellish your retelling. Demonstrate how imaging and metaphors help in memory. This establishes a clear model for students to follow.

▶ Keep moving among the groups while they are retelling, asking questions to assess their progress and to assist where needed.

▶ After the students complete their retelling sessions, call on them to relate what they have read and learned. Look for opportunities to ask "What if...?" questions.

▶ Write the student responses on the board or overhead transparency so that all can see. Point out any differences in the responses and ask students to discuss them.

■ **Some Options to Consider**

▶ Encourage students to gather information from other sources in addition to the text, such as the Internet, pictures, and charts.

▶ Within groups, give struggling students material to use that is written at an easier level.

▶ Follow-up activities can include going on a field trip, watching a video, observing an experiment, or listening to a guest speaker.

Using strategies in addition to reading is especially helpful to struggling learners whose difficulties with reading may become overly frustrating and turn them away from the learning experience.

Strategies to Consider

Assisting Gifted Students With Learning Disabilities

Educators who study the effectiveness of strategies on the education of gifted students with learning disabilities offer the following suggestions (Brody and Mills, 1997).

❑　**Use technology.** Technology helps talented students overcome their disabilities. For example:

- ▸ Students who are capable of high-level mathematics but have difficulty with computation can use calculators to move ahead in their area of strength
- ▸ A microcomputer with a word processing program and a spell checker can be very helpful to a student who has difficulties with writing or spelling
- ▸ Students with reading problems but having high auditory processing abilities can use tape recorders and other sources of information, such as films, that are not dependent on reading

❑　**Taking responsibility for their own learning.** This is a powerful strategy because it forces these students to use their gifts to recognize and shore up their weaknesses. It can include:

- ▸ Teaching them self-assessment techniques
- ▸ Exposing them to new and interesting methods of inquiry
- ▸ Assisting them in locating information
- ▸ Exposing them to a broad range of topics to stimulate new interests
- ▸ Providing experiential learning

❑　**Other considerations.**

- ▸ Gear curriculum to their strengths rather than their weaknesses
- ▸ Divide big tasks into small tasks and make them meaningful
- ▸ Give genuine praise where appropriate
- ▸ Use peer tutoring to compensate for areas of weakness
- ▸ Provide cooperative learning activities regularly

ATTENTION DISORDERS

As brain research slowly reveals more of how the brain learns, educators gain renewed hope in understanding problems that can arise during this complex process. Most learning requires the brain's attention (also called *focus*). Because emotions often drive attention, this activity occurs first in the brain's limbic area (Chapter 1) and requires the coordinated effort of three neural networks: *alerting*, *orienting*, and *executive control* (Posner and Raichle, 1994). Alerting helps the brain to suppress background stimuli and inhibit ongoing activity. Orienting

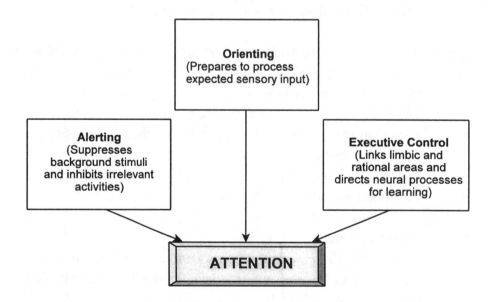

Figure 3.1 Attention for learning requires the coordinated efforts of three neural networks: alerting, orienting, and executive control.

mobilizes neural resources to process the expected input and inhibit all other input. Executive control links the limbic centers with the rational areas of the cerebrum, directing the various neural processes needed to respond to a specific learning objective. Problems can arise anywhere within the brain, and the resulting loss of attention may be accompanied by hyperactivity and impulsivity (see Figure 3.1).

Research Findings

What Is Attention-Deficit Hyperactivity Disorder (ADHD)?

Attention-deficit hyperactivity disorder (ADHD) is a syndrome that interferes with an individual's ability to focus (inattention), regulate activity level (hyperactivity), and inhibit behavior (impulsivity). It is one of the most common learning disorders in children and adolescents. It affects an estimated 4.1 percent of youths ages 9 to 17 for a period of at least six months. About 2 to 3 times more boys than girls are affected. ADHD usually becomes evident in preschool or early elementary years, frequently persisting into adolescence and occasionally into adulthood.

Although most children have some symptoms of hyperactivity, impulsivity, and inattention, there are those in whom these behaviors persist and become the rule rather than the exception. These individuals need to be assessed by health care professionals with input from parents and teachers. No specific test exists for ADHD. The diagnosis results from a thorough review of a physical examination, a variety of psychological tests, and the observable behaviors in the child's everyday settings. These behaviors are compared to a list of symptoms contained in the fourth edition of the *Diagnostic and Statistical Manual of Mental Disorders* (DSM-IV). A diagnosis of ADHD requires that 6 or more of the symptoms for inattention or for hyperactivity-impulsivity be present for at least six months, appear before the age of 7, and be evident across at least two of the child's environments (e.g., at home, in school, on the

---

Some Indicators of ADHD

(Not all indicators may be present in the same individual. Indicators should appear before the age of 7 and persist for at least six months in at least two of the child's environments.)

Inattention: Fails to attend to details; difficulty sustaining attention; does not seem to listen; fails to finish; has difficulty organizing tasks; avoids sustained effort; loses things; is distracted by extraneous stimuli; is forgetful.

Hyperactivity: Talks incessantly; leaves seat in classroom; may dash around or climb; difficulty playing quietly; fidgets with hands or feet; motor excess.

Impulsivity: Blurts out answers; difficulty waiting for turn; interrupts or intrudes.

playground, etc.). Recently, ADHD has been classified into three subtypes: Predominantly inattentive, predominantly hyperactive-impulsive, and the combined type.

Differences Between ADHD and ADD. Some children have no trouble sitting still or inhibiting their behavior, but they are inattentive and have great difficulty focusing. They tend to be withdrawn, polite, and shy. Because they lack the hyperactivity symptom, these children are often referred to as having Attention Deficit Disorder (ADD) without hyperactivity. The two conditions are categorized as different disorders because there are some symptomatic differences.

Table 3.1 shows some of the behavioral differences observed in students diagnosed with ADHD compared with those diagnosed with ADD. The descriptions may seem simplistic, but they do help to discriminate between two conditions that are very closely related. Although ADHD and ADD are separate disorders, many of the strategies suggested in this chapter can apply to both groups of students.

Table 3.1 Some Behavioral Differences Between ADHD and ADD		
	ADHD	**ADD**
Decision Making	Impulsive	Sluggish
Attention Seeking	Show off Egotistical Relishes in being the worst	Modest Shy Often socially withdrawn
Assertiveness	Bossy Often irritating	Underassertive Overly polite and docile
Recognizing Boundaries	Intrusive Occasionally rebellious	Honors boundaries Usually polite and obedient
Popularity	Attracts new friends but has difficulty bonding	Bonds but does not easily attract friends
Associated Diagnoses	Oppositional Defiance Conduct Disorder	Depression

What Causes ADHD?

The exact causes of ADHD are unknown. Scientific evidence indicates that this is a neurologically based medical problem for which there may be several causes. Some research studies suggest that the disorder results from an imbalance in certain neurotransmitters (most likely dopamine and serotonin) that help the brain regulate focus and behavior. One thing seems certain:

Parents and teachers do not *cause* ADHD. However, how they react to a child with ADHD symptoms may lessen or worsen the effects of the disorder.

ADHD has been associated with symptoms in children after difficult pregnancies and problem deliveries. Maternal smoking as well as exposure to environmental toxins, such as dioxins, during pregnancy also increase the risk of an ADHD child. Other studies indicate that the ADHD brain consumes less glucose—its main fuel source—than the non-ADHD brain, especially in the frontal lobe regions (Zametkin, Mordahl, Gross, King, Semple, Rumsey, Hamburger, and Cohen, 1990). Brain imaging studies have revealed structural differences in adults with ADHD, suggesting that the disorder may have a genetic component.

Is ADHD Inherited?

Probably. Genetic predispositions for ADHD are likely because the disorder tends to run in families. Children with ADHD usually have at least one close relative who also has ADHD, and at least one-third of all fathers who had ADHD as a youth have children with ADHD. Stronger evidence of a genetic connection comes from studies showing that if one identical twin has the disorder, the other is likely to have it also. One suspect cause is the gene responsible for coding the neuron receptors for the key neurotransmitter dopamine. A significant function of dopamine is to help the brain focus with intent to learn.

ADHD has probably been in the gene pool for thousands of years.

The genetic marker for ADHD behavior probably has been present in the gene pool for thousands of years, indicating that ADHD individuals had important roles to play in the survival of early societies. In prehistoric times, for example, individuals with ADHD behavior could have been valuable as scouts to protect a hunting party from sneak attack by predators. Success in this role required people who could rapidly scan a wide area looking for danger. Impulsiveness and quick-thinking were decided advantages in a hunting society. A scout who was too deeply focused on just one interesting tree or fixated on an attractive vista would likely miss the approaching predator and get eaten. ADHD traits became a mixed blessing, however, when societies became agrarian.

Although there may be a genetic predisposition for ADHD, this does not imply that parenting and schooling don't matter. On the contrary, these are likely to be susceptibility—rather than dominant—genes, so the child's environment plays a major role in determining whether the genetic traits appear. How the parents and school cope with a "problem" child will shape that child's development and interaction with the world (DeGrandpre and Hinshaw, 2000).

Can Brain Scans Reveal ADHD?

Maybe. Several neuroimaging studies have shown that the brains of those diagnosed with ADHD differ consistently from non-ADHD individuals. For example, two structures in the limbic area (the cordate nucleus and the globus pallidus) and one in the cerebellum (the vermis) are smaller in adults diagnosed with ADHD than in adults without the disorder (see Figure 3.2). Further, it seems that these structural differences are strongly associated with a genetic defect. The two limbic structures appear to be involved in the dopamine network. Dopamine is a neurotransmitter that, among other things, helps to control attention. In the ADHD individual, the smaller size of the globus pallidus and the cordate nucleus may decrease the effectiveness of dopamine, resulting in difficulty sustaining attention (Barkley, 1998). Another recent study reported that adults diagnosed with ADHD had abnormally low levels of an enzyme (DOPA decarboxylase) that produces dopamine (Swanson, Castellanos, Murias, LaHoste, and Kennedy, 1998).

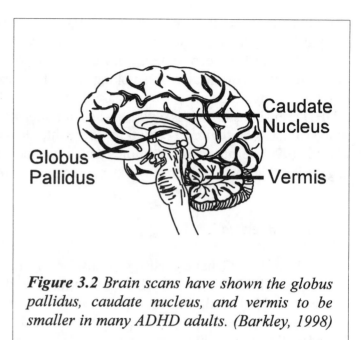

Figure 3.2 Brain scans have shown the globus pallidus, caudate nucleus, and vermis to be smaller in many ADHD adults. (Barkley, 1998)

Scans also show that the overall brain size of children with ADHD is about 5 percent smaller than normal. However, this size difference, while consistent, is too small to make a diagnosis of ADHD in a particular individual (Swanson et al., 1998). Besides, brain imaging techniques are expensive and thus will not likely be used as a standard diagnostic tool for ADHD in the foreseeable future.

Is ADHD on the Increase?

No one knows for sure. Although the number of children identified with the disorder has risen, no clear indication exists that the rise is due to greater prevalence of the disorder, to better diagnosis and identification, or both. Certainly, heightened media interest has led to increased awareness of the disorder and the availability of effective treatments. Some scientists suggest that the changing family patterns and child-rearing problems of today may have more to do with the rise in children labeled ADHD than any biological factors. As more children are raised by total strangers, video games, and television, ADHD-like behavior may become the norm rather than the exception.

As more children are raised by total strangers, video games, and television, ADHD-like behavior may become the norm rather than the exception.

Is It Possible to Have ADHD-Like Behavior and Not ADHD?

Yes. Some children diagnosed with ADHD early in life simply have the symptoms which mimic disorder but do not have the disorder. There are other factors that produce ADHD-like symptoms: Some children have not learned the acceptable and unacceptable rules of behavior in certain environments, such as school. Their behavior, therefore, looks like ADHD, but these children may benefit more from being taught the appropriate behavior than from medication. Other children sometimes develop allergic reactions to certain foods that result in, among other things, hyperactive behavior. Again, these children will benefit more from diet modification than medication to control behavior. Additional factors could be stress reactions, other medical conditions, or intolerant schools.

Can Schools Inadvertently Enhance ADHD-Like Behavior?

As discussed in Chapter 1, most children are growing up in an environment that is very different from just a few years ago. But many schools haven't changed their instructional approaches to accommodate the resulting new brain. The possibility exists, therefore, that school and classroom operations can inadvertently create or enhance ADHD-like behavior in students when

- ▸ teachers under pressure to *cover* curriculum move too fast (even with the realization that some students need more time)
- ▸ the main mode of instruction is teacher talk (when we know that more students have visual and kinesthetic learning preferences)
- ▸ room arrangements allow students to hide from the teacher and create mischief (the classic row-by-row formation is more conducive to isolation than collaboration)
- ▸ discipline is arbitrary and perceived as unfair (students in secondary schools encounter 6 to 8 teachers daily, each with a different set of rules and expectations)
- ▸ there are few or no opportunities to get up and move around (too much stuff to cover, so students just sit and listen)
- ▸ the classroom is too hot or too dark (studies show students achieve more in rooms that are well-lit with plenty of natural light)
- ▸ there are few opportunities for students to interact with each other (interactive learning reduces boredom and increases retention)
- ▸ the classroom emotional climate is neutral or tense (positive emotional climate enhances learning).

Modifying the preceding situations can often change ADHD-like behavior into more positive student participation and academic success.

What Is the Future of ADHD Research?

Promising. Additional studies will need to be conducted to differentiate true ADHD individuals from those whose symptoms mimic the disorder. Brain scans may eventually be an important part of this diagnosis. Brain imaging studies before and after the use of different medications may also help identify the behavioral and cognitive networks that cause the disorder, thereby leading to more effective treatment. Recently, a committee of the National Institutes of Health recommended a study to determine the long-term benefits and risks of stimulant medications, such as methylphenidate (known as Ritalin®), currently used to treat ADHD. Studies looking at the influence of certain risk factors as well as possible genetic links to the disorder are also underway.

What Do Educators Need to Consider?

Teachers need to pinpoint areas in which each student's difficulties occur. Otherwise, valuable intervention resources may be spent where they are not effective. For example, one ADHD student may have difficulty starting a task because the directions are not clear, while another may understand the directions but may have difficulty getting organized to begin a task. These two students need different types of interventions. Also, the sooner educational interventions begin, the better. They should be started when educational performance is affected and problems persist.

Teachers of these students need to be positive, upbeat, and highly organized problem solvers. Unpredictability is a classroom constant, but teachers who use praise liberally and who are willing to put in extra effort will often experience success with ADHD students. After all, most of these students want to succeed.

Impact on Learning

ADHD can affect a student in one or more of the following performance tasks:

- Starting tasks
- Staying on task
- Completing tasks
- Making transitions
- Interacting with others
- Following directions
- Producing work at consistently normal levels
- Organizing multistep tasks

Strategies to Consider

Avoiding School-Created ADHD-Like Behavior

Directions: Complete the profile below to determine whether some of your classroom or school structures can inadvertently create ADHD-like behavior in students. On a scale of 1 (lowest) to 5 (highest), circle the number that indicates the degree to which your teaching/school does the following. Connect the circles to see a profile.

1. I/We move quickly during instruction because I/we have a lot of curriculum to cover.   1----2----3----4----5

2. I/We use lecture as the main method of instruction.   1----2----3----4----5

3. I/We have classrooms arranged so it is possible for some students to be hidden from the teacher.   1----2----3----4----5

4. Each teacher determines the rules of behavior for the classroom.   1----2----3----4----5

5. I/We tend to keep students in their seats during lessons to avoid opportunities for behavior problems.   1----2----3----4----5

6. I/We usually turn down the lights when using the overhead projector or other visual aid.   1----2----3----4----5

7. I/We generally use the textbook as the main focus of instruction and classroom activity.   1----2----3----4----5

8. Copying information from the board is one of the main methods I/we use to give students information.   1----2----3----4----5

9. I/We tend to give more time to presenting information than to concern over students' emotional needs.   1----2----3----4----5

– Continued –

Avoiding School-Created ADHD-Like Behavior—Continued

Scoring. If most of the circles are in the 3 to 5 range, there is a reasonable probability that some students who do not have true ADHD could be displaying ADHD-like behaviors. Here's why:

Response 1: Moving too quickly can lose some students who are deep processors. They want to spend more time playing with a concept before going on to the next. If the teacher doesn't allow time for processing, these students may nonetheless stay with the first idea and would thus be off task or become defiant about moving on. Slowing down and allowing processing time is more likely to lead to retention of learning.

Response 2: Fewer of today's students learn best by listening. They have been raised in a culture that emphasizes rapidly changing visual impact. Too much teacher talk will drive some students to create visual representations of their own (doodling) and thus they will appear off task. Using a multisensory approach is more likely to keep more students focused.

Response 3: When some students are hidden from the teacher's sight, they can resort to off-task behavior or get into mischief, especially if there are no chances for student participation in the lesson. Classroom seating arrangements should ensure that every student can be seen by the teacher.

Response 4: When each teacher determines the rules of behavior in each classroom, chances are high for rules to change from one teacher to the next (elementary) or from classroom to classroom (secondary). Students may then perceive the application and enforcement of discipline as arbitrary, which can result in defiance. Schools with low disciplinary problems are generally those with a few rules that all teachers enforce.

Response 5: Brain research is showing the importance of movement in opening neural pathways. More students today need movement to focus. Keeping them in their seats for long periods of time may encourage some students to fidget, squirm, or get up on their own, typical signs of ADHD-like behavior.

Response 6: Many secondary students come to school with less sleep than they need. Low lights will cause them to get drowsy and thus appear inattentive. How many sleep-deprived teachers might nod off under the same circumstances? Would that mean that the teachers have ADHD? Keep the lights on!

Avoid School-Created ADHD-Like Behavior—Continued

Response 7:   Textbooks are helpful instructional tools, but they are rarely novel. When they are the main focus of instruction, students can drift and resort to other off-task behaviors. Using a variety of information sources, including the textbook, is far more interesting.

Response 8:   Many of today's students see the copying of information from a board as boring busywork. Discussing the information in groups with "What if...?" scenarios is far more intriguing and will less likely lead to off-task behavior.

Response 9:   More students are coming to school hoping to get their emotional needs met, mainly because this is not happening at home. Educators must recognize the importance of maintaining a purposeful, positive emotional climate in schools and classrooms. Brain research is showing us that survival ("Am I *safe* here?") and emotional needs ("Am I *wanted* here?") must be met before we can expect students to focus on the curriculum.

Changes in school operations and teacher behavior that adjust those responses in the 3 to 5 range toward the 1 to 2 range may decrease the incidence of ADHD-like behavior in students.

Strategies to Consider

General Guidelines for Working with ADHD/ADD Students

✓ **Provide the student with a structured, predictable, and welcoming environment.** As part of this environment,
- Display rules and make sure students understand them
- Post daily schedules and assignments in a clear manner
- Call attention to any schedule changes
- Set specific times for specific tasks
- Design a quiet workspace that students can use on request
- Seat problem students near positive peer models
- Plan academic subjects for the morning hours
- Provide regularly scheduled and frequent breaks during which students can stretch
- Use attention-getting devices, such as secret signals, color codes, etc.
- Do a countdown for the last several minutes of an activity
- If a student starts getting disruptive, ask the student to read or answer a question
- Sincerely praise students for constructive things they have done during the day
- Shift the focus away from competition to contribution, enjoyment, and satisfaction
- Contact parents to report good news and build a supportive relationship

✓ **Modify the Curriculum.** ADHD/ADD students (as all students) can often benefit from the notion that less is more. If a student can demonstrate proficiency after 10 problems, then don't assign 20. Curriculum modification can also include the following:
- Mixing activities of high and low interest
- Avoiding more than 20 minutes of seatwork or inactivity
- Providing computerized learning materials
- Simplifying and increasing visual presentations
- Teaching organization and study skills
- Using memory strategies, such as mnemonic devices
- Using visual references for auditory instruction
- Giving students simple decisions to make during the day to build this skill
- Explaining your decision to students and having them explain theirs to you
- Writing tests with easier questions dispersed throughout to keep motivation high

Strategies to Consider

Getting, Focusing, and Maintaining Attention

The greatest challenges for the teacher of ADHD/ADD students are to get their attention, focus it towards a learning objective, and maintain that attention during the learning episode. The following are some suggested activities for each of these steps (Rief, 1998).

Getting Student Attention

✓ Use auditory signals, such a ringing a bell, using a beeper or timer, or playing a bar of music on the piano.

✓ Use visual signals, such as raising your hand or flashing the lights, to indicate the time for silence; or say "Everybody...ready."

✓ Use color. Use colored markers on white board or on overhead transparencies. Colored paper can be used to highlight key words, steps, or patterns.

✓ Use eye contact. Students should face you when you are speaking to them, especially when you give instructions.

✓ Use story-telling and humor. Add a bit of mystery to your story and ask students to guess the ending (orally or in writing). Use props to pique interest.

✓ Start a lesson with an interesting question or problem, and model enthusiasm and excitement about the upcoming lesson.

✓ If using an overhead, place an object on it to get attention. Frame important points with your hands or a colored box.

– Continued –

Getting, Focusing, and Maintaining Attention—Continued

Focusing Student Attention

- Use the overhead projector frequently when giving direct instruction. It helps focus attention and you can write on it without turning your back to the students. You can write in color, place objects on it for interest, frame important points, and cover up irrelevant information. Be sure to remove any distracting material from the screen to avoid confusion. Use a stick or laser pointer to draw attention to the material on which you want students to focus.

- Use multisensory strategies during your presentation. Maintain your visibility and make sure you can be heard by all students.

- Be aware of competing sounds in your environment, such as noisy ventilators or outside traffic, and try to limit their distraction.

- Use illustrations and encourage students to draw as much as possible. The drawings do not have to be accurate or sophisticated, just clear enough to understand a concept. Have fun with this. Even silly illustrations can help students remember a series of events, key points, steps in problem solving, or abstract information.

- Use graphic organizers that are partially filled in. Have students enter information as you proceed through the lesson. Carefully choose the organizer that appropriately shows relationships between and among ideas contained in the lesson.

- Incorporate demonstrations and hands-on activities whenever possible.

- Position all students so they can easily see the board or screen. Encourage them to readjust their seating whenever their view is blocked.

Getting, Focusing, and Maintaining Attention—Continued

Maintaining Student Attention

☺ Present with a lively, brisk pace and keep moving to maintain your visibility. Avoid lag time in instruction.

☺ Talk less. Talk is a powerful memory device so give students opportunities to converse with each other about what they are learning. Maintain accountability by asking them to share with you what they learned from their partner.

☺ Use pictures, diagrams, manipulatives, gestures, and high-interest materials.

☺ Ask higher-order thinking questions that are open-ended, require reasoning, and stimulate critical thinking and discussion.

☺ Vary the way you call on students so they cannot predict who is next. Encourage them to share answers orally with a partner or a group, or write them down in a journal.

☺ Use the proper structure of cooperative learning groups. ADHD students do not usually function well without the clearly defined structures and expectations that cooperative learning techniques provide.

☺ Allow students to use individual chalk or dry-erase boards, which are motivating and effective in checking for understanding and in determining who needs extra help and practice.

☺ Use motivating computer programs that provide frequent feedback and self-correction for skill-building and practice.

Strategies to Consider

Strategies for Specific ADHD/ADD Behaviors

For Excessive Activity	For Inability to Wait	For Failure to Sustain Attention to Routine Tasks and Activities
Channel activity into acceptable avenues. For example, rather than attempting to reduce a student's activity, encourage directed movement in classrooms when this is not disruptive. Allow standing during seatwork, especially at the end of a task.	Give the student substitute verbal or motor responses to make while waiting. This might include teaching the student how to continue on easier parts of the task (or a substitute task) while waiting for the teacher's help.	Decrease the length of the task. There are many ways to do this, including breaking one task into smaller parts to be completed at different times, or just assigning fewer tasks or problems.
Use activity as a reward. For example, to reward appropriate behavior, allow the student to run an errand, clean the board, or organize the teacher's desk.	When possible, permit daydreaming or planning while the student waits. For example, the student might be allowed to doodle or play with some objects while waiting. Another option is to show the student how to underline or record relevant information.	Make tasks interesting. For example, allow students to work with partners or in small groups; use an overhead projector or other device; or alternate high and low interest activities. Novelty can often sustain interest. Make a game out of checking students' work, and use games to help in learning rote material.
Use active responses in instruction. Teaching activities that encourage active responses (e.g., moving, talking, organizing, writing in a diary, painting, or working at the board) are helpful to ADHD students.	When inability to wait becomes impatience, encourage leadership. Do not assume that impulsive statements or behavior are aggressive in intent. Cue the student when an upcoming task will be difficult and extra control will be needed.	

Strategies for Specific ADHD/ADD Behaviors—Continued

For Noncompliance and Failure to Complete Tasks	For Difficulty at the Beginning of Tasks	For Completing Assignments on Time
Make sure the tasks fit within the student's learning abilities and preferred response style. Students are more likely to complete tasks when they are allowed to respond in various ways, such as with a computer, on an overhead, on tape. Make sure that disorganization is not the reason the student is failing to complete tasks.	Increase the structure of the tasks and highlight the important parts. This includes encouraging more note-taking, giving directions orally as well as in writing, clearly stating the standards for acceptable work, and pointing out how tasks are structured (e.g., topic sentences, headers, table of contents, index).	Increase the student's use of lists and assignment organizers (notebook, folders). Write assignments on the board and make sure that the student has copied them.
Find ways to increase the choice and specific interest of tasks for the student. Consider allowing the student with ADHD a selection of specific tasks, topics, and activities. Determine which activities the student prefers and use these as incentives.	Ask the student to write down the steps needed to get the task started and have the student review the steps orally.	Establish routines to place and retrieve commonly used objects, such as books, assignments, and clothes. Pocket folders are helpful because new work can be placed on one side and completed work on the other. Parents can be encouraged to establish places for certain things (e.g., books, homework) at home. Students can be encouraged to organize their desk or locker with labels and places for certain items.
		Teach students that, upon leaving one place for another, they will ask themselves, "Do I have everything I need?"

(Adapted from Fowler, 1994)

Strategies to Consider

Using Mnemonics to Help Retention

Mnemonics (from the Greek *to remember*) are very useful devices for remembering unrelated information, patterns, or rules. They were developed by the ancient Greeks to recall dialogue in plays and for passing information to others when writing was impractical. There are many types of mnemonic schemes that will assist memory challenged ADHD/ADD students. Here are two examples that can be easily used in the classroom. Work with students to develop schemes appropriate for the content.

✓ **Rhyming Mnemonics.** Rhymes are simple yet effective ways to remember rules and patterns. They work because if you forget part of the rhyme or get part of it wrong, the words lose their rhyme or rhythm and signal the error. To retrieve the missing or incorrect part, you start the rhyme over again, which helps you relearn it because each line serves as the auditory cue for the next line.

Common examples of rhymes we have learned are "*I* before *e*, except after *c* ...," "Thirty days hath September ...," and "Columbus sailed the ocean blue ...." Here are some rhymes that can help students learn information in other areas:

**The Spanish Armada met its fate
In fifteen hundred and eighty-eight.**

**Divorced, beheaded, died;
Divorced, beheaded, survived.**
(the fate of Henry VIII's six wives, in chronological order)

**The number you are dividing by,
Turn upside down and multiply.**
(rule for dividing by fractions)

Using Mnemonics to Help Retention—Continued

This may seem like a clumsy system, but it works. Make up your own rhyme, alone or with the class, to help you and your students remember more information faster.

✓ **Reduction Mnemonics:** In this scheme, you reduce a large body of information to a shorter form and use a letter to represent each shortened piece. The letters are either combined to form a real or artificial word or are used to construct a simple sentence. For example, the real word **HOMES** can help us remember the names of the great lakes (Huron, Ontario, Michigan, Erie, and Superior). The name **ROY G BIV** aids in remembering the seven colors of the spectrum (red, orange, yellow, green, blue, indigo, and violet). The artificial word **NATO** recalls North Atlantic Treaty Organization. The sentence **My Very Earnest Mother Just Served Us Nine Pizzas** can help us remember the nine planets of the solar system in order from the sun (Mercury, Venus, Earth, Mars, Jupiter, Saturn, Uranus, Neptune, and Pluto). Here are other examples:

Please Excuse My Dear Aunt Sally.
(the order for solving algebraic equations: Parenthesis, Exponents, Multiplication, Division, Addition, Subtraction)

Frederick Charles Goes Down And Ends Battle.
(F, C, G, D, A, E, B: the order that sharps are entered in key signatures; reverse the order for flats)

In Poland, Men Are Tall.
(the stages of cell division in mitosis: Interphase, Prophase, Metaphase, Anaphase, and Telophase)

Krakatoa Positively Casts Off Fumes, Generally Sulfurous Vapors.
(the descending order of zoological classifications: Kingdom, Phylum, Class, Order, Family, Genus, Species, Variety)

King Henry Doesn't Mind Drinking Cold Milk.
(the descending order of metric prefixes: Kilo-, Hecto-, Deca-, (measure), Deci-, Centi-, and Milli-)

Note: This strategy is adapted from Sousa, D.A. (2001). *How the Brain Learns* (2nd ed.). Thousand Oaks, CA: Corwin Press, pp. 131-132.

Strategies to Consider

Tips for Parents of ADHD/ADD Children

Parents of children with ADHD/ADD sometimes feel overwhelmed by the challenges associated with these disorders. However, the following tips, suggested by the National Information Center for Children and Youth with Disabilities (Fowler, 1994), may give parents some help in dealing with their children. Teachers and parents should work together to develop a consistent plan for responding to the child's needs.

❑ Learn about ADHD/ADD. The more you know, the more you can help yourself and your child.

❑ Praise your child when he or she does well. Talk about your child's strengths and talents.

❑ Be clear, consistent, and positive. Set clear rules that tell your child what *to do*, not just what *not* to do. Be clear about what will happen if the rules are not followed. Praise good behavior and reward it.

❑ Learn about strategies for managing your child's behavior. These include the techniques of charting, having a reward program, ignoring behaviors, natural consequences, logical consequences, and time-out. Using these strategies will lead to more positive behaviors and cut down on problem behaviors.

❑ Talk with your doctor about whether medication will help your child, getting second opinions if your questions go unanswered. **Caution:** Some people claim that ADHD/ADD can be treated primarily with megavitamins, chiropractic scalp massage, allergy treatments, and unusual diets. Be aware that these treatments have not yet stood up to scientific scrutiny. However, as new evidence emerges, an integrated approach of various treatments might be considered.

❑ Pay attention to your child's mental health—and your own! Be open to counseling. It can help you deal with the challenges of raising a child with

Tips for Parents of ADHD/ADD Children—Continued

ADHD/ADD. It can also help your child deal with frustration, have greater self-esteem, and learn more about social skills.

❑ Talk to other parents whose children have ADHD/ADD and share practical advice and emotional support. Look at the resources and organizations at the end of this book for more help.

❑ Meet with school officials to develop an educational plan to address your child's needs. Both you and your child's teacher should get a written copy of this plan.

❑ Keep in touch with your child's teacher to find out how your child is doing in school. Offer support. Tell the teacher how your child is doing at home.

❑ Remember that as researchers continue their investigations, we may gain new knowledge that could change some of our current understandings and beliefs about the nature of ADHD and ADD, resulting in the development of alternative treatments. Keep abreast of what is happening in this field through some of the organizations listed in the resources section of this book.

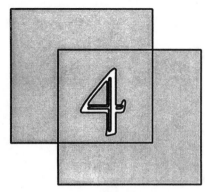

SPEECH DISABILITIES

Human beings have developed an elaborate and complex means of spoken communication that many say is largely responsible for our place as the dominant species on this planet. Spoken language is truly a marvelous accomplishment for many reasons. At the very least, it gives form to our memories and words to express our thoughts. The human voice can pronounce about 200 vowel and 600 consonant sounds that allow it to speak any of the estimated 6,500

Some Specialized Areas of the Brain

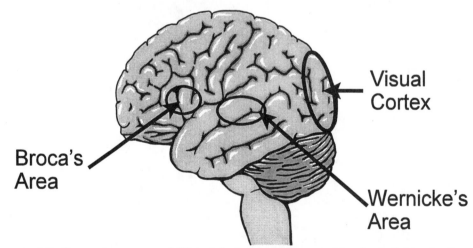

Figure 4.1 *Broca's area and Wernicke's area, located in the left hemisphere, are the two major language processing centers of the brain. The visual cortex, across the back of both hemispheres, processes visual stimuli.*

languages (not counting dialects) that exist today. With practice, the voice becomes so fine-tuned that it makes only about one sound error per million sounds and one word error per million words.

Before the advent of scanning technologies, we explained how the brain produced spoken language on the basis of evidence from injured brains. In 1861, French surgeon Paul Broca noted that damage to the left frontal lobe induced language difficulties generally known as *aphasia*, wherein patients muttered sounds or lost speech completely. Broca's area (just behind the left temple) is about the size of a quarter (Figure 4.1). A person with damage to Broca's area, for example, could understand language but could not speak fluently. In 1871, German neurologist Carl Wernicke described a different type of aphasia—one in which patients could not make sense of words they spoke or heard. These patients had damage in the left temporal lobe. Wernicke's area (above the left ear) is about the size of a silver dollar. Those with damage to Wernicke's area could speak fluently, but what they said was quite meaningless. The inferences, then, were that Broca's area stored vocabulary, grammar, and probably syntax of one's native language, while Wernicke's area was the site of native language sense and meaning.

But more recent research, using scanners, indicates that spoken language production is a far more complex process than previously thought. When preparing to produce a spoken sentence, the brain uses not only Broca's and Wernicke's areas, but also calls on several other neural networks scattered throughout the left hemisphere. Nouns are processed through one set of patterns; verbs are processed by separate neural networks. The more complex the sentence structure, the more areas that are activated, including the right hemisphere.

Learning Spoken Language

Is Language Prewired in the Brain?

In the 1950s, MIT linguist Noam Chomsky theorized that young children could not possibly learn the rules of language grammar and syntax merely by imitating adults. He proposed that nature endowed humans with the ability to acquire their native language by attaching what they hear to a language template that is prewired in the brain by birth—just as baby tigers are prewired to learn how to hunt. Other linguists now suggest that language acquisition may be the result of some genetic predisposition coupled with the baby brain's incredible ability to sort through the enormous amount of information it takes in—including language—and to identify regular patterns. Although the debate over how much language is prewired is far from over, researchers are gaining remarkable insights into how and when the young brain masters

> *The human brain is prewired at birth to learn all the languages on this planet.*

language. Figure 4.2 shows some of the major milestones of spoken language development during the first 36 months.

Spoken Language Development

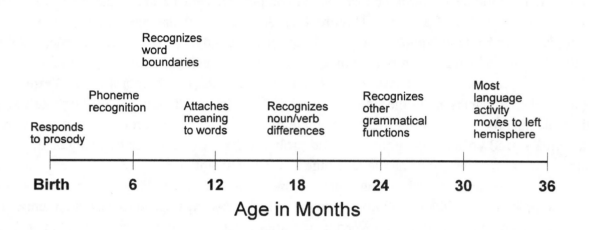

Figure 4.2 *An average timeline of spoken language development during the child's first 3 years. Considerable variation exists among individual children. (Sousa, 2001, p. 179)*

Learning Sounds Called Phonemes. The neurons in a baby's brain are capable of responding to the sounds of all the languages on this planet. At birth (some say even before) babies respond first to the *prosody*—the rhythm, cadence, and pitch—of their mother's voice, not the words. Spoken language consists of minimal units of sound, called *phonemes*, which combine to form syllables. For example, in English, the consonant sound "p" and the vowel sound "o" are both phonemes that combine to form the syllable *po-* as in *potato*.

Each language has its own set of phonemes. Surprisingly, however, the total number of phonemes used by all the world's languages is only about 90. This number represents the maximum number of sounds that the human vocal apparatus can produce. Although the infant's brain can perceive this entire range of phonemes, only those that are repeated get attention, and the neurons reacting to the unique sound patterns get continually stimulated and reinforced.

By the age of 10 to 12 months, the toddler's brain has begun to distinguish and remember phonemes of the native language and to ignore foreign sounds. For example, one study (Cheour, Ceponiene, Lehtokoski, Luuk, Allik, Alho, and Näätänen, 1998) showed that at the age of 6 months, American and Japanese babies are equally good at discriminating between the "l" and "r" sounds, even though Japanese has no "l" sound. However, by age 10 months, Japanese babies have a tougher time making the distinction, while American babies have become much better at it. During this and subsequent periods of growth, the ability to distinguish native sounds improves, while one's ability to distinguish nonnative speech sounds diminishes.

From Phonemes to Words. The next step for the brain is to detect words from the stream of sounds it is processing. This is not an easy task because people don't pause between words when speaking. Yet the brain has to recognize differences between, say, *green house* and *greenhouse*. Remarkably, babies begin to distinguish word boundaries by the age of 8 months even though they don't know what the words mean (Van Petten and Bloom, 1999). They begin to acquire new vocabulary words at the rate of about 10 a day. At the same time, memory and Wernicke's areas are becoming fully functional so the child can now attach meaning to words. Of course, learning words is one skill; putting them together to make sense is another, more complex skill.

Learning Grammar. Chomsky believed that all languages contain some common rules that dictate how sentences are constructed, and that the brain has preprogrammed circuits that respond to these rules. Modern linguists think that the brain may not be responding so much to basic language rules as to statistical regularities heard in the flow of the native tongue. They soon discern that some words describe objects while others describe actions. Toddlers detect patterns of word order—person, action, object—so they can soon say, "I want cookie." Other grammar features emerge, such as tense, and by the age of 3, over 90 percent of sentences uttered are grammatically correct. Errors are seldom random, but usually result from following perceived rules of grammar. If "I batted the ball" makes sense, why shouldn't "I holded the bat?" Regrettably, the toddler has yet to learn that nearly 200 of the most commonly used verbs in English are irregularly conjugated.

> *The more that children are exposed to spoken language in the early years, the more quickly they can discriminate between phonemes and recognize word boundaries.*

During the following years, practice in speaking and adult correction help the child decode some of the mysteries of grammar's irregularities and a sophisticated language system emerges from what once was babble. No one knows how much grammar a child learns just by listening, or how much is prewired. What is certain is that the more children are exposed to spoken language in the early years, the more quickly they can discriminate between phonemes and recognize word boundaries.

Effects of Television. Just letting the toddler sit in front of a television does not seem to accomplish this goal, probably because the child's brain needs live human interaction to attach meaning to the words. Moreover, television talk is not the slow, expressive speech that parents use with their infants, which infants like and want to hear. Although toddlers may be attracted to the rapidly changing sounds and images on a television, little or no language development is in progress. Further evidence indicates that prolonged television watching can impair the growth of young brains. Susan Johnson, a pediatrician at the University of California, San Francisco, cites several studies that raise concerns over the effects of television viewing on young minds (Johnson, 1999). These studies point out that the visual system is not stimulated properly by television viewing in that there is no pupil dilation and the eyes stare at the screen and do not move from one point to the next—a skill critical for reading. The images change every 5 to 6 seconds (even faster during commercials) robbing the higher-thought areas of the brain (in the frontal lobe) of time to process the images. The wavelengths of light produced by the television tube's phosphors are very limited compared to the full spectrum of light we receive when viewing objects outdoors. Furthermore, television reduces the opportunities for the child's brain to create internal images.

Putting It All Together. The successful use of oral language requires the brain to produce sounds that follow a certain set of patterns and rules for

- ▸ phonology—phonemes (the smallest sounds of language)
- ▸ morphology—word formation
- ▸ syntax—sentence formation
- ▸ semantics—word and sentence meaning, especially idioms
- ▸ prosody—intonation and rhythm of speech
- ▸ pragmatics—effective use of language for different purposes, following rules of conversation, and staying on topic

Amazingly, most brains get it right. But problems can occur anywhere along the way. Some problems may just be a matter of time, i.e., the brain needs more time to discern the patterns and figure out the rules. More persistent problems may be due to physiological difficulties (e.g., hearing loss), childhood trauma (physical or psychological), genetic influences, or other factors not yet understood.

Problems in Learning Spoken Language

Language Problems With Children and Pre-Adolescents

Language Delay. Most toddlers begin to speak words around the age of 10 to 12 months. However, in delayed speech, children may not speak coherent words and phrases until nearly 2 years of age. The evidence

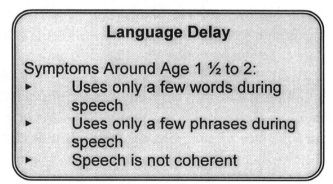

Language Delay

Symptoms Around Age 1 ½ to 2:
- ▸ Uses only a few words during speech
- ▸ Uses only a few phrases during speech
- ▸ Speech is not coherent

70

suggests that a language delay to 2 years is inherited, thus representing a distinct disorder not easily remedied by environmental interventions (Dale, Simonoff, Bishop, Eley, Oliver, Price, Purcell, Stevenson, and Plomin, 1998). This revelation diminishes the claim some people make that environmental influences cause most language delay. However, certain environmental factors, such as stress, *can* cause language delay in some children.

Specific Language Impairment. A broad range of problems in learning language are grouped in the category often referred to as specific language impairment (SLI). It describes a general condition in which a child's spoken language does not develop at the expected and acceptable rate, even though the person's sensory and cognitive systems appear normal and there is no apparent environmental problem. Parents may first become aware of SLI when their children fail to demonstrate the normal bursts of language development that occur around the age of two years. Many of these children will eventually achieve normal levels of language development during

> **Specific Language Impairment**
>
> Symptoms:
> - Complexity of speech not developing with age
> - Little or no growth in vocabulary
> - Consistently poor grammar with little or no improvement
> - Difficulty remembering recently used words

the subsequent two years. However, some will continue to display language difficulties at school age, having difficulty building vocabulary as well as difficulty acquiring written language.

Although most of the cognitive functions of children with SLI are normal, verbal memory deficits often occur. Montgomery (2000) tested the verbal memory of a group of SLI and non-SLI children on word recall and sentence comprehension. He found that children with SLI had less functional verbal working memory capacity and greater difficulty managing their working memory abilities than their non-SLI peers. A study by Weismer, Evans, and Hesketh (1999) also found similar verbal working memory deficits in word recall. However, the students with SLI showed no performance difference on language processing tasks involving true/false test items.

> **Expressive Language Disorder**
>
> Symptoms:
> - Below average vocabulary skills
> - Difficulty producing complex sentences
> - Improper use of correct tenses
> - Problems in recalling words

The question is whether SLI has a biological or an environmental basis, or some combination of both. Studies with a large group of SLI children tend to support the notion of a biological basis through genetic influences and seem to point to deficits in the brain systems responsible for grammar and vocabulary processing (Leonard, 1998; Tomblin and Buckwalter, 1998). Therefore, care must be taken in ascribing environmental factors or identifying a single intervention as a cure for SLI. Because many of the children with SLI have little or no cognitive deficit, it would seem that interventions should focus on cognitive strategies that help explain and practice the rules of grammar as well as acquire vocabulary in context.

Some children with SLI also display the symptoms of attention-deficit hyperactivity disorder (ADHD). Recent studies (Williams, Stott, Goodyer, and Sahakian, 2000), however, suggest that these two disorders are not directly connected and originate from deficits in different cerebral systems.

Expressive Language Disorder. Children with this disorder have trouble expressing themselves in speech. They often have a weak vocabulary and difficulty recalling words and constructing complex sentences. Although the cause is unknown, cerebral damage, head trauma, and malnutrition have been associated with the disorder. Treatment usually involves language therapy that focuses on increasing the number of phrases a child can use. The phrases are presented as blocks and the child practices building complex sentences from these blocks. Language therapy and similar treatments show an encouraging recovery rate, especially if interventions are started soon after diagnosis.

Receptive Language Disorder. Those with receptive language disorder have trouble understanding certain aspects of speech. They may not respond to their names, have difficulty following directions, or point to a bell when you say ball. Their hearing is fine, but they can't make sense out of certain sounds, words, or sentences they hear. Sometimes, they may appear inattentive.

Because receiving and using speech are closely related, many people with receptive language disorder also have symptoms of expressive language disorder. The combined symptoms are referred to as Receptive-Expressive Language Disorder.

> **Receptive-Expressive Language Disorder**
>
> Symptoms:
> - Impairment in language comprehension
> - Impairment in language expression
> - Speech contains many articulation errors
> - Difficulty recalling early visual or auditory memories

Language Problems With Adolescents

Problems with language can be particularly troublesome for adolescents because language plays such a major role in all secondary school subjects. The elementary years emphasize language development. The middle school grades begin to focus on specific subjects where mastery of language is assumed. But in high school, teachers expect students to have an increased vocabulary, more advanced sentence structure, and the ability to use different kinds of language for different situations.

Much effort goes into identifying and remediating language problems in young children. Yet less effort seems to be directed toward identifying adolescents with language problems. Such problems can lead to feelings of failure, low self-esteem, poor academic and social success, and a high drop-out rate. Adolescents with language disorders can be those

> ▶ who received no interventions;
> ▶ who initially received treatment through early intervention programs, but who still have some language difficulties;
> ▶ who had normal language development, but experienced a disruption because of some mental, physical, emotional, or traumatic event; and,
> ▶ who have some other learning disability.

Adolescent Language Disorder

Symptoms:
▶ Failure to understand or follow rules of conversation, such as taking turns and staying on topic
▶ Difficulty using different language for different needs of the learner or situation
▶ Difficulty requesting further information to aid understanding
▶ Incorrect use of grammar
▶ Poor or limited vocabulary
▶ Difficulty with instructions, especially those that are long or grammatically complex
▶ Extreme forgetfulness
▶ Difficulty understanding puns, idioms, jokes, riddles

Working with adolescents with language difficulties requires more direct instruction aimed at treating the identified language weakness. Consistent practice is important, but the practice should not be so repetitive as to be perceived as boring. Practice using computer programs creates interest, and success in mastering these programs can enhance self-esteem.

Language and Cognitive Thought. Several studies are providing strong evidence that language and cognitive thought are separated in the brain. One study involved patients with Williams syndrome, a rare genetic disorder first described in 1961. Children with this disorder have difficulty with simple spatial tasks, and many have IQ scores in the 40 to 50 range and cannot read or write above the first-grade level.

Because evidence exists that language and cognitive thought are separated in the brain, we should not assume that students with language problems are not intelligent.

Despite these inadequacies, they develop extraordinary spoken language skills. They amass large vocabularies, can speak in complex, grammatically correct sentences, and often have the gift of gab, and engaging personalities. Coincidently, many children with Williams syndrome exhibit extraordinary musical talent (Lenhoff, Wang, Greenberg, and Bellugi, 1997).

Implications at Home. Given the evidence that the brain's ability to acquire spoken language is at its peak in the early years, parents should create a rich environment that includes lots of communication activities, such as talking, singing, and reading. However, the acquisition of speech and language can be affected by a number of factors, including muscular disorders, hearing problems, or developmental delays. These factors should be investigated if a child demonstrates significant delay or difficulty in speech.

Can Students With Language Deficits Learn a Second Language?

As foreign language study becomes more common in our schools, the question arises: Should students with language difficulties be expected to learn a second language? For students without language difficulties, learning another language can be a rewarding experience that can enrich their lives forever. But for students with language problems, it can be a stressful, if not painful, experience.

Continued research on how the brain learns is revealing some insights into the neural systems responsible for language acquisition. During the 1960s, Kenneth Dinklage (1971) at Harvard University was investigating why some of the brightest students at Harvard could not pass their foreign language classes. The students were highly motivated and devoted enormous amounts of time and effort to studying their languages, but many were still failing. Furthermore, their anxiety over the situation only made the situation worse. After interviews and testing, Dinklage found that some of these students had been diagnosed with language disabilities which they had overcome with considerable effort and tutoring; others had undiagnosed language problems. Taking the university's language classes revealed these problems.

In an unorthodox experiment, Dinklage convinced native language speakers with learning disabilities to teach the troubled students. Most of the students taught in this experiment were able to pass their foreign language classes. Dinklage's work highlighted the basic problem facing language disabled students in foreign language classrooms: The problem is related to being learning disabled, not to any lack of motivation or effort or even to the anxiety produced by the situation. Anxiety was not the cause of failure but the result. Students not previously diagnosed as having language difficulties showed up as such in the foreign language classroom. However, once the instructional methods addressed the language difficulties issues, the students could learn.

In the 1980s, Leonore Ganschow (1995) and Richard Sparks (1993) studied Dinklage's work as well as related research that described language as having three component parts or linguistic codes: phonological, semantic, and syntactic. From this, they developed their own theory, called the Linguistic Coding Deficit Hypothesis. It states that difficulties with the acquisition of foreign language originate from problems in one or more of these linguistic codes in the student's native language system. These problems can result in mild to extreme deficiencies with specific oral and written aspects of language.

> *Language deficits that arise when learning a first language are very likely to arise when learning a second language.*

Not surprisingly, Ganschow and Sparks assert that most learners who experience difficulty with foreign language learning have problems with phonological awareness—the ability to recognize and manipulate the basic sounds of language, called phonemes. Consequently, students who have difficulty recognizing phonemes will also have problems with the interpretation and production of language that is needed for basic understanding, speaking, and spelling.

Ganschow and Sparks maintain that individuals who are very strong in all three linguistic codes will be excellent language learners. Conversely, those who are weak in all three codes will be very poor language learners. In between these extremes lies a spectrum of students who may be very good at spoken language but poor at written language, and other students with the opposite characteristics, and still others with combinations of all the possible linguistic variations.

Because of these great variations in the capabilities of students with language deficits, the following question arises: What do we mean when we say they have *learned* the second language? Some students may become excellent readers of the language but not be able to carry on a simple conversation. Others may have difficulty reading the language but be very fluent in conversation and have a near-native accent. Still others may be able to speak correctly but with an accent that is not even close to that of native speakers.

The important point, nonetheless, is that the difficulties these students have in acquiring a foreign language stem from deficits in their first language. With this knowledge in hand, Ganschow and Sparks developed two approaches to foreign language instruction that have been effective (see **Strategies to Consider** at the end of this chapter).

What Is the Future of Language Disorders Research?

Brain imaging technology is revealing much more about the relationship between exposure to speech and language, brain development, and communication skills. Genetic studies are investigating whether at least some language problems may be inherited. The effect of frequent ear infections on the development of speech and language is also under investigation.

Scientists are trying to distinguish those language problems that may be overcome by maturation alone from those that may require some type of intervention or therapy. Some research is focusing on characterizing dialects that belong to certain ethnic and regional groups. This knowledge will help professionals distinguish a language dialect from a language disorder. The success of these efforts would spare children who are merely slower in developing or speaking a dialect the embarrassment of unnecessary labeling, while concentrating treatment on those who really need it. Another area of study is the effect of language development on later school performance.

Finally, some studies are exploring how the brain acquires a second language either during or after learning one's native language. Understanding which neural systems are involved in learning native and second languages can guide the development of instructional practices that will make it easier for all students to learn more than one language.

What Do Educators Need to Consider?

Educators need to do all of the following:

▸ Address any language-learning problems quickly to take advantage of the brain's ability to rewire improper connections during this important period of growth.

▸ Give more attention to the language problems of adolescents and train secondary school teachers in identifying and addressing language weaknesses.

▸ Accept the notion that students with language difficulties may still be able to learn a second language when taught with the appropriate instructional approaches.

▸ Not assume that children with language-learning problems are going to be limited in cognitive thought processes as well.

The acquisition of oral language is a natural ability that comes more easily to some children than to others. Functional imaging technologies, such as PET and fMRI scans, are allowing a more detailed study of the parts of the brain that are activated during the processing of spoken language. As research reveals more about the amazing process by which we learn to speak languages, parents, educators, and other professionals will be better able to give help to those with language-learning problems.

Impact on Learning

Language disorders can affect learning in the following ways:

- Some language delays are simply the result of delayed maturation and do not represent a permanent disorder.

- Language deficits affecting the acquisition of a native language will likely affect the acquisition of a second language.

- Language deficits will not usually affect a student's cognitive thought processes.

Strategies to Consider

Speech and Language Patterns by Age

The human brain is programmed to learn spoken language during the child's earliest years. As language learning progresses, certain behavior patterns emerge over time forming the building blocks to continued language growth and development. Early language development occurs in context with other skills, such as cognition (thinking, understanding, and problem solving), gross and fine motor coordination (stacking, throwing, catching, and jumping), social interaction (peer contact and group play), and taking care of one's self (washing, eating, and dressing).

The National Institute on Deafness and Other Communication Disorders (NIDCD, 2000) and the Learning Disabilities Association of America (LDA, 2000) have compiled from the research a list of speech and language behaviors that emerge for most children from birth through the age of six years. Each child is different, but the list is a good indicator of speech and language progress for most children.

Birth to 5 Months

- ☺ Reacts to loud sounds
- ☺ Turns head towards a sound source
- ☺ Watches your face when you speak
- ☺ Vocalizes pleasure and displeasure sounds (laughs, giggles, or cries)
- ☺ Makes noise when talked to

Between 6 and 11 Months

- ☺ Recognizes name
- ☺ Says 2-3 words besides "mama" and "dada"
- ☺ Understands simple instructions
- ☺ Imitates familiar sounds
- ☺ Recognizes words as symbols for objects: cat—meows; car—points to garage

Speech and Language Patterns by Age—Continued

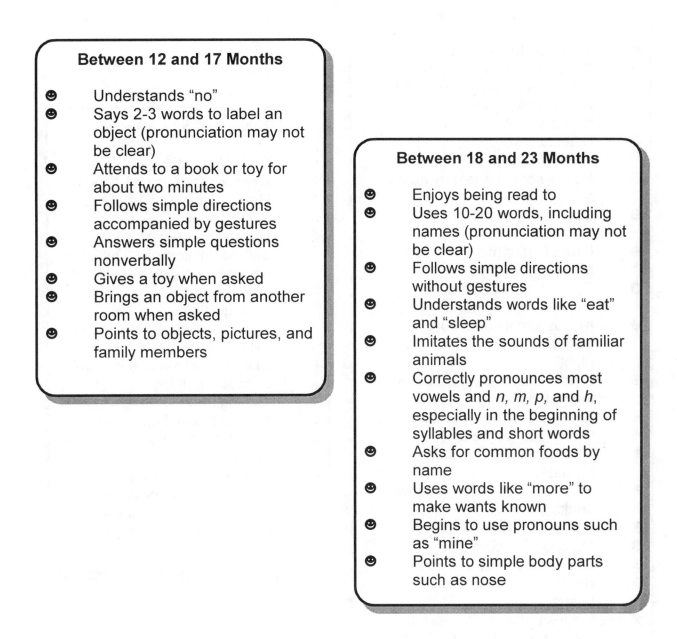

Between 12 and 17 Months

☻ Understands "no"
☻ Says 2-3 words to label an object (pronunciation may not be clear)
☻ Attends to a book or toy for about two minutes
☻ Follows simple directions accompanied by gestures
☻ Answers simple questions nonverbally
☻ Gives a toy when asked
☻ Brings an object from another room when asked
☻ Points to objects, pictures, and family members

Between 18 and 23 Months

☻ Enjoys being read to
☻ Uses 10-20 words, including names (pronunciation may not be clear)
☻ Follows simple directions without gestures
☻ Understands words like "eat" and "sleep"
☻ Imitates the sounds of familiar animals
☻ Correctly pronounces most vowels and *n, m, p,* and *h,* especially in the beginning of syllables and short words
☻ Asks for common foods by name
☻ Uses words like "more" to make wants known
☻ Begins to use pronouns such as "mine"
☻ Points to simple body parts such as nose

– Continued –

Speech and Language Patterns by Age—Continued

Between 2 and 3 Years

- ☺ Identifies body parts
- ☺ Converses with self and dolls
- ☺ Has a vocabulary of over 400 words. Asks questions, such as "What's that?"
- ☺ Uses two-word negative phrases such as "no want"
- ☺ Forms some plurals by adding an "s" to words
- ☺ Uses more pronouns, such as "you" and "I"
- ☺ Gives first name and holds up fingers to tell age
- ☺ Combines nouns and verbs, such as "daddy go"
- ☺ Knows simple time concepts, such as "tomorrow" and "last night"
- ☺ Refers to self as "me" rather than by name
- ☺ Tries to get adult attention with "watch me" phrases
- ☺ Likes to hear same story repeated
- ☺ Talks to other children as well as adults
- ☺ Answers "where" questions
- ☺ Matches 3-4 colors
- ☺ Understands big and little
- ☺ Names common pictures and things
- ☺ Solves problems by talking instead of hitting or crying
- ☺ Uses short sentences, such as "Me want cookie."

Between 3 and 4 Years

- ☺ Can tell a story
- ☺ Uses sentences of 4-5 words
- ☺ Has a vocabulary of about 1000 words
- ☺ Uses most speech sounds but may distort more difficult sounds such as *l, r, s, sh, ch, y, v, z,* and *th*
- ☺ Strangers begin to understand much of what is said
- ☺ Uses verbs that end in "ing," such as "walking" and "talking"
- ☺ Names at least one color
- ☺ Understands "yesterday," "tonight," "summer"
- ☺ Begins to obey requests, like "Put the toy under the chair."
- ☺ Knows last name, name of street, and several nursery rhymes

Speech and Language Patterns by Age—Continued

Between 4 and 5 Years

- ☺ Uses past tense correctly
- ☺ Uses sentences of 4-5 words
- ☺ Has a vocabulary of about 1500 words
- ☺ Defines words
- ☺ Speech is understandable but makes mistakes pronouncing long words such as "hippopotamus"
- ☺ Uses some irregular past tense verbs such as "ran"
- ☺ Names and points to colors red, blue, yellow, and green
- ☺ Identifies triangles, circles, and squares
- ☺ Understands "in the morning," "next," and "noontime"
- ☺ Can talk of imaginary conditions, such as "I hope"
- ☺ Asks many questions, including "who" and "why"

Between 5 and 6 Years

- ☺ Uses sentences of 6-8 words
- ☺ Has a vocabulary of about 2000 words
- ☺ Defines objects by their use (you eat with a fork) and can tell what objects are made of
- ☺ Understands spatial relations like "on top," "behind," "far," and "near"
- ☺ Understands time sequences (what happened first, second)
- ☺ Knows home address
- ☺ Identifies penny, nickel, and dime
- ☺ Understands common opposites like big/little and same/different
- ☺ Counts ten objects
- ☺ Asks questions for information
- ☺ Distinguishes the left and right hand
- ☺ Uses complex sentences, for example, "Let's go to the park after we eat"
- ☺ Uses imagination to create stories

As a precaution, a child who is more than a year delayed should be examined by medical professionals for possible systemic problems, such as hearing loss. Remember that many children who have early speech and language delays eventually catch up to their developmental stage by the time they enter school.

Strategies to Consider

Developing Oral Language Skills

Spoken language comes naturally to the young brain. But to master the language, the brain must first consistently *hear* it. Infants and young children hear the sounds of language and begin to make connections between words and objects or actions. At this point, speech is not necessary. The brain is acquiring vocabulary and making the associations that will give the child the words and patterns it will later need to speak the language. *Listening*, then, is the groundwork for speech and eventually for reading skills.

Recent research confirms that the young brain is fully ready to learn through tactile (touch) interaction by nine months of age. The neural networks for abstract thinking, including math and logic, are set to begin shortly thereafter. Thus, the ability to process language, sounds, music, and rhythms is functional before the age of one year. The parent is the first teacher, and what the parent does to nurture oral language skills in the early years may well set the stage for the child's future success in school. Because some language deficits are eventually overcome, the sooner the child's language skills are engaged and practiced, the greater the likelihood that the time required to correct the deficits will be reduced. Parents, teachers, and staff in early childhood centers can enhance the development of the child's oral language skills through the following activities suggested by Diamond and Hopson (1998) and the Learning Disabilities Association of America.

1. Talk to the child

- ◆ Talk to the child whenever you are together.
- ◆ Talk about the day's events, a book the child has read, a story the child has heard, or the traffic signs along the highway. Tell the child whatever you are doing.
- ◆ Ask the child to explain any activity you are doing at home, such as ironing, trimming bushes, or sorting laundry. Don't settle for single-word or short answers.
- ◆ Ask the child to point out objects in the environment and name them. Describe the characteristics of an object (long, yellow, and tasty), and ask the child to name it (banana).

Developing Oral Language Skills—Continued

2. Read to the child	♦ Read aloud at least 20 minutes every day while the child is sitting in your lap. ♦ Take turns talking about what was read. ♦ For a child with limited attention span, provide books with large, colorful pictures and few words. ♦ Ask the child to point out objects in the book as you read its name. Vary some of the phrases, like "cat in the hat" and "cat on the mat," to see if the child can hear the difference.
3. Reading books should be an interactive experience	♦ Discuss the book's pictures and paraphrase its story. ♦ Let the child make up a version of what will happen next in the story. ♦ If the story is familiar, allow the child to finish telling key events or to give the succeeding rhyme. ♦ Give the child an opportunity to correct you by purposely misreading or omitting items and events. ♦ Have the child point out words as you read them. ♦ Act out the story or create a puppet show. ♦ Reinforce sequential reading by starting at the beginning of the page and showing the direction of written text, from left to right and top to bottom of page.
4. Cultivate phonological awareness with auditory and visual word games	♦ Play rhyming games: If a child does not hear the rhyme, try a game with words that begin with the same sound. ♦ Play the broken record game: Say a word very slowly and break it into syllables, then have the child repeat the word at a normal speed. ♦ Pick a game the child enjoys, such as matching letters or copying the names of famous people. ♦ Have the child draw pictures and make up a story while you write it down.

– Continued –

Developing Oral Language Skills—Continued

5. Learning starts with a one-to-one match, followed by patterns and sequence

♦ Children learn to count and learn the letters of the alphabet long before they make connections to arithmetic and reading. Use activities with the child that involve counting: "Bring me one cup and two plates. Put the napkin next to one plate." Have the child repeat the instructions and match the items to the number you requested.

♦ Have the child match letters to items in the room that begin with that letter, such as *l* for lamp and *p* for pencil. Make sure the child repeats the letter and the word aloud and walks or points to the object.

♦ Move on to activities that involve patterns and sequence. Posters, checkers, dominos, and playing cards are strong symbols of patterns and sequence. The child doesn't have to learn the game to be able to identify patterns and sequences in the game pieces.

6. Provide a print-rich home and school environment

♦ Children with oral language difficulties are very likely to have problems learning to read. The sooner that they can make connections between oral language and the written word, the better. Other media, such as videotapes, audiotapes, and the computer, can help with the effort of learning to read by making it fun and worthwhile.

♦ Keep television watching to a minimum.

Strategies to Consider

Teaching Foreign Languages to Students With Language Disabilities

Research studies are identifying the problems language disabled students have with acquiring a second language. Armed with this knowledge, we can design instructional approaches that address the underlying causes and increase the chances for student success. Specifically, two approaches to foreign language instruction for language disabled students emerged from the work of Ganschow and Sparks (1995).

1. The Phonological Deficits Approach. This approach springs from the notion that most students having difficulty in acquiring a foreign language have phonological deficits in their native (first) language. Consequently, the following guidelines are suggested:

♦ **Teach the sound system of the foreign language explicitly.** The Orton-Gillingham method (explained in Ganschow and Sparks, 1995) is a particularly effective way to accomplish this. This method presents sounds in a highly structured fashion, accompanied by considerable visual, kinesthetic, and tactile practice and input. Studies using this method showed that students who were taught phonological skills in one language had improved their phonological awareness in English as well.

♦ **Teach the fundamentals of phonology in the student's native language before beginning instruction in the foreign language.** This step helps to address the students' native language deficits, which we already noted as necessary for success in acquiring the foreign language. Here students are taught to recognize phonemes, to read words efficiently, and to apply the sounds to the written language. They are learning the sounds and components of language structure and how these sounds and components are manipulated for meaning.

♦ **Apply the fundamentals of phonology to the foreign language.** In this step, the sounds and components of the foreign language are identified. The

– Continued –

85

Teaching Foreign Languages to Students With Language Disabilities —Continued

students can then transfer the knowledge they have about phonology from their first language to the second language.

2. The Course Adaptation Approach. Essentially, this approach adapts the foreign language courses to conform to those principles of instruction suitable for students with learning disabilities. It can be done in two ways:

♦ **Changing the Instructional Strategies.** Teachers in these courses reduce the syllabus to the essential components, slow the pace of instruction, reduce the vocabulary demand, provide constant review and practice, and incorporate as many multisensory activities as possible.

♦ **Designing Courses to Address Specific Deficits.** Courses can be adapted to respond to the specific requests of the foreign language students who are having difficulties in their classes. For example, one course might be designed for students who are strong in listening and speaking skills but weak in reading and writing, while another course might be more appropriate for students whose skills are in the reverse order.

For either of these approaches to work effectively, students need to undergo a realistic assessment of their language learning problems. It becomes important to ensure that the learning environment is consistent with students' needs. For example, a student who is able to do oral language well should not be placed in a situation where passing grammar and translation tests is the main requirement. Nor should a student who reads and translates proficiently be placed with a teacher who values pronunciation and conversation. Reasonable accommodations need to be made.

It is perhaps unrealistic to assume that most high schools have the capacity or will to devote foreign language classes solely to students with language disabilities. And even if the will were there, finding teachers who are trained in the methods of instruction for these students might be more of a problem. Nonetheless, the purpose of this book is to identify what current research is telling us about the learning process and to suggest ways of providing instructional settings that translate the research into educational practice.

READING DISABILITIES

Renewed emphasis in recent years on improving the basic skills of students has increased pressure to start reading instruction sooner than ever before. In many schools, reading instruction starts in kindergarten. Some neuropsychologists are now debating whether kindergartners are developmentally ready for this challenging task. Are we creating problems for these children by trying to get them to read before their brains are ready? Because boys' brains are physiologically one or two years less mature than girls' brains at this age, are boys at greater risk of failure? To answer these questions, let's examine what researchers have discovered about how the brain learns to read, and the problems that can develop.

Learning to Read

Is Reading a Natural Ability?

Not really. The brain's ability to acquire spoken language with amazing speed and accuracy is the result of genetic hard-wiring and specialized cerebral areas that focus on this task. But there are no areas of the brain that specialize in reading. In fact, reading is probably the most difficult task we ask the young brain to undertake. Reading is a relatively new phenomenon in the development of humans. As far as we know, the genes have not incorporated reading into their coded structure, probably because reading—unlike spoken language —has not emerged over time as a survival skill.

Many cultures (but not all) do emphasize reading as an important form of communication and insist it be taught to their children. And so the struggle begins. To get that brain to read, here's what we are saying, for example, to the English-speaking child: "That language you have been speaking quite correctly for the past few years can be represented by abstract symbols called the *alphabet*. We are going to disrupt that sophisticated spoken language protocol you have already developed and ask you to reorganize it to accommodate these symbols, which, by the way, are not very reliable. There are lots of exceptions, but you'll just have to adjust." Some

> *Reading is probably the most difficult task for the young brain to do.*

children—perhaps 50 percent—make this adjustment with relative ease once exposed to formal instruction. It appears, however, that for the other 50 percent, reading is a much more formidable task, and for about 20 to 30 percent, it definitely becomes the most difficult task they will ever undertake in their lives.

How Does the Brain Read?

To read, the brain must eventually learn to connect abstract symbols to sound bits it already knows. In English, the brain must first learn the alphabet, whose letter names do not always represent their sounds in words. When are *f* or *l* ever pronounced as *ef* or *el* in English? Then the brain must connect those 26 letters to the 44 sounds of spoken English (phonemes) that the child has been using successfully for years. Thus, reading involves a recognition that speech can be broken into small sounds (phonemes) and that these segmented sounds can be represented in print (phonics). Just as the brain thinks it knows what letter represents a phoneme sound, it discovers that the same symbol can have *different* sounds, such as the *a*'s in *cat* and in *father*. Next it learns that a group of letters makes a syllable, but that the same group of letters, say *-ough*, can have multiple sounds, as in *cough, bough, dough,* and *through*. Simple, isn't it?

Unfortunately, the human brain is not born with the insight to make these sound-to-symbol connections, nor does it develop naturally without instruction. Children of literate homes may encounter this instruction before coming to school. Others, however, do not have this opportunity before coming to school. For them, classroom instruction needs to focus on making the phoneme-phonics connections before reading can be successful. If children cannot hear the "-at" sound in *bat* and *hat* and perceive that the

> *Just because some children have difficulty understanding that spoken words are composed of discrete sounds doesn't mean that they have brain damage or dysfunction.*

difference lies in the first sound, then they will have difficulty decoding and sounding out words quickly and correctly.

Researchers using brain imaging techniques are getting a clearer picture of the cerebral processes involved in reading: The word (for example, *dog*) is first recorded in the visual cortex (Figure 5.1), then decoded by a structure on the left side of the brain called the angular gyrus, which separates it into its basic sounds, or phonemes (e.g., the letters *d-o-g* are pronounced "duh, awh, guh"). This process activates Broca's area so that the word can be identified. The brain's vocabulary store and reasoning and concept formation abilities, along with activity in Wernicke's area, combine to provide meaning, producing the thought of a furry animal that barks (Shaywitz, 1996). All this occurs in a fraction of a second.

Keep in mind that although the process outlined in Figure 5.1 appears linear and singular, it is really bidirectional and parallel, with many phonemes being processed at the same time. That the brain learns to read at all attests to its remarkable ability to sift through seemingly confusing input and establish patterns and systems. For a few children, this process comes naturally; most have to be taught (Sousa, 2001).

How the Brain Reads

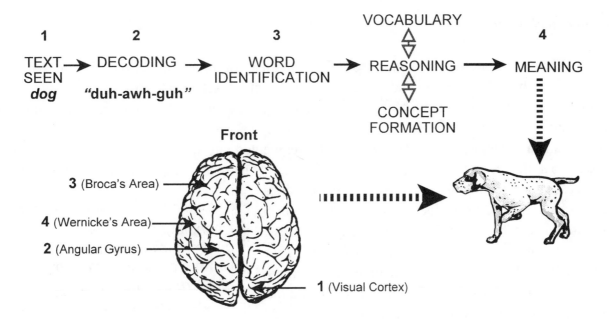

Figure 5.1 *In reading the word* dog *it is first seen (1), then decoded into its phonological elements (2), and identified (3). The higher-level functions of reasoning and concept formation provide the meaning (4) and produce the thought of a furry animal that barks. (Sousa, 2001, p. 184)*

The neural systems that perceive the phonemes in our language are more efficient in some children than in others. Just because some children have difficulty understanding that spoken words are composed of discrete sounds doesn't mean that they have brain damage or dysfunction. The individual differences that underlie the efficiency with which one learns to read can be seen in the acquisition of other skills, such as learning to play a musical instrument, playing a sport, or building a model. To some extent, neural efficiency is related to genetic composition, but these genetic factors can be modified by the environment.

Learning to read, therefore, starts with phoneme awareness, a recognition that written spellings represent sounds (called the alphabetic principle), and that this combination applies phonics to the reading and spelling of words. These skills are *necessary* but not *sufficient* to learn to read the English language with meaning. The reader must also become proficient in grasping larger units of print, such as syllable patterns, whole words, and phrases. The ultimate goal of reading is for children to become sufficiently fluent to understand what they read. This understanding includes literal comprehension as well as more sophisticated reflective understandings, such as "Why am I reading this?" and "What is the author's point?"

Phonological Awareness

What Is Phonological Awareness? Phonological awareness is the recognition that oral language can be divided into smaller components, such as sentences into words, words into syllables and, ultimately, individual phonemes. Being phonologically aware means having an understanding of all these levels. In children, phonological awareness usually starts with initial rhyming and a recognition that sentences can be segmented into words. Next comes segmenting words into syllables and blending syllables into words. The most complex level of phonological awareness is phonemic awareness—the understanding that words are made up of individual sounds and that these sounds can be manipulated to create new words.

Phonological awareness is different from phonics. Phonological awareness involves the auditory and oral manipulation of sounds. Phonics builds on the alphabetic principle and associates letters and sounds

> *Phonological awareness is different from phonics. The two are closely related, but they are not the same.*

with written symbols. The two are closely related, but they are not the same. Recognition of rhyming and alliteration are usual indications that a child has phonological awareness, which develops when children are read to from books based on rhyme or alliteration. But this awareness does not easily develop into the more sophisticated phonemic awareness, which is so closely related to a child's success in learning to read (Chard and Dickson, 1999).

How Does Phonological Awareness Help in Learning to Read? New readers must recognize the alphabetic principle and that words can be separated into individual phonemes, which can be reordered and blended into words. This enables learners to associate the letters with sounds in order to read and build words. Thus, phonological awareness in kindergarten is a strong predictor of reading success that persists throughout school (Shankweiler, Crain, Katz, Fowler, Liberman, Brady, Thornton, Lunquist, Dreyer, Fletcher, Steubing, Shaywitz, and Shaywitz, 1995). Early instruction in reading, especially in letter-sound association, strengthens phonological awareness and helps in the development of the more sophisticated phonemic awareness (Snow, Burns, and Griffin, 1998).

Phonics Versus Whole-Language Approaches to Reading.

Throughout the history of teaching reading, a great debate has existed between whether it is better to start with word sounds (phonics) or to teach words as they derive their meaning from a larger context (whole language). Unfortunately, some schools that adopted the whole-language approach abandoned the teaching of phonics altogether. In fact, in any school that exclusively adopted one approach, there was always a block of students who still did not learn to read. Even those schools that purported to use a "blended" or "eclectic" approach often failed to include systematic instruction in phonological awareness, phonics, and their component skills.

Nonetheless, the research is clear: successful reading starts with phonemic awareness of sound-symbol correspondences and the blending of sound-spellings until almost any unknown word can be accurately decoded (Moats, 2000). Starting with the phonemic awareness approach is one of the few aspects of reading supported by a substantial and long-term body of research.

An exclusively whole-language approach minimizes or omits the systematic teaching of phoneme awareness, spelling patterns, and rules of grammar. Whole language appears to be primarily a system of intentions and beliefs from the late 1960s proposing that early reading instruction should focus on purpose and meaning and that word analysis skills should arise only incidently to contextual reading. However, its philosophy was derived from an analysis of how *adults* read and long before the development of brain imaging technologies. The whole language approach gained great popularity in the late 1970s, and by the early 1980s, school districts were replacing phonics-based programs with programs based on individual reading instruction with children's literature. Yet no solid body of research existed then or exists now to support the effectiveness of *exclusively* using the whole-language approach with beginning readers. Almost every basic premise that whole language advocates about how we *learn* to read is contradicted by recent scientific studies that show the following:

> *The research is clear: Successful reading starts with phonemic awareness.*

- ◆ Learning to read is not a natural ability for the human brain.
- ◆ The alphabetic principle is not learned merely by exposure to print.
- ◆ Spoken language and written language are very different, and thus require the mastery of different skills.
- ◆ The most important skill at the beginning stages of reading is the ability to read single words accurately, completely, and fluently.
- ◆ Context is not the primary factor in beginning word recognition.

Children bring a knowledge of spoken language when they encounter the printed page. They need to learn the written symbols that represent speech, and to use them accurately and fluently. Reading instruction should begin with phonemic awareness and then move to contextual and enriched reading as the student gains competency and confidence. Thus some of the principles of whole language can be incorporated later as part of reading development (Moats, 2000).

Difficulties in Learning to Read

Reading is so complex that any small problem along the way can slow or interrupt the process. It is small wonder that children have more problems with reading than with any other skill we ask them to learn. Difficulties result essentially from either environmental or physi-

> *Successful reading involves the coordination of three neural networks: visual processing, sound recognition, and word interpretation.*

cal factors, or some combination of both. Environmental factors include limited exposure to language in the preschool years, resulting in little phoneme sensitivity, letter knowledge, print awareness, vocabulary, and reading comprehension. Physical factors include speech, hearing, and visual impairments and substandard intellectual capabilities. Any combination of environmental and physical factors makes diagnosis and treatment more difficult. Neuroimaging, however, is showing great promise as a tool for diagnosing reading and language difficulties.

As we can see from Figure 5.2, successful reading involves the coordination of three neural networks: visual processing (orthography), sound recognition (phonology), and word interpretation (semantics). In reading the word *dog*, the visual processing system puts the symbols together. The decoding process alerts the auditory processing system that recognizes the alphabetic symbols to represent the sound "dawg." Other brain regions, including the frontal lobe, search long-term memory sites for meaning. If all systems work correctly, a mental image emerges of a furry animal that barks (Patterson and Lambon Ralph, 1999). Problems can occur almost anywhere along the way. Many variations of reading disorders exist, but here are some of the more common ones that teachers encounter.

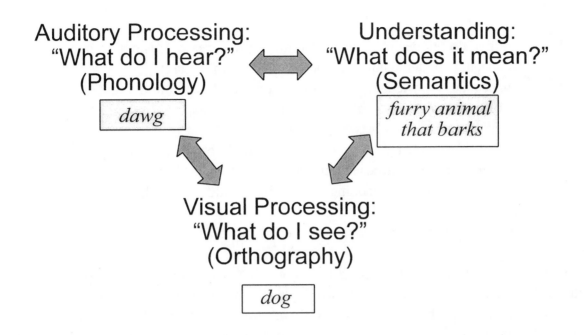

Figure 5.2 *Successful reading requires the coordination of three systems: visual processing to see the word, auditory processing to hear it, and semantic processing to understand it.*

Deficits in Phoneme Awareness and the Alphabetic Principle

If the brain cannot understand that words are made up of segmented sounds that can be connected to letters (the alphabetic principle), then reading becomes extremely difficult. For children with this problem, reading is hesitant and characterized by

> *Understanding phonemes, more than any other factor, is a critical part of successful reading.*

frequent starts and stops and multiple mispronunciations. Their comprehension is low because they take too much time to read, and memory cannot retain the words long enough to understand what has been read. This condition is referred to as *phonological alexia.*

This deficit may have genetic and neurobiological origins in that the decoding process in the angular gyrus (Figure 5.1) is defective. It also may be caused by lack of exposure to spoken language patterns and usage during the preschool years. In either case, the result is the same—difficulty in linking speech sound to letters, decoding that is labored and weak, and a lack of comprehension.

Deficits in Reading Comprehension

Some children do not derive meaning from what they read. This deficit may relate to

- ▶ inadequate understanding of the words used in the text,
- ▶ inadequate knowledge about the domains represented in the text,
- ▶ a lack of familiarity with the semantic and syntactic structures that help predict relationships between words,
- ▶ a lack of knowledge about different writing conventions that are used to achieve different purposes (humor, explanation, dialogue, etc.),
- ▶ a deficit in verbal reasoning ability that would enable the reader to read between the lines, and
- ▶ a lack of the ability to remember verbal information.

This condition is referred to as *surface alexia*. Although a large number of research studies have investigated vocabulary acquisition and syntactic development, no clear answers are available at this time to explain exactly how that occurs. Thus our understanding of how to help students use reading comprehension strategies in different situations is not well developed, but new research areas seem promising.

Dysfunction in the Timing of Speech Sounds

Recent studies of young children with language-learning difficulties indicate that they may have a dysfunction in brain-timing mechanisms, which makes processing of certain speech sounds difficult. Researchers discovered that by using computer-processed language programs that pronounced words more slowly, some children (ages 5 to 10) were able to advance their reading levels by two years after just four weeks of training. This improvement was maintained for at least a year (Tallal, Miller, Bedi, Byma, Wang, Nagarajan, Schreiner, Jenkins, and Merzenich, 1996).

Researchers discovered that by using computer-processed language programs, some children were able to advance their reading levels by two years after just four weeks of training.

Another revelation from brain scans is that poor readers' brains show more frontal lobe activity than do good readers' brains. This means that the poor readers are putting forth additional effort—perhaps subvocalizing—to pronounce and interpret the word correctly (Merzenich, Jenkins, Johnston, Schreiner, Miller, and Tallal, 1996; Tallal et al., 1996). So it doesn't make sense to say to a poor reader, "Try harder." The problem is not the effort, but the accuracy with which that effort is processing sounds.

Dyslexia

About 2 to 5 percent of elementary-age children have some form of developmental reading disorder known as dyslexia, which results from a defect in the ability to process graphic symbols. The disorder is not attributable to eye problems or to low intelligence.

Newer research is shedding more light on dyslexia. Because dyslexics often confuse *b* and *d*, psychologists thought for many years that dyslexia was merely a vision problem. Researchers now believe that the letters can also be confused because they sound alike. This is the brain's inability to process what it *hears*, not what it *sees*. The problem seems to lie in the decoding process,

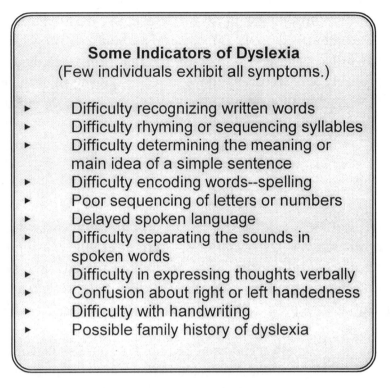

Some Indicators of Dyslexia
(Few individuals exhibit all symptoms.)

- Difficulty recognizing written words
- Difficulty rhyming or sequencing syllables
- Difficulty determining the meaning or main idea of a simple sentence
- Difficulty encoding words--spelling
- Poor sequencing of letters or numbers
- Delayed spoken language
- Difficulty separating the sounds in spoken words
- Difficulty in expressing thoughts verbally
- Confusion about right or left handedness
- Difficulty with handwriting
- Possible family history of dyslexia

which occurs in the angular gyrus (see Figure 5.1). Brain imaging studies have shown a significantly reduced blood flow to the left angular gyrus in people diagnosed with dyslexia. The studies also indicated that the amount of blood flow to this area was highly correlated with the severity of the dyslexia—the less blood flow, the worse the dyslexia (Rumsey, Horwitz, Donohue, Nace, Maisog, and Andreason, 1999).

Other imaging studies show an imperfectly functioning system for dividing words into their phonological units—a critical step for accurate reading. Letter reversals can be the result of phonological missteps in the decoding of print to sound and back to print. It is likely that the learner has problems in assigning what he says or hears in his head (the phoneme) to the letters he sees on paper (the grapheme) (Shaywitz, Shaywitz, Pugh, Fulbright, Constable, Mencl, Shankweiler, Liberman, Skudlarski, Fletcher, Katz, Marchione, Lacadie, Gatenby, and Gore, 1998). So, for many individuals, dyslexia may really be *dysphonia*—an incorrect auditory-visual association between phoneme and grapheme. If so, then remedial strategies should focus on reestablishing correct phonemic connections with intense practice.

Some people diagnosed with dyslexia probably have a form of visual impairment. One type of impairment, called *visual magnocellular-deficit* (see page 97), may cause the visual images of letters to be held longer than usual and subsequent images are superimposed onto them. Letters become blurred, causing confusion for the reader. This theory is the focus of ongoing research studies (Stein, Talcott, and Walsh, 2000).

Convincing evidence exists that dyslexia is largely inherited (Fagerheim, Raeymaekers, Tønnessen, Pedersen, Tranebjaerg, and Lubs, 1999). Thus it is a life-long chronic problem and not just a "phase." The stereotype that nearly all dyslexics are boys is not true, although it probably persists because boys are more likely to show their frustration with reading by acting out. Studies indicate that many girls are affected as well and are not getting help.

Nonlinguistic Perceptual Deficits

Recent research indicates that some people, who are otherwise unimpaired, have extreme difficulties in reading because of deficits in *nonlinguistic* auditory and visual perception. This revelation was somewhat of a surprise because conventional wisdom held that impairments in reading (and also in oral language) were restricted to problems with *linguistic* processing. Wright, Bowen, and Zecker (2000) have reviewed the research in nonlinguistic deficits. They cite six major developments that promise a better understanding of and treatment for this type of disorder.

1. **Perception of Sequential Sounds.** The inability to detect and discriminate sounds presented in rapid succession seems to be a common impairment in individuals with reading and language disorders. These individuals also have difficulty in indicating the order of two sounds presented in rapid succession. Hearing words accurately when reading or from a stream of rapid conversation (phonology, see Figure 5.2) is critical to understanding.

2. **Sound-Frequency Discrimination.** Some individuals with reading disorders are impaired in their ability to hear differences in sound frequency. This condition can affect the ability to discriminate tone and pitch in speech. At first glance, this may seem like only an oral language-related impairment. However, it also affects reading proficiency because reading involves sounding out words in the auditory processing system.

3. **Detection of Target Sounds in Noise.** The inability to detect tones within noise is another recently discovered nonlinguistic impairment. When added to the findings in 1 and 2 above, this evidence suggests that

> *Evidence is growing that auditory functions play a much greater role in reading disorders than previously thought.*

auditory functions may play a much greater role in reading disorders than previously thought.

4. **Visual Magnocellular-Deficit Hypothesis.** The interpretation of some research studies has lead to a hypothesis about the functions of the visual processing system. This proposes that certain forms of reading disorders are caused by a deficit in the visual processing system, which leads to poor detection of coherent visual motion and poor discrimination of the speed of visual motion. This part of the visual system involves large neurons and so is referred to as the magnocellular system. Impairment in this system may cause letters on a page to bundle and overlap, or appear to move—common complaints from some dyslexics.

5. **Individual Differences.** The large number of possible deficits in visual and auditory perception on various reading tasks accounts for the wide range of individual differences observed among those with reading disorders. Analyzing these differences leads to a better understanding of the multidimensional nature of reading disorders and possible treatment.

6. **Remediation.** Efforts to remediate nonlinguistic reading and language problems are showing some encouraging results. Tallal (1996) and Merzenich (1996) tested a treatment that improved the ability of children with language disorder to hear brief sounds presented in rapid succession —a skill necessary for speech perception and reading. Other studies using specially designed eyeglasses to assist eye control helped students improve their reading at twice the rate of control groups (Stein, Richardson, and Fowler, 2000).

These developments are contributing to a greater understanding of factors that contribute to nonlinguistic reading disorders and to effective remediation treatments. Research will continue to attempt to identify all nonlinguistic perceptual deficits to determine their impact on reading and language processing.

Voices of Disagreement

In fairness, it should be noted that not all researchers are in agreement that scientific evidence strongly supports a phonemic awareness approach to learning to read. Coles (2000), for example, criticizes the scientific research as subject to different interpretations and too limited in trying to explain such a complex process as reading. Although he offers no alternative, he suggests that scientific studies do not address broader questions such as, "What kind of emotions, feelings, and thinking should the teaching of reading encourage?" He also is concerned that this scientific approach will prevent the useful components of whole language from being incorporated into the teaching of reading.

What Educators Need to Consider

Because reading does not come naturally to the human brain, children learning to read have to put much effort into associating their spoken language with the alphabet and with word recognition. To do this successfully, phonemic awareness is essential. Educators should give second thought to reading programs that delay phonemic awareness or that treat it as an ancillary skill to be learned in context with general reading. All teachers are teachers of reading, and thus should have the training to strengthen the reading skills of students at every grade level.

Significant progress is being made in understanding the connection between the visual and auditory processing systems during reading. Research-based reading programs that use computers to help students coordinate these systems have substantially benefitted slower readers.

Impact on Learning

- Reading problems are the most common difficulties that children have in school and their lack of confidence in reading can affect all their school work.

- Learning to read requires a systematic process of several steps, some of which are not acquired without direct instruction.

- The visual and auditory impact of the technology (e.g., computers, toys, and games) that young children use today is subtly eroding the argument that reading is a necessary skill.

Strategies to Consider

Developing Phonological Awareness

Training in phonological awareness needs to be more intense for children with reading disabilities. Reading programs are filled with activities for separating words into phonemes, synthesizing phonemes into words, and deleting and substituting phonemes. Research suggests that the development of phonological awareness is more likely to be successful if it follows these general principles (Chard and Osborn, 1998):

❑ **Continuous Sounds Before Stop Sounds.** Start with continuous sounds such as *s, m,* and *f* that are easier to pronounce than the stop sounds of *b, k,* and *p.*

❑ **Modeling.** Be sure to model carefully and accurately each activity when it is first introduced.

❑ **Easy to Complex Tasks.** Move from easier tasks, such as rhyming, to more complex tasks such as blending and segmenting.

❑ **Larger to Smaller Units.** Move from the larger units of words and onset-rimes to the smaller units of individual phonemes.

❑ **Additional Strategies.** Use additional strategies to help struggling readers, such as concrete objects (e.g., bingo chips or blocks) to represent sounds.

Strategies to Consider

Phonemic Awareness and Guidelines

Research shows that early phoneme awareness is a strong indicator of later reading success. Further, the research on interventions clearly demonstrates the benefits of explicitly teaching phonemic awareness skills. No students benefit more from this instruction than those already burdened with reading problems.

The development of phonological awareness occurs over several years. It is the last step in a developmental continuum that begins with the brain's earliest awareness of rhyme. Figure 5.3 illustrates the continuum from rhyming to full phoneme manipulation (Chard and Dickson, 1999).

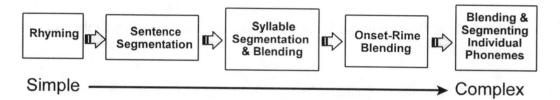

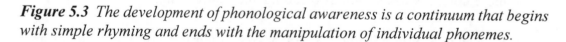

Figure 5.3 *The development of phonological awareness is a continuum that begins with simple rhyming and ends with the manipulation of individual phonemes.*

The first four steps, from rhyming to onset-rime blending, can occur during the preschool years in the appropriate environment. If the parent sings rhyming songs and reads to the child from rhyming books (e.g., Dr. Seuss' *There's a Locket in My Pocket*), the child's brain begins to recognize the sounds that comprise beginning language.

However, many children begin school with a very weak phonological base. Teachers must then assess where students lie on the phonological continuum and select appropriate strategies to move them toward phoneme awareness. Edelen-Smith (1998) offers teachers some guidelines to consider when selecting strategies to help students recognize and successfully manipulate phonemes.

Phoneme Awareness and Guidelines—Continued

General Guidelines

1. **Be Specific.** Identify the specific phonemic awareness task and select the activities that are developmentally appropriate and that keep the students engaged in the task. Select words, phrases, and sentences from curricular materials to make this meaningful. Look for ways to make activities enjoyable so students see them as fun and not as monotonous drills.

2. **Avoid Letter Names.** Use the phoneme sounds of the alphabet when doing activities and avoid letter names. Letters sounded as they are named only confuse the learner. Keep in mind that one sound may be represented by two or more letters. Target specific sounds and practice beforehand so students can hear them clearly.

3. **Treat Continuant and Stop Sounds Differently.** Continuant sounds are easier to manipulate and hear than the stop sounds. When introducing each type, treat them differently so students become aware of their differences. Exaggerate continuant sounds by holding on to them: *sssssssing* and *rrrrrrun*. Use rapid repetition with the stop consonants: */K/-/K/-/K/-/K/-/K/-/K/-athy*.

4. **Emphasize How Sounds Vary With Their Position in a Word.** Generally, the initial position in the word is the easiest sound. The final position is the next easiest and the middle position is the most difficult. Use lots of examples to make this clear, such as *mop*, *pin*, and *better*.

5. **Be Aware of the Sequence for Introducing Combined Sounds.** When introducing the combined sounds, a consonant-vowel pattern should come first, then a vowel-consonant pattern, and finally, the consonant-vowel-consonant pattern. For example: first *tie*, next *add*, and then *bed*.

– Continued –

Phoneme Awareness and Guidelines—Continued

Onset and Rime

The brain's awareness of onsets, rimes, and syllables develops before an awareness of phonemes (Goswami, 1994). Onsets are the initial consonants that change the meaning of a word; rimes are the vowel-consonant combinations that stay constant in a series. For example, in *bend*, *lend*, and *send*, the onsets are *b, l,* and *s*; the rime is *-end*. Using literature, word families, and direct instruction are strategies that focus on word play designed to enhance onset and rime recognition (Edelen-Smith, 1998).

♦ **Literature.** Books with rhyming patterns (like many books by Dr. Seuss) are easily recalled through repeated exposure. Almost any literary source that plays with word sounds is valuable. Books that particularly develop awareness of sound patterns associated with onset and rime are those using alliteration (the repetition of an initial consonant across several words, e.g., *Peter Piper picked a peck of peppers*) and assonance (the repetition of vowel sounds within words, e.g., *The rain in Spain stays mainly on the plain*).

♦ **Word Families Charts.** Using words from a story or book, construct a chart that places a different beginning letter in front of a rime. For example, start with the rime *-at* and add *f, h, b,* and *s* to form *fat, hat, bat,* and *sat*. Have the students make up a story line whenever the word changes, e.g., "The fat cat chased a hat." Encourage the students to make their own charts with different rimes and to keep them for future reference.

♦ **Direct Instruction.** Students who have difficulties distinguishing the sounds among rhyming words need more direct instruction. Model rhyming pairs (e.g., *sun-fun* and *hand-band*) using flash cards so students match what they see with what they hear. Be sure they repeat each rhyming pair several times to reinforce auditory input. Another activity includes three cards, only two of which have rhyming words. Ask students to pick out and say the two that rhyme, or the one that doesn't. Later, change the rhyming words to two rhyming pictures out of three (e.g., a nose, a rose, and a horse).

Strategies to Consider

Simple Phonemic Awareness

Young students are usually unaware that words are made of sounds that can be produced in isolation. This leaves it up to the teacher to find ways to emphasize the concept of speech sounds. Here are some ways to do this (Edelen-Smith, 1998):

- **Recognizing Isolated Sounds.** Associate certain speech sounds with an animal or action that is familiar to the students. For example, the buzzing sound of a bee or snoring in sleep is "zzzzzzzz–," the hissing of a snake, "sssssss," the sound of asking for quiet, "shhhhhhhh–," or the sound of a motor scooter or motor boat, "pppppppp–."

  Alliteration, mentioned earlier, also helps with this task. Talking about Peter Piper picking a peck of peppers affords the valuable combination of sound recognition, story telling, and literary context. It also provides self-correcting cues for initial-sound isolation and for sound-to-word matching.

- **Counting Words, Syllables, and Phonemes.** It is easier for a child's brain to perceive words and syllables than individual phonemes. Thus word and syllable counting is a valuable exercise for sound recognition that can lead later to more accurate identification of phonemes. Start with a sentence from the curriculum and say it aloud. Do not write it out because the students should focus on listening. Ask the students to count the number of words they think are in the sentence. They can use markers or tokens to indicate the word number. Then show or write the sentence and have the students compare the number of words to their own count.

  Syllable counting can be done in many ways. Students can count syllables in the same way they identified the word count. Also, they can march around the room while saying the syllables, they can clap hands, tap pencils, or do any other overt activity that indicates counting.

– Continued –

103

Simple Phonemic Awareness—Continued

- **Synthesizing Sounds.** Sound synthesis is an essential yet easily performed skill for phonemic awareness. Start with using the initial sound and then saying the remainder of the word. For example, the teacher says, "It starts with 'b' and ends with '-and,' put it together and it says 'band'." The students take turns using the same phrasing to make up their own words. Variations include limiting the context to objects in the classroom or in the school, or to a particular story that the class has recently read.

    Guessing games can also be productive and fun activities for playing with sounds. One game involves hiding an object in a bag or some other place and then giving clues to its name sound-by-sound or syllable-by-syllable. When a student guesses the word correctly, you reveal the object. Songs can also be used. Blending the music with the sounds of words increases the chances that the phonemes will be remembered.

- **Matching Sounds to Words.** This activity asks the learner to identify the initial sound of a word, an important skill for sound segmentation. Show the student a picture of a kite and ask, "Is this a dddd-ite, or a llll-ite, or a kkkk-ite?" You could also ask, "Is there a *k* in kite?," or "Which sound does kite start with?" This allows the students to try three onsets with three rimes and to mix and match until they get it correct. Consonants make a good beginning because they are easier to emphasize and prolong during pronunciation. Have students try other words in threes. Be sure to use the phoneme sound when referring to a letter, not the letter name.

- **Identifying the Position of Sounds.** Segmenting whole words into their components is an important part of phonemic awareness. This ability is enhanced when learners recognize that sounds occur in different positions in words: initial, medial, and final. Edelen-Smith (1998) suggests explaining that words have beginning, middle, and end sounds just like a train has a beginning (engine), middle (passenger car), and end (caboose). Slowly articulate a consonant-vowel-consonant (CVC) word at this time, such a *c-a-t,* and point to the appropriate train part as you sound out each phoneme. Then have the students sound out other CVC words from a list or recent story, pointing to each train part as they say the parts of the word.

Simple Phonemic Awareness—Continued

■ **Segmenting Sounds.** One of the more difficult phonemic tasks for children is to separately pronounce each sound of a spoken word in order. This process is called sound segmentation. Developing this skill should start with isolating initial phonemes. The previous activities—matching sounds to words and identifying the position of sounds—help the learner identify and recognize initial phonemes. Visual cues can also play an important part in segmenting sounds. Research on Elkonin (1973) boxes, for example, indicates that they are particularly effective in developing this important skill. Show a card with the picture of a common object, say a dog (Figure 5.4). Below the object is a series of three boxes that represent the three sounds in the word, *dog (duh, awh,* and *guh)*. Model the process by saying the word slowly and placing a token into each box as you say the sound aloud. Then have the students practice it first with this picture and then with other pictures. Select words that are familiar to the students (or have the students select the words) so that they can use contextual clues for meaning. After sufficient practice, eliminate the cards so that students can perform the sound segmenting task without visual cues.

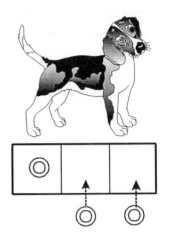

Figure 5.4 An example of using Elkonin boxes. Students move tokens into boxes when hearing each of the phonemes. (Elkonin, 1973)

■ **Associating Sounds With Letters.** For the reading process to be successful, the brain must associate the sounds that it has heard during the prereading years of spoken language with the written letters that represent them. This is particularly difficult for students with disabilities that hamper the learning of reading. Consequently, extensive practice is essential. Nearly all of the activities mentioned above —especially those involving visual cues—can be modified to include associations between sounds and

– Continued –

Simple Phonemic Awareness—Continued

letters. As the students master individual sounds, their corresponding letter names can then be introduced. A type of bingo game can also be used to practice sound-with-letter association. Each student gets a card with letters placed into a bingo grid. Draw a letter from a container and call out the phoneme. Students place tokens on the letter that corresponds to the phoneme. The student who first gets "phoneme bingo" names the letters aloud. Teachers can devise all types of variations to this bingo game to maintain the practice while keeping the task interesting and fun.

Strategies to Consider

Compound Phonemic Awareness

In compound phonemic awareness, the learner must hold one sound in memory while matching it to a second sound. For example, "Do dog and deer begin with the same sound?" The two activities that develop compound phonemic awareness involve matching one word to a second word and the deleting of sounds in a word.

❑ **Matching One Word to Another Word.** Byrne (1991) has suggested three games to develop phonemic word matching skills. The words and pictures used in each of these games should relate to themes and readings done in the classroom. One involves making a set of dominoes that have two objects pictured on each tile. The students have to join the tiles that share the same beginning or ending sounds.

A second game uses picture cards that are placed face down in a pile. Each student draws a card from the pile and places it face up. Students continue to draw cards and place them in the face-up pile. The first student to match the beginning or ending sound of a drawn card with the top card on the face-up pile says the match aloud and collects the pile.

The third game is a variation of bingo. Each bingo card contains pictures, which the students mark when their picture has the same beginning or ending sounds as the word said by the caller (student or teacher).

❑ **Deleting Sounds.** Deleting sounds from words and manipulating phonemes within words are more difficult tasks for the young brain to accomplish. Studies show that children must attain the mental age of seven years before this task can be accomplished adequately (Cole and Mengler, 1994). Furthermore, segmentation skills and letter names must be mastered before sound deletion tasks can be successfully learned.

– Continued –

Compound Phonemic Awareness—Continued

Three tasks seem to be particularly important to mastering this skill: deleting parts of a compound word, identifying a missing sound, and deleting a single sound from a word.

Deleting Parts of a Compound Word. To illustrate deleting parts of a compound word, point to a picture or an object that is a compound word and demonstrate how each word can be said with one part missing. For example, "This is a classroom. I can say *class* without the *room*. And this is a farmhouse (or greenhouse). I can say *farm* (*green*) without *house*. Now you try it. This is a playground." Use other common examples, such as *lighthouse, airplane, grandmother, seashore, sandbox, toothpaste,* and *nightlight*.

Identifying the Missing Sound. In this task, focus on deleting the initial and final sounds instead of the medial sounds, which is the first step to master for the young brain. Take word pairs, such as *ate-late*, and ask "What's missing in *ate* that you hear in *late*?" Other examples are *ask-mask*, *able-table*, and *right-bright*. After a few trials, have the students make up their own word pairs, preferably from lesson material.

Deleting a Single Sound From a Word. This task should begin with segmentation practice. First, separate the sound for deletion. For example, separate "g" from *glove*. "*Glove*. It starts with *g* and ends with *love*. Take the first sound away and it says *love*." Use words for which a sound deletion results in another real word. Other examples are *spot-pot*, *train-rain*, *scare-care*, and *snap-nap*. After practicing this skill, say a word aloud and ask students to say the word with the initial sound missing: "Say *mother* without the 'm'." Visual clues can help those who have difficulty saying a word with the deleted sound.

Strategies to Consider

What Teachers and Students Need to Know About Reading

Here is what the latest research is saying that teachers and students need to know for the successful teaching of reading to children with reading difficulties (Foorman et al., 1998):

What Teachers Need to Know About Teaching Reading

♦ How the brain learns to read
♦ The relationship between reading and spoken language
♦ Direct instruction in phonics
♦ Direct instruction in the alphabetic principle
♦ How to diagnose spelling and reading skills
♦ How to use a variety of reading intervention strategies

What Beginning Readers Need to Learn

✓ *Phonological Awareness*: Rhyming, alliteration, deleting and substituting sounds, sound patterns
✓ *Phonemic Awareness*: Segmenting words into individual sounds, manipulating phonemes
✓ *Alphabetic Principle*: Correlating letter-sound patterns with specific text
✓ *Orthographic Awareness*: Understanding spelling rules and writing conventions
✓ *Comprehension Monitoring Strategies*: Identifying the main idea, making inferences, using study skills that assist reading

Strategies to Consider

Reading Strategies for Students With Reading Difficulties

Studies have shown that both children with reading disabilities and other low achievers can master the learning strategies that improve reading comprehension skills. For students with learning problems, learning to use questioning strategies is especially important because these students do not often spontaneously self-question or monitor their own reading comprehension.

Here are three strategies that researchers and teachers have found particularly effective. Some of the strategies have been around for nearly 20 years, but their fundamental premises have been reaffirmed by recent research.

Questioning and Paraphrasing. Reciprocal Teaching is a strategic approach that fosters student interaction with the text being read. In Reciprocal Teaching, students interact deeply with the text through the strategies of questioning, summarizing, clarifying, and predicting. Organized in the form of a discussion, the approach involves one leader (students and teacher take turns being the leader) who, after a portion of the text is read, first frames a question to which the group responds. Second, participants share their own questions. Third, the leader then summarizes the gist of the text, and participants comment or elaborate upon that summary. At any point in the discussion, either the leader or participants may identify aspects of the text or discussion that need to be clarified, and the group joins together to clarify the confusion. Finally, the leader indicates that it's time to move on and solicits predictions about what might come up next in the text.

The value of paraphrasing, self-questioning, and finding the main idea are well researched strategies (Deshler, Shumaker, Alley, Clark, and Warner, 1981). Students divide reading passages into smaller parts, such as sections, subsections, or paragraphs. After reading a segment, students are cued to use a self-questioning strategy to identify main ideas and details. The strategy requires a high level of attention to reading tasks because students must alternate their use of questioning and paraphrasing after reading each section, subsection, or paragraph.

Reading Strategies for Students With Reading Difficlties—Continued

Questioning to Find the Main Idea. Wong and Jones (1982) developed a self-questioning strategy focused primarily on identifying and questioning the main idea or summary of a paragraph. Here's how it works. Students are first taught the concept of a main idea and how to do self-questioning. Students then practice, asking themselves questions aloud about each paragraph's main idea. They can use a cue card for assistance. Following the practice, the teacher provides immediate feedback. Eventually, following successful comprehension of these short paragraphs, students are presented with more lengthy passages, and the cue cards are removed. Continuing to give corrective feedback, the teacher finishes each lesson with a discussion of students' progress and of the strategy's usefulness. Wong and Jones found that students with learning disabilities who were trained in a self-questioning strategy performed significantly higher (i.e., demonstrated greater comprehension of what was read) than untrained students.

Story-Mapping. Idol (1987) studied the effectiveness of story maps. In this strategy, students read a story, generate a map of its events and ideas, and then answer questions. (Figure 5.5 is one example of a story map.) In order to fill in the map, students have to identify the setting, characters, time, and place of the story; the problem, the goal, the action that took place; and the outcome. The teacher models for students how to fill in the map, then gives many opportunities to practice the mapping technique for themselves and receive corrective feedback. The map is an effective visual tool that provides a framework for understanding, conceptualizing, and remembering important story events. Idol also found that the reading comprehension of students improved significantly when the teacher gave direct instruction on the use of the strategy, expected frequent use of the strategy, and encouraged students to use the strategy independently.

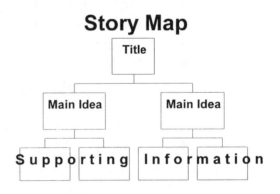

Figure 5.5 *This is just one example of a story map. (Sousa, 2001, p. 198)*

Strategies to Consider

Teaching for Reading Comprehension – Part I

Students with reading disorders often have difficulty deriving meaning from what they read. If little or no meaning comes from reading, students lose motivation to read. Furthermore, meaning is essential for long-term retention of what they have read. Strategies designed to improve reading comprehension have been shown to improve students' interest in reading and their success.

One such successful strategy, suggested by Deshler, Ellis, and Lenz (1996), is a four-step process called by the acronym **PASS** (**P**review, **A**sk, **S**ummarize, and **S**ynthesize). The teacher guides the students through the four steps, ensuring that they respond orally or in writing to the activities associated with each step. Grouping formats, such as cooperative learning, can be used to encourage active student participation and reduce anxiety over the correctness of each student's response.

1. *Preview, Review, and Predict:*
- Preview by reading the heading and one or two sentences.
- Review what you already know about this topic.
- Predict what you think the text or story will be about.

2. *Ask and Answer Questions:*
- Content-focused questions:
  Who? What? Why? Where?
  How does this relate to what I already know?
- Monitoring questions:
  Does this make sense?
  Is my prediction correct?
  How is this different from what I thought it was going to be about?

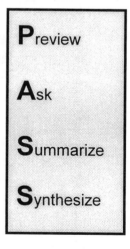

Preview

Ask

Summarize

Synthesize

Teaching for Reading Comprehension – Part I—Continued

- Problem-solving questions:
  Is it important that it make sense?
  Do I need to reread part of it?
  Can I visualize the information?
  Does it have too many unknown words?
  Should I get help?

3. *Summarize*:
- Explain what the short passage you read was all about.

4. *Synthesize*:
- Explain how the short passage fits in with the whole passage.
- Explain how what you learned fits in with what you knew.

If students have difficulty with any particular step, they can go back to the previous step to determine what information they need in order to proceed.

Strategies to Consider

Teaching for Reading Comprehension – Part II

Another excellent technique for helping students comprehend what they read and build vocabulary is called collaborative strategic reading (CSR). It is particularly effective in classrooms where students have many different reading abilities and learning capabilities. The strategy is compatible with all types of reading programs.

CSR uses direct teaching and the collaborative power of cooperative learning groups to accomplish two phases designed to improve reading comprehension (Klingner, Vaughn, and Schumm, 1998). The first phase is a teacher-led component that takes students through four parts of a reading plan: Preview, Click and Clunk, Get the Gist, and Wrap-Up. The second phase involves using cooperative learning groups to provide an interactive environment where students can practice and perfect their reading comprehension skills.

PHASE ONE
Teacher-Led Activities

◆ **Preview the Reading.** Students know that previews in movies give some information about coming events. Use this as a hook to the new reading. The learners preview the entire reading passage in order to get as much as they can about the passage in a just a few minutes time. The purpose here is to activate their prior knowledge about the topic and to give them an opportunity to predict what they will learn.

Refer to student experiences about a movie, television program, or a prior book that might contain information relevant to the new reading. Also, give clues to look for when previewing. For example, pictures, graphs, tables, or call-out quotes provide information to help predict what students already know about the topic and what they will learn.

114

Teaching for Reading Comprehension – Part II—Continued

- ◆ **Click and Clunk.** Students with reading problems often fail to monitor their understanding while they read. Clicks and clunks are devices to help students with this monitoring. Clicks are parts of the reading that make sense; clunks are parts or words that don't.

     Ask students to identify clunks as they go along. Then the class works with the teacher to develop strategies to clarify the clunks, such as
  - ▸ Rereading the sentences while looking for key words that can help extract meaning from the context
  - ▸ Rereading previous and following sentences to get additional context clues
  - ▸ Looking for a prefix or suffix in the word that could help with meaning
  - ▸ Breaking the word apart to see if smaller words are present that provide meaning

- ◆ **Get the Gist.** The goal of this phase is twofold. First, ask the readers to state in their own words the most important person, place, or thing in the passage. Second, get them to tell in as few words as possible (i.e., leaving out the details) the most important *idea* about that person, place, or thing. Because writing often improves memory, occasionally ask the students to write down their gists. Students can then read their gists aloud and invite comments from the group about ways to improve the gist. This process can be done so that all students benefit by enhancing their skills.

- ◆ **Wrap-Up.** Wrap-up is a closure activity that allows students to review in their mind what has been learned. Focus students on the new learning by asking them to generate questions whose answers would show what they learned from the passage. They should also review key ideas.

     Start with questions that focus on the explicit material in the passage, such as *who*, *what*, *where*, and *when*. Afterward, move to questions that stimulate higher-order thinking, such as "What might have happened if___?" and "What could be another way to solve this problem?" Writing down the response will help students sort out and remember the important ideas.

– Continued –

Teaching for Reading Comprehension – Part II—Continued

PHASE TWO
Cooperative Learning Groups

This phase puts the students into cooperative learning groups to practice CSR in an interactive environment. True cooperative learning groups are usually made up of about five students of mixed ability levels who learn and perform certain roles in the group to ensure completion of the learning task (Johnson and Johnson, 1989). The roles rotate among the group members so that every student gets the opportunity to be the leader and use the various skills needed to perform each task. Although there are many roles that students can perform, here are the most common (assuming five members per group):

- ▸ **Leader.** Leads the group through CSR by saying what to read next and what strategy to use.
- ▸ **Clunk Expert.** Reminds the group what strategies to use when encountering a difficult word or phrase.
- ▸ **Announcer.** Calls on different group members to make certain that everyone participates and that only one person talks at a time.
- ▸ **Encourager.** Gives the group feedback on behaviors that are to be praised and those that need improvement.
- ▸ **Reporter.** Takes notes and reports to the whole class the main idea that the group has learned and shares a question that the group generated during its wrap-up.

Other suggestions for using the cooperative learning groups with this strategy are as follows:

Cue Sheets. Giving all group members a cue sheet to guide them through the CSR provides a structure and focus for the group. The cue sheet should be specific for each role. For example,

Teaching for Reading Comprehension – Part II—Continued

the leader's sheet contains statements that steer the group through each step of CSR (e.g., "Today's topic is___." "Let's predict what we might learn from this." "Let's think of some questions to see if we really understand what we learned.") and also direct other group members to carry out their role (e.g., "Announcer, please call on others to share their ideas." "Encourager, tell us what we did well and what we need to do better next time.").

CSR Learning Logs. Recording in logs helps students to keep track of what was learned. Students can keep separate logs for each subject. The log serves as a reminder for follow-up activities and can be used to document a student's progress as required by the individualized education plan.

Reading Materials. CSR was originally designed for expository text, but has also been used successfully with narrative text. For the strategy to be successful, select reading passages that are rich in clues, that have just one main idea per paragraph, and that provide a context to help students connect and associate details into larger ideas. Weekly readers are sources that often meet these needs.

6 WRITING DISABILITIES

Once the enormous challenge of learning to read is undertaken, the brain is faced with the daunting task of directing fine muscle movements to draw the abstract symbols that represent the sounds of language. For many years, researchers thought that the mental centers responsible for speech and writing were located in the same (left) side of the brain. Recent research, however, indicates that these two processes are related yet separate, sometimes residing in different cerebral hemispheres (Baynes, Eliassen, Lutsep, and Gazzaniga, 1998). This finding, which suggests that spoken and written language develop differently, is not surprising when we realize that human beings have been speaking for over 10,000 years but writing for only 3,000 years. Thus, spoken language has become innate and usually develops with ease, but writing does not develop without instruction.

Learning to Write

Writing is a highly complex operation requiring the coordination of multiple neural networks. It involves the blending of attention, fine motor coordination, memory, visual processing, language, and higher-order thinking. When an individual is writing, the visual feedback mechanisms are at work checking the output, adjusting fine motor skills, and monitoring eye-hand coordination. Meanwhile, kinesthetic monitoring systems are conscious of the position and movement of fingers in space, the grip on the pencil, and the rhythm and pace of the writing.

Cognitive systems are also busy, verifying with long-term memory that the symbols being drawn will indeed produce the sounds of the word that the writer intends. Accomplishing this task requires visual memory for symbols, whole-word memory, and spelling rules. Hence, the

118

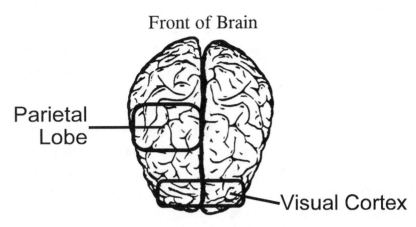

Front of Brain

Parietal
Lobe

Visual Cortex

Figure 6.1 *In a right-handed individual, writing involves mainly the left parietal lobe. For a left-handed person, the right parietal lobe is the area of main activation. Regardless of which hand is used, the visual cortex involvement is the same.*

phoneme-to-grapheme match is a continuous feedback loop ensuring that the written symbols are consistent with oral language protocols the writer has previously learned.

Recent brain imaging studies have shown the labor-intensive nature of writing. The parietal lobe, which includes the motor cortex, and the occipital lobe, where visual processing occurs, were the areas of highest activity (Figure 6.1) when an individual was writing (Wing, 2000). Not surprising was the discovery that spoken language areas in the left hemisphere were also activated. Writing relies heavily on speech because most of us sound out words in our head as we write them down.

After reviewing numerous scanning studies on the writing process, Alan Wing (2000) pieced together a

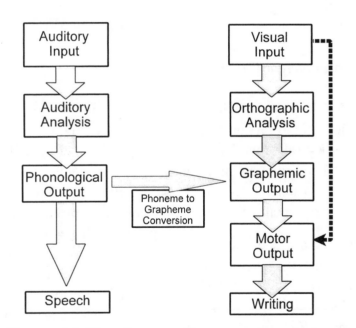

Figure 6.2 *The diagram illustrates the relationship between speech and handwriting. The writer hears the word (phonological output) and converts the sounds to the appropriate letters (graphemes). The dotted arrow shows how motor adjustments are made as the visual system judges the legibility of the writing.*

complex flow diagram illustrating the relationships between the neurological networks responsible for both speech and writing. Figure 6.2 is a simplified version of Wing's diagram. The visual systems analyze the spelling and grammar as it is written out on paper (orthography) and adjust the motor output to form the letters correctly. Simultaneously, the auditory system is sounding out the words in the brain (phonological output), associating and converting the sounds to letters (phoneme-to-grapheme conversion) for writing (motor output).

At a minimum, the ability to write requires a properly functioning central nervous system, intact receptive and expressive language skills, and the related cognitive operations. To write accurately and clearly also requires emotional stability; application of the concepts of organization and flow; an understanding of the rules of pronunciation, spelling, grammar and syntax; visual and spatial organization; and simultaneous processing.

When all these operations fall into place, writing becomes a valuable tool for learning. Writing encourages mental rehearsal, reinforces long-term memory, and helps the mind sort and prioritize information. However, for some students, the process of writing becomes an arduous task that actually interferes with learning.

Problems With Writing

Environmental Causes

Difficulties with writing can be environmental, that is, too little time was spent in the child's early years on practicing correct writing, or they can stem from deficits within one or more of the neural networks needed for legible and clear writing to occur. Let's deal first with how the school environment may contribute inadvertently to writing problems.

Teachers of writing should realize that, like reading, the brain does not perceive writing to be a survival skill. That is, the brain has no "writing centers" comparable to those for spoken language. Instead, writing requires the coordination of numerous neural networks and systems, all of which have to learn new skills. Learning to write therefore requires direct instruction—it is not innate to the brain. Hard work and lots of practice are needed just to learn the fine motor skills for reproducing the printed and cursive letters of the alphabet. In some schools, little time is given to formal instruction in writing. To conserve time, it is often taught as an ancillary activity to other learning tasks. Some of the difficulties students experience with writing may be due to an unfortunate combination of learning the difficult skills of writing with very little practice time. Further, more students are questioning the need to write well because they have access to computers at an early age and typing into a word processing program seems so much easier.

> *There are no areas of the brain specialized for writing.*

What About Inventive Spelling and Avoiding the Teaching of Writing Mechanics?
Some writing programs even advocate teaching the mechanics of writing only as student interests dictate and only in the course of writing compositions. Or, they may suggest that spelling need not be taught formally and that students will be more likely to write when they are allowed to use inventive spelling. As well-intended as that may be, long-term research findings are questioning this approach. For example,

❑   Descriptive research shows that the spelling and handwriting difficulties of students can actually interfere with their learning how to write compositions (Graham, 1990).

❑   The inventive spelling approach dramatically reduces the possibility that students will learn writing mechanics in such a way that this knowledge will transfer to their other school subjects.

❑   Shifting away from teaching writing mechanics is apt to produce long-term deficits in the knowledge of how to write successfully.

❑   This approach assumes that writing mechanics and learning to spell correctly will take care of themselves as the students write more compositions. However, no research exists to support this notion (Stein, Dixson, and Isaacson, 1994).

❑   Because practice makes permanent, the more frequently students use inventive spelling to write words incorrectly, the more likely they are to store the incorrect spelling in memory, thereby making it more difficult later to learn the correct spelling (Sousa, 2001).

All teachers need to emphasize that writing is more than *hand*writing. The notion of transferring thoughts and ideas from inside the brain to an outside device—paper or computer—requires teaching how to organize thoughts, analyze material, and sort out material differently, depending on whether students plan to relate an incident or persuade another person. To write an initial draft requires instruction in penmanship and learning the rules of written language including spelling, capitalization, punctuation, and sentence structure. Unfortunately, complex rules in the English language are loaded with exceptions and require substantial practice for mastery. Even after the initial draft is written, students need to learn how to edit and revise their material for clarity.

> *Because practice makes permanent, the more frequently students use inventive spelling to write words incorrectly, the more likely they are to store the incorrect spelling in memory, thereby making it more difficult later to learn the correct spelling.*

121

The point here is that students who demonstrate difficulty with writing need a full assessment to determine whether their obstacles are environmental or systemic. Teachers should look first at the learner's background knowledge of writing and assess the type and degree of writing instruction that has been provided in the past. Simply by providing more and sustained practice of writing skills and written language rules, teachers can help many students to eventually overcome their writing difficulties.

Neurological Causes

Given that such a complex order of operations involving several neural systems is necessary for accurate writing, difficulties can arise anywhere along the way. Because writing is so dependent on the brain's parietal lobes, for instance, problems (e.g., lesions or stroke) in this area are especially significant. On the other hand, research on brain functioning has not found much evidence to support the notion of a visual basis for most writing difficulties, even though conventional wisdom has pointed in that direction.

Whatever the neurological cause of writing difficulties, some children struggle because so much time is spent on the *process* that they often lose track of the *content* they are working on. The persistent condition of not being able to put thoughts into writing or accomplish other parts of the writing process (such as letter formation) is known as *dysgraphia*.

Dysgraphia

This is a spectrum disorder describing major difficulties in mastering the sequence of movements necessary to write letters and numbers. The disorder exists in varying degrees and is seldom found in isolation without symptoms of other learning problems.

Many students have difficulty with writing as they progress through the upper elementary grades. But those with dysgraphia

---

Dysgraphia

Symptoms:

- Inconsistencies in letter formation; mixture of upper and lower cases, of print and cursive letters
- Unfinished words or letters
- Generally illegible writing (despite time given to the task)
- Talking to self while writing
- Watching hand while writing
- Inconsistent position on page with respect to margins and lines
- Slow copying or writing
- Omitted words in writing
- Inconsistent spaces between letters and words
- Struggle to use writing as a communications tool
- Cramped or unusual grip on pencil
- Unusual body, wrist, or paper position

are inefficient at *handwriting* more than anything else, and this inefficiency establishes a barrier to learning. Their handwriting is usually characterized by slow copying, inconsistencies in letter formation, mixtures of different letters and styles, and poor legibility. Specific symptoms of the disorder are shown in the box titled *Dysgraphia*. Teachers must realize that dysgraphia is a disorder and is *not* the result of laziness, not caring, not trying, or just carelessness in writing.

What Causes Dysgraphia?

Dysgraphia is a neurological disorder that can stem from several causes. Figure 6.2 illustrates the numerous cerebral systems and stages involved in handwriting. Problems can occur almost anywhere. McCarthy and Warrington (1990) have suggested that a deficit in the phoneme-to-grapheme conversion is one of the main causes of handwriting disorders. This can lead to poorly legible written text with severely abnormal spelling, also referred to as dyslexic dysgraphia.

Problems with muscles controlling motor output to the hands, wrists, and fingers lead to a motor clumsiness that also produces poorly legible handwriting and copying, but with mostly correct spelling. Sometimes, deficits in the spatial processing functions of the brain's right hemisphere cause poorly legible text, but with accurate spelling (Deuel, 1994). Table 6.1 summarizes these three types of dysgraphia. Determining which type of writing disorder a child has requires the assessment of various factors, such as fine motor coordination, writing speed, organization, knowledge and use of vocabulary, spelling, and the degree of attention and concentration.

Table 6.1 Different Types of Dysgraphia		
Type	**Symptoms**	**Possible Cause**
Dyslexic Dysgraphia	Spontaneously written text is poorly legible with severely abnormal spelling. Copying of text is satisfactory.	Deficits in phoneme-to-grapheme conversion
Motor Clumsiness Dysgraphia	Spontaneously written text is poorly legible but spelling is satisfactory. Copying of text is poorly legible.	Deficits in muscle control of motor output to fingers, wrist, and hand
Spatial Dysgraphia	Spontaneously written text is poorly legible but spelling is satisfactory. Copying of text is satisfactory.	Deficits in spatial processing systems of the brain's right hemisphere

We now know that the centers for processing spoken language and written language are separated in the brain. Teachers should not assume, therefore, that a student with symptoms of dysgraphia will have other language problems as well. In fact, students with dysgraphia but who are otherwise linguistically talented find enormous frustration when trying to convert their thoughts into written expression. Their frustration can eventually turn them away from writing. Teachers sometimes misinterpret this behavior as laziness, carelessness, or poor motivation. Administering assessment instruments will be useful in determining whether the cause of poor writing is of neurological or some other origin.

Associating Dysgraphia With Other Disorders

Sequencing Problems. Some individuals have a cerebral deficit that makes it difficult for them to process sequential and rational information. Students with this difficulty will have problems with the sequence of letters, numbers, and words as they write. Usually they slow down their writing to focus on the mechanics of spelling, punctuation, and word order. As a result, they may get so bogged down with the details of writing that they lose the thoughts they are trying to express.

Attention-Deficit Hyperactivity Disorder (ADHD). Students with ADHD (Chapter 3) often have difficulty with writing in general and with handwriting in particular. They are processing information at a very rapid rate and don't possess the fine motor skills needed to write down their thoughts legibly.

Auditory Processing Disorders. Students who have language disorders (Chapter 5) as a result of auditory processing deficits will usually have difficulty with writing. Those with expressive language disorder are particularly weak at writing because it is the most difficult form of expressive language.

Visual Processing Disorders. Most students with dysgraphia do not have visual processing problems. However, the small percentage of students who *do* will have difficulty with writing speed and legibility simply because they are not able to fully process the visual information as they are transferring it to paper.

> *Students with dysgraphia have problems with the writing process. They are often frustrated and are not necessarily lazy or unmotivated.*

What Do Educators Need to Consider?

One of the main goals of writing is to help individuals express their knowledge and ideas. Students with dysgraphia have writing problems that lead to excessively rapid or slow writing, messy and illegible papers, and frustration. It is wrong to label them as lazy or unmotivated. Rather, educators should look for ways to help these students cope with their writing difficulties.

Regina Richards (1998) and Susan Jones (2000) suggest that educators develop three types of strategies for helping students with dysgraphia: accommodation (also called compensation) strategies, modification strategies, and remediation strategies. Accommodations bypass the problem by avoiding the difficulty and by reducing the impact that writing has on learning. Modification looks to change the types and the expectations of assignments. Remediation strategies focus on reteaching the concept or skill or providing additional structural practice that more closely matches the student's needs and learning style.

To help students, educators must first determine the point at which a student begins to struggle. Does the problem occur as the student begins to write or does it appear later in the writing process? Is there a problem with organization of thoughts? Is the struggle more evident when the student changes from just copying material to generating complex ideas and trying to commit those to writing? Is the struggle because of confusion over printed and cursive letters, over grammar, or because of punctuation? Once the struggle area is identified, then it becomes a matter of selecting the appropriate combination of accommodation, modification, and remedial techniques for the student.

Impact on Learning

- Because technology allows writing to be done on computers, students need to have reasons for learning, practicing, and improving their handwriting.

- Writing difficulties can be so frustrating that the student avoids all learning.

- Because practice makes perfect, practicing inventive spellings for too long will lead to the permanent storage of misspellings, which will be difficult to change later.

Strategies to Consider

Suggestions to Build Confidence in Students With Writing Disorders

Lack of confidence is one of the major difficulties of students with writing disorders. Here are a few suggestions to give to students with dysgraphia to help them regain confidence and overcome the frustrations they often experience when writing.

✓ **Organize Your Thoughts.** First try to get your major ideas down on paper. Then go back and fill in the details.

✓ **Use a Tape Recorder.** If you are feeling frustrated with your writing, stop and dictate what you want to write into a tape recorder. Listen to the tape later and write down your major ideas.

✓ **Use the Computer.** Even if you are not great at the beginning, it is important to practice your keyboarding skills. You will get better and faster at it once you have learned the pattern of the keys. Computers can help you organize your thoughts, put them in the proper sequence, and even check your spelling. In the long run, it will be faster and clearer than handwriting.

✓ **Continue to Practice Handwriting.** No matter how frustrating handwriting is, you will need to be able to write things down in the future. Like any other skill, your handwriting will get better with continued practice.

✓ **Talk While Writing.** Talk to yourself while writing. This auditory feedback is a valuable tool to help you monitor what and how you write.

✓ **Use Visual Aids.** Drawing a picture or diagram can help you organize your thoughts. Some computer programs also have the capability of producing your graphic organizers.

Strategies to Consider

Accommodation Strategies for Students With Writing Disorders

Accommodation strategies help bypass writing difficulties and reduce the impact that writing has on the learning process so that students can focus more completely on the content of their writing. The accommodations can adjust the rate and volume of writing, the complexity of the task, and the tools used to create the final product. Here are some accommodating strategies to consider in each of these areas (Richards, 1998; Jones, 2000).

Accommodating the Rate of Work Produced

◆ **Allow more time** for students to complete written tasks, such as note-taking, written tests, and copying. Also, allow these students to begin written projects earlier than others. Consider including time in the student's schedule for acting as an aide, and then have the student use that time for making up or starting new written work.

◆ **Encourage developing keyboarding skills and using the computer.** Students can begin to learn keyboarding in first grade. Encourage them to use various word processing programs. Teaching handwriting is still important, but students may be more likely to produce longer and more complex writing with the computer.

◆ **Have students prepare worksheets in advance,** complete with the required headings, such as name, date, and topic. Provide a standard template for them with this information already on it.

– Continued –

Accommodation Strategies—Continued

Accommodating the Volume of Work Produced

- ◆ **Provide partially completed outlines** and ask students to fill in the missing details. This is a valuable, but not burdensome, exercise in note taking.

- ◆ **Allow students to dictate to another student.** One student (scribe) writes down what another student says verbatim and then allows the dictating student to make changes without help from the scribe.

- ◆ **Correct poor spelling in first drafts,** but do not lower the grade because of it. However, make clear to the students that spelling does eventually count, especially in assignments completed over time.

- ◆ **Reduce copying of printed work.** Avoid having students copy over something already printed in a text, like entire mathematics problems. Provide a worksheet with the text material already on it or have the students just write down their original answers or work.

- ◆ **Allow students to use abbreviations** in some writing, such as b/4 for before, b/c for because, and w/ for with. These are also helpful shortcuts during note taking.

Accommodating the Complexity of the Work Produced

- ◆ **Allow students to use print or cursive writing.** Many students with dysgraphia are more comfortable with print (manuscript) letters.

Accommodation Strategies—Continued

◆ **Teach students the stages of writing,** such as brainstorming, drafting, editing, and proofreading.

◆ **Encourage students to use a spell checker.** Using the spell checker decreases the demands on the writing process, lowering frustration and diverting more energy to thought production. For students who also have reading difficulties, concurrently using a computer reading program also decreases the demands on the writer.

◆ **Have students proofread after a delay** when they are more likely to catch writing errors. This way, they will see what they *actually* wrote rather than what they *thought* they wrote.

Accommodating the Tools of Work Production

◆ **Allow students to use lined and graph paper.** Lined paper helps students keep their writing level across the page. Have younger students use graph paper for mathematics calculations to keep columns and rows straight. Older students can turned lined paper sideways for column control.

◆ **Allow students to use different writing instruments.** Students should use the writing instrument they find most comfortable. Some students have difficulty writing with ballpoint pens, preferring thin-line marker pens that have more friction with the paper. Others prefer mechanical pencils.

◆ **Have pencil grips available** in all styles. Even high school students enjoy these fun grips and some like the big pencils usually associated with primary school.

◆ **Allow some students to use speech recognition programs.** For students with very difficult writing problems, using a speech recognition program within a word processing program allows them to dictate their thoughts rather than type them. However, this is not a substitute for learning handwriting.

Strategies to Consider

Modification Strategies
for Students With Writing Disorders

For some students, accommodation strategies will not remove the barriers that their writing difficulties pose. Teachers may need to make modifications in these students' assignments. Here are some suggested modifications in the volume, complexity, and format of written work.

Modifying the Volume of Work Produced

❏ **Limit the amount of copying that students do.** For example, to copy definitions, have the students rewrite and shorten them without affecting the meaning. Another option is to have them use drawings or diagrams to answer questions.

❏ **Reduce the length** of written assignments. Emphasize quality over quantity.

Modifying the Complexity of Work Produced

❏ **Prioritization of tasks.** Stress or de-emphasize certain tasks for a complex activity. For example, students could focus on complex sentences in one activity and on using descriptive words in another. Evaluate the assignment based on the prioritized tasks.

Modification Strategies—Continued

❏ **Encourage graphic organizers.** Preorganization strategies such as the use of graphic organizers will help students get their main ideas in line before tackling the writing process.

❏ **Use cooperative learning groups** to give students a chance to play different roles, such as brainstormer, encourager, organizer of information, etc.

❏ **Provide intermittent deadlines** for long-term assignments. Work with other teachers when setting due dates, especially those involving writing assignments. Parents may also be able to monitor the student's work at home so that it can comply with deadlines.

Modifying the Format of the Work Produced

❏ **Allow students to submit alternative projects,** such as an oral report or visual project. Ask for a short written report to explain or expand on the oral or visual work. However, these alternatives should not replace all writing assignments.

Strategies to Consider

Remediation Strategies for Students With Writing Disorders

Students should not be allowed to avoid the process of writing, no matter how severe their dysgraphia. Writing is an important skill that they will eventually use to sign documents, write checks, fill out forms, take messages, or make a grocery list. Thus, they need to learn to write even if they can do so for just a short time.

Remediation strategies focus on reteaching information or a particular skill to help students acquire mastery and fluency. Substantial modeling of all strategies is essential for the students to be successful. Here are some suggested areas for remediation (Richards, 1998; Jones, 2000).

★ **Teaching Handwriting Continuously.** Many students would like to have better handwriting. Build handwriting instruction into the students' schedule. Provide opportunities to teach them this, keeping in mind the age, aptitude, and attitude of each student.

★ **Helping With Spelling.** Spelling difficulties are common for students with dysgraphia, especially if sequencing is a major problem. The students with dysgraphia who also have dyslexia need structured and specific instruction in learning to spell phonetically. This skill can help them use technical tools that rely on phonetic spelling to find a word.

★ **Correcting the Pencil Grip.** Young children should be encouraged to use a proper pencil grip from the beginning of their writing experience. Descriptive research indicates that, for the best results, the grip should be consistently between 3/4 inch to 1 inch from the pencil tip. Moderate pressure should be applied and the angle of the pencil to the paper should be about 45 degrees and slanted toward the student's writing arm. Accomplishing the proper slant will be difficult for left handed writers.

Remediation Strategies—Continued

A poor pencil grip can be changed to the appropriate form by using plastic pencil grips, which are commercially available. Obviously, it is easier to encourage the correct grip as soon as the student begins writing; older students with poor grip posture find it very difficult to make changes. The teacher needs to consider whether it is worth the time and effort to get the student to change the grip to be more efficient. If not, identify compensatory strategies that are available for the student.

★ **Writing a Paragraph.** Students can be taught this eight-step process for writing a paragraph. The eight steps can be easily remembered by using the acronym, **POWER**.

1. Plan the paper by thinking about the ideas that you want to include in it.

2. Organize the idea by using a graphic organizer or mind map. This places the main idea in the center and supporting facts are written on lines coming out from the center, much like the spokes of a wheel. Other visual formats can be used depending on the paragraph's topic.

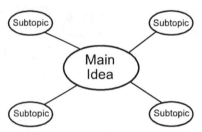

3. Analyze the graphic organizer to ensure that all your ideas have been included. Check your spelling.

4. Write a draft of the paragraph, focusing on the main ideas.

5. Edit your work for punctuation, capitalization, grammar, and spelling.

6. Use the corrections made in step 5 to revise the paragraph.

7. Proofread again, editing and revising as needed.

8. Develop a final product in written or typed form.

P...... Plan the paper (Step 1)
O...... Organize your thoughts and ideas (Steps 2 and 3)
W...... Write the draft (Step 4)
E...... Edit your work (Steps 5, 6, and 7)
R...... Revise your work and produce a final copy (Step 8)

– Continued–

Remediation Strategies—Continued

★ **Increasing the Speed of Writing.** Many students with dysgraphia write very slowly. To identify the appropriate remediation strategy, teachers need to determine the cause of the slowness.

▸ Is it the actual formation of the letters? If so, the students need more practice on this skill, perhaps by saying the letters aloud while writing. Air writing can be helpful because it uses many more muscles to form the letters. Also, have the students write large letters on a big surface, such as a chalkboard or dry-erase board.

▸ Is it in the organization of ideas? If so, provide the students with graphic organizers to help them sort and prioritize their thoughts and facts.

★ **Dealing With Fatigue.** Poor motor sequencing or an incorrect pencil grip can lead to fatigue with the writing process. The following can help students relieve the stress of writing and relax the writing hand.

▸ Take writing breaks at regular intervals. Students should realize that it is permissible to stop occasionally and relax the muscles of the hand. This break also gives them a chance to review what has been written and to continue to organize their thoughts.

▸ Shake the hands quickly to relax the muscles. This increases blood flow to the finger and hand muscles.

▸ Rub the hands on some texture, like the carpet or clothes.

▸ Rub the hands together and focus on the feeling of warmth. The rubbing also helps to restore blood flow to the area.

★ **Giving Praise, Being Patient, and Encouraging Patience.** Genuinely praise the positive aspects of students' work. Be patient with their efforts and problems, and encourage them to have patience with themselves.

Strategies to Consider

Expressive Writing for Students With Learning Disabilities

One of the goals of teaching writing is to help students express their thoughts and ideas in personal narratives and persuasive essays. Students whose learning disabilities include problems with writing often have great difficulty with this. Finding ways of helping these students has been the subject of considerable research.

A recent analysis studied the effectiveness of research-based instructional approaches for teaching expressive writing to students with learning disabilities. The following three components of instruction consistently led to improving student success in learning expressive writing (Gersten, Baker, and Edwards, 1999):

1. Adhering to a basic framework of planning, writing, and revision

Most of the successful interventions used a basic framework of planning, writing, and revision. Each step was taught explicitly, followed by multiple examples and the use of memory devices, such as prompt cards or mnemonics.

Planning. Advance planning results in better first drafts. One way of helping students develop a plan of action is to provide a planning think sheet that uses structured and sequential prompts. It specifies the topic and poses questions to guide the student's thought processes. See the sample sheet at the right.

Planning Think Sheet

TOPIC:_____

Who am I writing for?

Why am I writing this?

What do I already know about this?

How can I group my ideas?

How will I organize my ideas?

– Continued –

Expressive Writing—Continued

Creating a First Draft. The planning think sheet helps students create first drafts by serving as a guide through the writing process. The guide also gives the student and teacher a common language for an ongoing discussion about the assignment. This student-teacher interaction emphasizes cooperative work rather than the recent method of writing mainly in isolation.

Revising and Editing. The skills of revising and editing are critical to successful writing. Some researchers found a peer editing approach to be particularly effective (Gersten and Baker, 1999). Here's how it worked:

- Pairs of students alternated their roles as student-writer and student-critic.
- The student-critic identified ambiguities and asked the writer for clarification. The writer then made revisions, with the teacher's help if needed.
- Once the clarifications were made, the student pair then moved on to correct capitalization, punctuation, and spelling.
- Throughout the process, the student writers had to explain the intent of their writings and continue revising their essays to reflect their intent accurately. These clarifying dialogues helped the student pairs to understand each other's perspective.

2. Teaching explicitly the critical steps in the writing process

Because different types of writing (e.g., personal narrative or persuasive essay) are based on different structures, explicitly teaching text structures provides the students with a specific guide to complete their writing task. For example, writing a persuasive essay requires a thesis and supporting arguments. Narrative writing focuses on character development and a story climax. Teach these structures, using explicit models of each text type.

Expressive Writing—Continued

3. Providing feedback guided by the information explicitly taught

The researchers found that successful interventions always included frequent feedback to the students on the quality of their overall writing, strengths, and missing elements (Gersten and Baker, 1999). Combining feedback with instruction strengthens the dialogue between student and teacher, thereby helping students to develop a sensitivity to their own writing style. This sensitivity may lead students to reflect on, realize, and correct writing problems as well

> *Researchers found that frequent feedback was a powerful tool for improving students' writing.*

as perceive their ideas from another's perspective. The research studies also showed that student gains were more likely to occur when the teachers and other students provided feedback mainly in the areas of organization, originality, and interpretation.

MATHEMATICAL DISABILITIES

Learning to Calculate

How and when the young brain begins to deal with number logic and arithmetic calculations are unknown. However, mounting evidence shows that toddlers have a sense of numbers and can already deal with limited arithmetic operations (e.g., simple adding and subtracting) before the age of one year (Diamond and Hopson, 1998). This early ability makes sense in terms of our past development as a species. In primitive societies, a youngster going for

a stroll out of the cave needed to determine quickly if the number of animals in an approaching pack might spell danger or just an opportunity for play. Young hunters had to determine how *many* individuals would be needed to take down a large animal. Recognizing that three apples provide more nourishment than one was also a valuable survival asset. Numeration, then, persisted in the genetic code.

For many years, educators recognized that some children were very adept in mathematical calculations while others struggled despite much effort and motivation. But the percentage of school-age children who experience difficulties in learning mathematics has been steadily growing in the last three decades. Why is that? Is the brain's ability to perform arithmetic calculations declining? If so, why? Does the brain get less arithmetic practice because technology has shifted computation from brain cells to inexpensive electronic calculators?

It is only in the past few years that brain scanning studies have revealed clues about how the brain performs mathematical operations. Functional MRI scans indicate that the parietal and

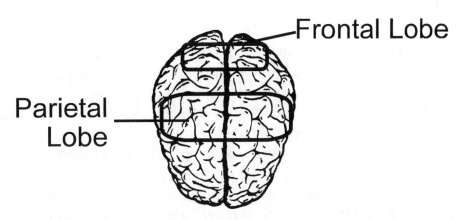

Figure 7.1 *Mathematical calculations primarily activate the brain's frontal and parietal lobes. Other areas may be activated as the calculations become more complex.*

frontal lobes (Figure 7.1) are primarily involved in basic mental mathematics (e.g., counting forward or doing serial calculations). However, other areas of the brain are recruited into action when dealing with more complex calculations (Rueckert, Lange, Partiot, Appollonio, Litvan, LeBihan, and Grafman, 1996).

Mathematical Disabilities

In previous chapters, we have referred to the considerable amount of research that has been conducted in an effort to understand how the human brain learns. As a result, we also have a greater understanding of the diagnosis and remediation of learning disorders, especially in areas of language, reading, and writing. In addition, a few researchers have been studying why students have problems with learning early mathematics, despite normal intelligence and adequate instruction.

About 6 percent of school-age children have some form of difficulty with processing mathematics. This is about the same number as children who have reading problems. However, because of the strong emphasis that our society places on the need to learn reading, many more research studies have focused on problems in this area than on mathematics. Nonetheless, the growing number of students who are having problems with mathematics has renewed research interest in how the brain does calculations and the possible causes of mathematical disorders. The condition that causes persistent problems with processing numerical calculations is often referred to as *dyscalculia*.

Environmental Causes

Even individuals with normal abilities in processing numerical operations can display mathematical disorders. Because they have no inherent mathematical deficits, their difficulties most likely arise from environmental causes. In modern American society, reading and writing have become the main measures of a good student. Mathematics ability is regarded more as a specialized function rather than as a general indicator of intelligence. Consequently, the stigma of not being able to do mathematics is reduced and becomes socially acceptable. Just hearing their parents say "I wasn't very good at math" allows children to embrace the social attitudes that regard mathematics failure as acceptable and routine. A recent Harris poll revealed that although more than 90 percent of parents expect their children to go to college and almost 90 percent of kids want to go to college, fully half of those kids want to drop mathematics as soon as they can (USDE, 1998). To help these students, educators and parents must recognize the importance of more study in this field.

Fear of Mathematics. Some children develop a fear (or phobia) of mathematics because of negative experiences in their past or a simple lack of self-confidence with numbers. No doubt, mathematics phobia can be as challenging as any learning disability, but it is important to remember that these students have neurological systems for computation that are normal. They need help primarily in replacing the memory of failure with the possibility of success. Students with mathematical disorders, on the other hand, have a neurological deficit that results in persistent difficulty in processing numbers.

Quality of Teaching. One critical factor in how well students learn mathematics is the quality of the teaching. Recent studies show that student achievement in mathematics is strongly linked to the teacher's expertise in mathematics. Students of an expert teacher perform up to 40 percent better on achievement tests compared to students of a teacher with limited training in mathematics. The average K-8 teacher has taken only three or fewer mathematics or mathematics education classes in college. Partly because of the current teacher shortage, less than half of eighth grade mathematics teachers have taken a single class on how to teach mathematics, and 28 percent of high school mathematics teachers do not have a major or minor in mathematics (USDE, 1998).

Neurological and Other Causes

Because the parietal lobe is heavily involved with number operations, damage to this area can result in difficulties. Studies of individuals with Gerstmann syndrome—the result of damage to the parietal lobe—showed that they had serious problems with mathematical calculations as well as right-left disorientation, but no problems with oral language skills (Suresh and Sebastian, 2000).

Individuals with visual processing weaknesses almost always display difficulties with mathematics. This is probably because success in mathematics requires one to visualize numbers and mathematical situations, especially in algebra and geometry. Students with sequencing difficulties also may have dyscalculia because they cannot remember the order of mathematical operations nor the specific formulas needed to complete a set of computations.

Genetic factors also seem to play a role. For example, studies of identical twins reveal close mathematics scores. Children from families with a history of mathematical giftedness or retardation show common aptitudes with other family members. Girls born with Turner syndrome—a condition caused by the partial or complete absence of one of the two X chromosomes normally found in women—usually display dyscalculia, among other learning problems (Mazzocco, 1998).

> **Mathematical Disorders**
>
> General Symptoms:
> - Inconsistent results with addition, subtraction, multiplication, and division
> - Inability to remember mathematical formulas, rules, or concepts
> - Difficulty with abstract concepts of time and direction
> - Consistent errors when recalling numbers including transpositions, omissions, and reversals
> - Difficulty remembering how to keep score during games

Types of Mathematical Disorders

The complexity of mathematics makes the study of mathematical disorders particularly challenging for researchers. Learning deficits can include difficulties in mastering basic number concepts, counting skills, and processing arithmetic operations as well as procedural, retrieval, and visual-spatial deficits (Geary, 2000). As with any learning disability, each of these deficits can range from mild to severe.

Number Concept Difficulties. As mentioned before, the understanding of small numbers and quantity appears to be present at birth. The understanding of larger numbers and place value, however, seems to develop during the preschool and early elementary years. Studies show that most children with mathematical disorders nevertheless have their basic number competencies intact (Geary, 2000).

Counting Skill Deficits. Studies of children with mathematical disorders show that they have deficits in counting knowledge and counting accuracy. Some may also have problems keeping numerical information in working memory while counting, resulting in counting errors.

Difficulties With Arithmetic Skills. Children with mathematical disorders have difficulties solving simple and complex arithmetic problems. Their difficulties stem mainly from deficits in both numerical procedures (solving 6+5 or 4 x 4) and working memory. Moreover, deficits in visual-spatial skills can lead to problems with arithmetic because of misalignment of numerals in multicolumn addition. Although procedural, memory, and visual-spatial deficits can occur separately, they are often interconnected.

Procedural Disorders. Students displaying this disorder
  ▸ use arithmetic procedures (algorithms) that are developmentally immature,
  ▸ have problems sequencing the steps of multi-step procedures,
  ▸ have difficulty understanding the concepts associated with procedures, and
  ▸ make frequent mistakes when using procedures.
The cause of this disorder is unknown. However, researchers suspect a dysfunction in the left hemisphere, which specializes in procedural tasks.

Memory Disorders. Students displaying this disorder
  ▸ have difficulty retrieving arithmetic facts,
  ▸ have a high error rate when they do retrieve arithmetic facts, and
  ▸ retrieve incorrect facts that are associated with the correct facts.
Here again, a dysfunction of the left hemisphere is suspected, mainly because these individuals frequently have reading disorders as well. This association further suggests that memory deficits may be inheritable.

Visual-Spatial Deficits. Students with this disorder
  ▸ have difficulties in the spatial arrangement of their work, such as aligning the columns in multicolumn addition;
  ▸ often misread numerical signs, rotate and transpose numbers, or both;
  ▸ misinterpret spatial placement of numerals, resulting in place value errors; and,
  ▸ have difficulty with problems involving space in areas, as required in algebra and geometry.
This disorder is more closely associated with deficits in the right hemisphere, which specializes in visual-spatial tasks. Some studies suggest that the left parietal lobe also may be implicated.

Many students eventually overcome procedural disorders as they mature and learn to rely on sequence diagrams and other tools to remember the steps of mathematical procedures. Those with visual-spatial disorders also improve when they discover the benefits of graph paper and learn to solve certain algebra and geometry problems with logic rather than through spatial analysis alone. However, memory deficits do not seem to improve with maturity. Studies indicate that individuals with

> *Children often outgrow procedural and visual-spatial difficulties, but memory problems may continue throughout life.*

this problem will continue to have difficulties retrieving basic arithmetic facts throughout life. This finding may suggest that the memory problem exists not just for mathematical operations, but may signal a more general deficit in retrieving information from memory.

What Is the Future of Research in Mathematics Disorders?

Many questions remain unanswered regarding the environmental and innate causes of mathematical disorders. For example, we now believe that infants are born with an innate sense of number logic and the ability to perform simple arithmetic operations. Some researchers believe that toddlers can even communicate with each other about their counting through a form of "toddler arithmetic" (Diamond and Hopson, 1998). How do they do that? By learning more about exactly how infants' brains process arithmetic calculations, we can build on this foundation when exposing children to more complex mathematics. Likewise, researchers need to determine which types of mathematical disorders are simply delays in development and which may represent more fundamental problems.

Other questions for research include the following: What genetic factors affect the neural networks and cognitive skills that support mathematical operations? What types of mathematical disorders are related to reading disorders, and why?

The ultimate goal of research is to develop remedies to help individuals deal with their problems. Remediation becomes difficult when a disorder is not well understood. Nonetheless, enough is now known to suggest some strategies that are likely to help those challenged by mathematical processing. Further research can only improve on this situation.

What Do Educators Need to Consider?

Determining the Source of the Problem. The first task facing educators who deal with children with mathematics disorders is to determine the nature of the problem. Obviously,

143

environmental causes require different interventions than developmental causes. Low performance on a mathematics test *may* indicate that a problem exists, but tests do not provide information on the exact source of the poor performance. Standardized tests, such as the *Brigance Comprehensive Inventory of Basic Skills—Revised*, are available that provide more precise information on whether the problems stem from deficits in counting, number facts, or procedures.

> *Seven prerequisite skills can help **all** students learn mathematics more successfully.*

Prerequisite Skills. Examining the nature of mathematics curriculum and instruction may reveal clues about how the school system approaches teaching these topics. A good frame of reference is the recognition that students need to have mastered a certain number of skills before they can understand and apply the principles of more complex mathematical operations. Mahesh Sharma (1989) and other mathematics educators have suggested that the following seven skills are prerequisites to successfully learning mathematics. They are the ability to

1. Follow sequential directions.
2. Recognize patterns.
3. Estimate by forming a reasonable guess about quantity, size, magnitude, and amount.
4. Visualize pictures in one's mind and manipulate them.
5. Have a good sense of spatial orientation and space organization, including telling left from right, compass directions, horizontal and vertical directions, etc.
6. Do deductive reasoning, that is, reason from a general principle to a particular instance, or from a stated premise to a logical conclusion.
7. Do inductive reasoning, that is, come to a natural understanding that is not the result of conscious attention or reasoning, easily detecting the patterns in different situations and the interrelationships between procedures and concepts.

Sharma notes, for example, that those who are unable to follow sequential directions will have great difficulty understanding the concept of long division, which requires retention of several different processes performed in a particular sequence. First one estimates, then multiplies, then compares, then subtracts, then brings down a number, and the cycle repeats. Those with directional difficulties will be unsure which number goes inside the division sign or on top of the fraction. Moving through the division problem also presents other directional difficulties: One reads to the right, then records a number up, then multiplies the numbers diagonally, then records the product down below while watching for place value, then brings a number down, and so on.

Less Is More. Another lesson that research has taught us is that students with special needs are likely to be more successful if taught fewer concepts in more time. The notion that "less is more" can apply to all students, and is particularly important for those with learning problems. Studies of mathematics (as well as science) courses in the United States and other countries show that spending more time on fewer key concepts leads to greater student achievement in the long run. Yet, our mathematics curriculum does not challenge students to study topics in depth. We tend to present a large number of ideas but develop very few of them (National Center for Education Statistics, 1996). Students with special needs should focus on mastering a few important ideas and learn to apply them accurately.

Use of Manipulatives. Students with special needs who use manipulatives in their mathematics classes outperform similar students who do not. Manipulatives support the tactile and spatial reinforcement of mathematical concepts, maintain focus, and help students develop the cognitive structures necessary for understanding arithmetic relationships. In addition to physical manipulatives (e.g., Cuisenaire rods and tokens), computers and software also help these learners make connections between various types of knowledge. For example, computer software can construct and dynamically connect pictured objects to symbolic representations (such as cubes to a numeral) and thus help learners generalize and draw abstract concepts from the manipulatives.

Search for Patterns. One of the more surprising research findings is that many children with learning disabilities—including those with mathematical disorders—can learn basic arithmetic concepts. What is needed for these children is an approach that relies less on intensive drill and practice and more on searching for, finding, and using patterns in learning the basic number combinations and arithmetic strategies.

Build on Students' Strengths. As obvious as this statement seems, teachers can often turn a student's failure into success if they build on what the student already knows how to do. Too often teachers get so focused on looking for ways to improve an area of weakness that they unintentionally overlook an individual's learning strengths. Yet many years of research into learning styles has demonstrated effective ways of recruiting style strengths to build up weaknesses.

Most people learn mathematics best in the context of real-world problems. School systems will increase all their students' chances for learning mathematics successfully if they plan curriculum content and instructional strategies that enhance prerequisite skills while developing knowledge and application of mathematical concepts and operations. Students are more comfortable with mathematics when they perceive it as a practical tool and not as an end unto itself. Integrated curriculum units provide opportunities for mathematics to be threaded through diverse and relevant topics. Finally, if the notion that babies are born with a sense of number logic continues to be supported by further research, then educators will need to reconsider how and when we teach mathematics in schools.

Mathematics for Students Studying English as a Second Language

Little attention or research has been devoted to studying the problems of learning mathematics for students with learning disabilities who are also studying English as a second language (ESL). Yet, mathematics is one of the first subjects where these students are mainstreamed. One explanation for this lack is the perception that mathematics is a universal language and, thus, should transcend the language barriers posed by other subjects.

The few studies that have investigated this situation have indicated that language factors are indeed a concern. Although the language of mathematics is precise, it is not always translated accurately by ESL students. Those who also have learning disabilities already have problems understanding mathematical concepts in their native language. When faced with mathematical statements in English, these difficulties are compounded. The students have to cope with applying the rules of vocabulary, syntax, and grammar to both the English language *and* to mathematics. Consequently, they may have problems distinguishing differences in mathematical relationships, such as size, time, speed, and space.

Cultural differences also play a role, especially in the interpretation of story problems. The values, mores, and customs of different cultures can vary significantly from those represented in American textbooks. One study found that problems written for American children often contained biases of values and gender that caused confusion in children from other cultures (Fellows, Koblitz, and Koblitz, 1994).

Differences in algorithms—the procedures used to find the solution to a mathematical problem—also pose difficulties for ESL students. Asian and South American students, for example, learn algorithms that are different in

> *The algorithms that an ESL student uses to make calculations may be misinterpreted as a mathematics disorder.*

sequence from those taught in American schools. The algorithms that an ESL student uses to make calculations may be misinterpreted as a mathematics disorder. Rather than being concerned about differing algorithms, teachers should determine whether the student can explain the procedure and arrive at the correct answer. See the Strategies to Consider at the end of this chapter for more suggestions on helping ESL students.

Impact on Learning

- Students with difficulties in mathematics are likely to focus when the mathematics instruction forms patterns and has meaning.

- Mathematics will be very difficult to master if certain prerequisite skills are not in place.

- Some students can learn successfully if they process mathematics more as a language than as a collection of formulas and theorems.

- ESL students can have difficulties because of language problems and cultural differences.

Strategies to Consider

General Guidelines for Teaching Mathematics to Students With Special Needs

What we have learned about how students in general education learn mathematics can apply as well, with appropriate modifications, to students with mathematical disorders. Here are some recommendations gleaned from the research (Clements, 2000).

❑ **Help students develop conceptual understanding and skills.** These students need time to look at concrete models, understand them, and link them to abstract numerical representations. Allow them more time for mathematics study and for completing assignments.

❑ **Consider giving more oral and fewer written tests.** The stress of written tests increases the mental burden on these students who often are better at telling you what they know than writing it.

❑ **Develop meaningful (relevant) practice exercises.** No one questions the value of practice—it makes permanent! But extensive practice that has little meaning for students is perceived as boring and may actually be harmful to special needs students (Baroody, 1999). Practice solving problems that are purposeful and meaningful.

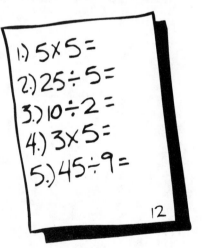

1.) 5 × 5 =
2.) 25 ÷ 5 =
3.) 10 ÷ 2 =
4.) 3 × 5 =
5.) 45 ÷ 9 =

12

❑ **Maintain reasonable expectations.** If we really want all students to have basic competencies in mathematics, then we must establish expectations that are reasonable. This should include problem-based learning, solving authentic problems, and showing the applications of mathematics to other

General Guidelines for Teaching Mathematics—Continued

subject areas, such as science. Similarly, setting expectations that are too low—explicitly or implicitly—increases the burden that children with all types of special needs may need to carry as adults.

❑ **Build on children's strengths.** In all areas of learning, teachers can often turn a student's failure into success if they build on what the student already knows how to do. Many years of research into learning styles has demonstrated effective ways of recruiting style strengths to build up weaknesses.

❑ **Use manipulatives appropriately.** Manipulatives can be valuable tools if students are able to connect what they are handling with what they are thinking. Have students explain aloud the connections they are making and make sure they refer to the mathematical concepts and skills they are learning.

❑ **Help students make connections.** Students perceive meaning when they are able to connect what they are learning to prior knowledge or to future usefulness. Help students connect symbols to verbal descriptions. Find ways to link social situations to solving practical mathematical problems (e.g., splitting a restaurant check, determining an appropriate tip).

❑ **Determine and build on a student's informal learning strategies.** All learners develop informal strategies for dealing with their world. Determine what strategies the student is using and build on them to develop concepts and procedures.

❑ **Accommodate individual learning styles as much as practicable.** Use as many multisensory approaches as possible. Include modeling, role-playing, demonstrations, simulations, and cooperative learning groups to provide variety and maintain student interest. Use mnemonic devices and games to help students remember number combinations and other important facts. Limit direct instruction (i.e., teacher talk) and use more interactive teaching strategies.

– Continued –

General Guidelines for Teaching Mathematics—Continued

❏ **Use technology appropriately.** All students should have access to electronic tools. They can use them to understand mathematical concepts as well as how to benefit their adult lives. Using computer software that includes speech recognition and three-dimensional design, for instance, can be very helpful for students with special needs.

Strategies to Consider

Diagnostic Tools for Assessing Learning Difficulties in Mathematics

Research studies over the last 15 years suggest that five critical factors affect the learning of mathematics. Each factor can serve as a diagnostic tool for assessing the nature of any learning difficulties students may experience with mathematical processing.

1. **Level of Cognitive Awareness.** Students come to a learning situation with varying levels of cognitive awareness about that learning. The levels can range from no cognitive awareness to high levels of cognitive functioning (Sharma, 1989). The teacher's first task is to determine the students' level of cognitive awareness and the strategies each brings to the mathematics task. This is not easy, but it can be accomplished if the teacher does the following:

   ▸ Interviews the students individually and observes how each one approaches a mathematical problem that needs to be solved.

   ▸ Asks "What is the student thinking?" and "What formal and informal strategies is the student using?"

   ▸ Determines what prerequisite skills are in place and which are poor or missing.

   ▸ Determines if a mathematics answer is correct or incorrect and asks students to explain how they arrived at the answer.

   Knowing the levels of the students' cognitive awareness and prerequisite skills will give the teacher valuable information for selecting and introducing new concepts and skills.

– Continued –

Diagnostic Tools—Continued

2. **Mathematics Learning Profile.** Researchers agree that each person processes mathematics differently and that these differences run along a continuum from primarily quantitative to primarily qualitative (Sharma, 1989; Marolda and Davidson, 1994).

Quantitative learners:

▸ Prefer to deal with entities that have definite values such as length, time, volume, and size.

▸ Prefer procedural approaches to problem-solving and tend to be very methodical and sequential in all they do.

▸ Approach mathematics as though following a recipe.

▸ Prefer to break down problems into their parts, solve them, and then reassemble the components to deal with larger problems.

▸ Are better at deductive reasoning, that is, reasoning from the general principle to a particular instance.

▸ Learn best when mathematics is presented as a highly structured subject and with a continuous linear focus.

▸ Prefer hands-on materials with a counting basis, such as base-10 blocks and number lines.

▸ Stick with one standardized way of solving problems because alternative solutions are often perceived as uncomfortable and distracting.

Qualitative learners:

▸ Approach mathematics tasks holistically and intuitively.

▸ Describe mathematical elements in terms of their qualities rather than by separate parts.

▸ Are social learners who reason by talking through questions, associations, and examples.

▸ Learn by seeing relationships between concepts and procedures.

▸ Draw associations and parallels between familiar situations and the current task.

▸ Focus on visual-spatial aspects of mathematical information.

Diagnostic Tools—Continued

> ▸ Have difficulty with sequences, algorithms, elementary mathematics, and precise calculations.
>
> ▸ In their work, tend to invent shortcuts, bypass steps, and consolidate procedures with intuitive reasoning.
>
> ▸ Often do not practice enough to attain levels of automaticity.

Because both types of learning styles are present in mathematics classes, teachers need to incorporate multiple instructional strategies. Teaching to one style alone leaves out students with the other style, many of whom may do poorly in mathematics as a result. In fact, some may even exhibit the symptoms of mathematics disorders.

3. **Language of Mathematics.** Mathematical disorders often arise when students fail to understand the language of mathematics, which has its own symbolic representations, syntax, and terminology. Solving word problems requires the ability to translate the language of English into the language of mathematics. The translation is likely to be successful if the student recognizes English language equivalents for each mathematical statement. For example, if the teacher asks the class to solve the problem "76 take away 8," the students will correctly write the expression in the exact order stated, "76 - 8." But if the teacher says, "Subtract 8 from 76," a student following the language order could mistakenly write, "8 - 76." Learning to identify and correctly translate mathematical syntax becomes critical to student success in problem solving.

$$31 - X = 19$$
$$Y + 2\,{}^1\!/_{15} = ?$$
$$Y = 7$$
$$x + 21^3 =$$

Language can be an obstacle in other ways. Students may learn a limited vocabulary for performing basic arithmetic operations, such as "add" and "multiply," only to run into difficulties when they encounter expressions asking for the "sum" or "product" of numbers. Teachers can avoid this problem by introducing synonyms for every function: "Let us *multiply* 6 and 5. We are finding the *product* of 6 and 5. The product of 6 *times* 5 is 30."

– Continued –

Diagnostic Tools—Continued

4. **Prerequisite Skills.** The seven prerequisite skills necessary to learn mathematics successfully are non-mathematical in nature. However, they must be mastered before even the most basic understandings of number concepts and arithmetic operations can be learned. Teachers need to assess the extent to which these seven skills are present in each student.

Teachers might consider using this simple profile diagram to assist in their assessment. After assessing the student's level on each skill, analyze the results and decide on a plan of action that will address any areas needing improvement.

Prerequisite Skills Profile for Mathematics

Student's Name:_____ Date:_____

Directions: On a scale of 1 (lowest) to 5 (highest), circle the number that indicates the degree to which the student displays mastery of each skill. Connect the circles to see the profile.

Skill

Skill					
Follows sequential directions	5	4	3	2	1
Recognizes patterns	5	4	3	2	1
Can estimate quantities	5	4	3	2	1
Can visualize and manipulate mental pictures	5	4	3	2	1
Sense of spatial orientation and organization	5	4	3	2	1
Ability to do deductive reasoning	5	4	3	2	1
Ability to do inductive reasoning	5	4	3	2	1

Action Plan: As a result of this profile, we will work together to_____
by doing_____

Diagnostic Tools—Continued

Students with four or more scores in the 1 to 2 range will have significant problems learning the basic concepts of mathematics. They will need instruction and practice in mastering these skills before they can be expected to master mathematical content.

5. **Levels of Learning Mastery.** How does a teacher decide when a student has mastered a mathematical concept? Certainly, written tests of problem solving are one of the major devices for evaluating learning. However, they are useful tools only to the extent that they actually measure mastery rather than rote memory of formulas and procedures. Cognitive research suggests that a person must move through six levels of mastery to truly learn and retain mathematical concepts. For mastery, the student

   ▸ Level One. Connects new knowledge to existing knowledge and experiences.

   ▸ Level Two. Searches for concrete material to construct a model or show a manifestation of the concept.

   ▸ Level Three. Illustrates the concept by drawing a diagram to connect the concrete example to a symbolic picture or representation.

   ▸ Level Four. Translates the concept into mathematical notation using number symbols, operational signs, formulas, and equations.

   ▸ Level Five. Applies the concept correctly to real world situations, projects, and story problems.

   ▸ Level Six. Can teach the concept successfully to others, or can communicate it on a test.

Too often, paper-and-pencil tests assess only level 6. Thus, when the student's results are poor, the teacher may not know where learning difficulties lie. By designing separate assessments for each level, teachers will be in a much better position to determine what kind of remedial work will help each student.

Strategies to Consider

Teaching Strategies in Mathematics for Different Learning Styles

Cognitive researchers are suggesting that students approach the study of mathematics with different learning styles that run the gamut from primarily quantitative to primarily qualitative (Sharma, 1989; Marolda and Davidson, 1994). The implication of this research is that students are more likely to be successful in learning mathematics if teachers use instructional strategies that are compatible with the students' cognitive styles. Tables 7.1 and 7.2 illustrate teaching strategies that are appropriate for the mathematical behaviors exhibited by quantitative and qualitative learners, respectively. Table 7.3 suggests a sequence for using inductive and deductive approaches when introducing a new mathematical concept.

Table 7.1 Teaching Strategies for Learners With Quantitative Style	
Mathematical Behaviors	Teaching Strategies to Consider
Approaches situations using recipes	Emphasize the meaning of each concept or procedure in verbal terms.
Approaches mathematics in a mechanical, routine-like fashion	Highlight the concept and overall goal of the learning.
Emphasizes component parts rather than larger mathematical constructs	Encourage explicit description of the overall conceptual framework. Look for ways to link parts to the whole.
Prefers numerical approach rather than concrete models	Use a step-by-step approach to connect the model to the numerical procedure.
Prefers the linear approach to arithmetic concept	Start with the larger framework and use different approaches to reach the same concept.
Has difficulty in situations requiring multistep tasks	Separate multiple tasks into smaller units and explain the connections between the units.

Teaching Strategies for Different Learning Styles—Continued

Table 7.2 Teaching Strategies for Learners With Qualitative Style	
Mathematical Behaviors	Teaching Strategies to Consider
Prefers concepts to algorithms (procedures for problem solving)	Connect models first to the concept, and then to procedures before introducing algorithms.
Perceives overall shape of geometric structures at expense of missing the individual components	Emphasize how the individual components contribute to the overall design of the geometric figure.
Difficulties with precise calculations and in explaining procedure for finding the correct solution.	Encourage explicit description of each step used.
Can offer a variety of approaches or answers to a single problem.	Use simulations and real word problems to show application of concept to different situations.
Prefers to set up problems but can not always follow through to a solution	Provide opportunities for the student to work in cooperative learning groups. To ensure full participation, give the student one grade for problem approach and set-up and one grade for exact solution.
Benefits from manipulatives and enjoys topics related to geometry	Provide a variety of manipulatives and models (e.g., Cuisenaire rods, tokens, or blocks) to support numerical operations. Look for geometric links to new concepts.

Tables 7.1 and 7.2 are meant to help teachers address specific mathematical behaviors that they identify in individual students. Such strategies target specific needs and, with practice, can strengthen a student's weakness. It is perhaps unrealistic, however, to expect teachers to identify and select individual strategies for problems encountered by all their students during a single learning episode.

– Continued –

Teaching Strategies for Different Learning Styles—Continued

Table 7.3 suggests an instructional sequence for introducing a new mathematical concept. The order first accommodates qualitative learners and then moves to techniques for quantitative learners (Sharma, 1989).

Table 7.3 Inductive to Deductive Approach for Introducing a New Concept	
Steps of the Inductive Approach for Qualitative Learners	■ Explain the linguistic aspects of the concept.
	■ Introduce the general principle or law that supports the concept.
	■ Provide students opportunities to use concrete materials to investigate and discover proof of the connection between the principle and the concept.
	■ Give many specific examples of the concept's validity using concrete materials.
	■ Allow students to discuss with each other what they discovered about how the concept works.
	■ Demonstrate how these individual experiences can be integrated into a general principle or rule that applies equally to each example.
Steps for the Deductive Approach for Quantitative Learners	■ Reemphasize the general principle or law that the concept relates to.
	■ Demonstrate how several specific examples obey the general principle or law.
	■ Allow students to state the principle and suggest specific examples that follow it.
	■ Ask students to explain the linguistic elements of the concept.

By understanding the different approaches to the learning of mathematics, teachers are more likely to select instructional strategies that will result in successful learning for all students.

Strategies to Consider

Mathematics for ESL Students
With Learning Disabilities

Researchers in the area of mathematics education offer the following recommendations for teachers of students with learning disabilities who are also studying English as a second language (ESL)(Raborn, 1995).

♦ **Appraising Abilities in Mathematics.** ESL students may have high abilities in mathematics but have problems expressing these because of difficulties with the English language. To appraise mathematics ability, teachers need to use measurement and assessment instruments that can distinguish mathematics competency and cognitive ability separately from the student's proficiency in English or from any language-based learning disability. Measurement is designed to compare the performance of one individual to others, generally through norm-referenced instruments. Assessments are used to highlight the student's strengths and weaknesses in mathematical content so that school officials can make a decision on appropriate class placement. Subsequent diagnostic procedures will help focus on patterns of performance in specific areas.

♦ **Selecting the Language of Instruction.** Educators should determine proficiency in *all* languages to which the student has been exposed. Although bilingual education regulations vary from state to state, if the student is stronger in his or her native language than in English, then mathematics instruction should start in the native language. This allows students to learn developmentally appropriate mathematical content without requiring English language proficiency. That is, students who are stronger in mathematics content than in English competency should be taught at their level of mathematics ability, not at their level of English proficiency.

– Continued –

159

Mathematics for ESL Students—Continued

♦ **Moving From Concrete Experiences to Abstract Concepts.** Tying concrete models with verbal descriptions (in English) to mathematical concepts is a valuable way of helping ESL students bypass language barriers. This verbal labeling can demonstrate the language sense of a mathematical concept through context. Ask students to practice using English to explain the concrete concept and to demonstrate with manipulatives where appropriate. Finally, remove the manipulatives and ask students to imagine the concept while explaining it aloud.

♦ **Using Strategies for Concept Development.** The strategy of concept attainment has proven very effective for ESL students. Students compare and contrast examples that *do* contain the concept's attributes (positive exemplars) with examples that *do not* contain the attributes (negative exemplars). In this way, the students must determine for themselves the attributes of the concept or category. Concept attainment is appropriate for any age level and is most effective if the following steps are employed (adjusted, of course, for student age):

  ▸ Begin by presenting a category that includes the concept. For example, if the concept is that of rectangles, then perhaps start with the category of "shape."

  ▸ Present information in the form of words, concrete materials, or diagrams that introduce an approximately equal number of positive and negative exemplars. Separate the exemplars into "yes" and "no" categories and ask students to examine them. Students will need to determine what the positive exemplars have in common and show how they differ from the negative exemplars.

  ▸ Ask the students to develop a hypothesis and explain how they got it. Following this discussion, the students must name the concept that was presented.

  ▸ When the concept has been correctly identified and named, the students offer their own exemplars as a check of their understanding. In a further test, the teacher can offer an exemplar and ask the students to place it in the "yes" or "no" category.

Mathematics for ESL Students—Continued

♦ **Using Mathematics to Develop Language.** The language of mathematics offers students the opportunity to deal with precise vocabulary, sequence, and syntax that can be helpful in acquiring both their native and a second language. Mathematics teaches predictable patterns and can develop proficiency in social and academic language skills. Give students the opportunity to talk to their peers and to adults so they can validate their ideas in mathematics while also practicing native and secondary language skills.

♦ **Using Students' Strengths.** Teacher observations and testing often reveal students' strengths as well as their weaknesses. Strengths should be pointed out to students and used in planning a variety of instructional techniques. Address visual and kinesthetic learning strengths by incorporating visual materials, manipulatives, and opportunities for movement in the classroom throughout each lesson. Demonstrations, models, and simulations are also helpful, although they are more appropriate for learning mathematics skills than mathematical concepts. They also aid in maintaining interest and student motivation. Cooperative learning groups have been shown to be particularly effective for ESL students because the group structure helps students attain intellectual and social goals. Further, the group format affords students an opportunity to take responsibility for cooperative roles and obligations.

SLEEP DISORDERS

The idea that the amount of sleep an individual gets each night can have an impact on learning is not shocking, yet it has probably been the most overlooked factor affecting student performance in school. Lack of sleep has become a national affliction and fiscal estimates of how much toll it takes on productivity range in the billions of dollars per year. Apart from these losses, researchers are just beginning to understand the negative repercussions that lack of sleep has on the learning process. Before we get into the problems of sleep deprivation, we need a brief review of the biology of sleep.

What Is Sleep?

How Does Sleep Occur?

Before the advent of brain imaging technology, most scientists thought of sleep as the time when the brain was quiet, dormant, and passive. We now know that our brains are very active during sleep, and we are just beginning to understand the ways that sleep affects our daily functioning and our mental and physical health.

Sleep is controlled by a biological clock that resides deep within the brain. Called the *suprachiasmatic nucleus* (SCN), it is a pair of pinhead-sized structures containing about 20,000 neurons. It actually rests near the *hypothalamus*, just above the point where the *optic nerves* cross. Light from the eye's *retina* creates signals that travel along the optic nerve and are monitored by the SCN (Figure 8.1). When darkness falls, the light signals decrease and the SCN prompts the *pineal gland* to produce the hormone *melatonin*. As the amount of melatonin in the blood

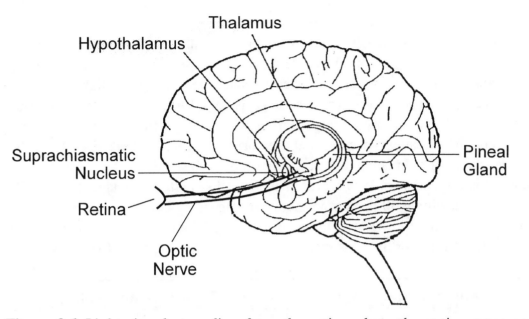

Figure 8.1 *Light signals traveling from the retina along the optic nerves are monitored by the suprachiasmatic nucleus (SCN). When the light signals decrease, the SCN prompts the pineal gland to release melatonin into the blood, beginning the sleep cycle.*

increases, we feel drowsy. Meanwhile, the SCN is altering and synchronizing other body functions, such as blood pressure, body temperature, and urine production, in preparation for sleep. In the morning, the melatonin concentration drops and the waking phase begins. This sleep-wake cycle is one of our daily rhythms, called a *circadian* (from Latin, about a day) rhythm.

Because sleep and wakefulness are regulated by different neurotransmitter signals in the brain, foods and medicines can alter the balance of these signals and affect our sleep patterns. For example, caffeinated products (e.g., coffee, soda, diet pills, and decongestants) stimulate parts of the brain that can interfere with sleep. Antidepressant drugs can also prevent deep sleep. Heavy smokers tend to wake up several times during the night because of nicotine withdrawal. Some people try to improve their sleep by drinking alcohol just before bedtime. Although alcohol does help people fall into light

> **A Word About Melatonin**
>
> Some people with chronic sleep problems (or jet lag) rely on melatonin supplements to improve their sleep. Because of the high dosage of melatonin in these pills, the long-term use of this supplement may create new problems. Because the potential side effects of long-term melatonin usage are unknown, medical experts do not recommend their use by the general public. See the Strategies to Consider at the end of this chapter for suggestions on how to deal with sleep problems.

sleep, it also robs them of the restorative value of deep sleep. Instead, it keeps them in the light sleep stages where they can be easily awakened.

Stages of Sleep. Sleep has five successive phases, called stages 1, 2, 3, 4, and REM. We progress through the five stages and the cycle repeats itself several times during the night. The Stage 1 is a transitional period where we are easily awakened. Stage 2 is light sleep. In stages 3 and 4, we move into deeper sleep. The last stage is called REM, for Rapid Eye Movement. Although brain and body activity increase during REM, this is the restorative stage in which neurons are repaired, dreaming occurs, and memories are consolidated and stored. Table 8.1 shows the five stages of sleep and the characteristics of each stage.

Most people spend about 50 percent of their total sleep time in stage 2, about 20 percent in REM, and the remaining 30 percent in the other stages. By contrast, infants spend about 50 percent of their sleep time in REM. This may be because infants fall into deeper sleep faster, allowing more REM time for the consolidation of rapidly growing neural networks.

Table 8.1 Five Stages of Sleep and Their Characteristics	
Stage 1 (Transitional sleep) 15 to 20 minutes	• Eyes move very slowly • Muscle activity slows • Drift in and out of sleep • Easily awakened • When awakened, can remember pieces of visual images
Stage 2 (Light sleep) 10 to 15 minutes	• Eye movements stop • Brain waves slow down
Stage 3 (Deep sleep) 15 to 20 minutes	• Very slow brain waves (called delta waves) appear with occasional faster waves • No muscle activity or eye movement
Stage 4 (Deepest sleep) 15 to 20 minutes	• Almost exclusively delta waves • No muscle activity or eye movement • Very difficult to awaken • When awakened, feel groggy and disoriented
REM (Rapid eye movement) 4 to 5 REM cycles per night, varying 10 to 40 minutes per cycle	• Breathing becomes more rapid, irregular, and shallow • Eyes jerk rapidly in various directions • Limb muscles become temporarily paralyzed • Heart rate and blood pressure increase • When awakened, can describe dreams • Long-term memory consolidation occurs for storage

How Much Sleep Do We Need?

Age is one of the more important factors determining the amount of sleep a person needs. Infants need about 16 hours a day. Between the ages of 1 to 3 years, the sleep requirement drops to 10 to 12 hours a night. From then until the preteen years, 9 to 10 hours is normal. Teenagers need 8 to 9 hours. For these pre-adult age groups, we are talking about *sleep time*, not *bedtime*.

Most adults do well with between 7 and 8 hours a night, although the range is about 5 to 10 hours. The length of sleep needed does not correlate with intelligence or personality, despite the often-cited fact that Thomas Edison slept very little. Albert Einstein, on the other hand, was notorious for sleeping long hours (Restak, 2000).

If we do not get enough sleep, our bodies begin to create a sleep debt. Eventually, the body will demand that the debt be paid. If we continue to get less sleep than we need, our judgment, reaction time, and other functions become impaired.

What Happens If We Don't Get Enough Sleep?

Adequate sleep is so important to normal body maintenance that undesirable repercussions appear if we do not get enough sleep. Yet, many school-age children and adults are sleep deprived. Recent research studies have highlighted the dangers of sleep deprivation. For example, tests of driving skills in a simulator and monitored eye-hand coordination tasks of people who were sleep deprived showed that they performed as bad as or worse than those who were intoxicated with alcohol. Moreover, sleep deprivation intensifies alcohol's affect on the body, so a fatigued person who drinks will likely become much more impaired than someone who is well rested (NINDS, 2000).

Why Do We Need Sleep?

The best evidence that sleep is an important and necessary biological function is what happens if we don't get enough of it. For instance, sleep-deprived rats die at the age of five weeks (rather than two to three years) and develop sores on their bodies, probably because their immune systems are impaired.

Hence, sleep must be necessary for the health of our nervous system. When we get too little sleep, we have difficulty concentrating, physical performance declines, and our memory is impaired. If sleep deprivation continues, hallucinations and severe mood swings may develop. These symptoms lead researchers to believe that sleep allows the neurons (used while we are awake) the time to shut down and repair themselves. Without sleep, the neurons become depleted of energy and so polluted with the byproducts of cellular metabolism that they begin to malfunction. Some research evidence strongly suggests that sleep also gives the brain a chance to exercise important neural connections that might otherwise deteriorate from inactivity (Schacter, 1996).

In children and young adults, deep sleep coincides with the release of growth hormones. Deep sleep is also the time when cell production increases and protein breakdown decreases. Because proteins are the building blocks of cells, this fact may indicate that the body is repairing cellular damage resulting from the day's activities and other harmful factors, such as stress and ultraviolet rays. Further, the parts of the brain that control decision making, emotions, and social interactions are much quieter during this time, suggesting that deep sleep helps us maintain our emotional and social balance when awake.

Recent brain imaging studies reveal that the parts of the brain used for learning are very active during REM sleep. One study found that REM sleep affects the learning of certain mental skills. People taught a skill and then deprived of non-REM sleep still remembered the skill, but people deprived of REM sleep could not (Restak, 2000). We spend more time in REM sleep while we are learning new things. Apparently, REM sleep is a time to consolidate memories already in the system. Consequently, students who are sleep deprived may be memory deprived as well.

Sleep Deprivation

As with most disorders, the problems associated with sleep can have environmental or neurological origins. Both types affect school-age children, although environmental causes affect far more students. The primary environmental cause of problems with sleep is just not getting enough of it each night.

Preteens

We know that preteens need about 9 to 10 hours of sleep, that is, of *sleep*, not of *time in bed*. Too many preteens with televisions in their bedrooms stay awake watching TV for hours, robbing them of needed sleep. Some children lose sleep because of family situations, such as parents coming home late at night, or other household disturbances. As a result of not enough sleep, children often doze off in school.

Sleep Deprivation
Symptoms:
▸ Difficulty waking in the morning
▸ Falling asleep spontaneously during the day
▸ Irritability later in the day
▸ Sleeping for extra long periods on weekends

If children are sleep deprived, they can become distracted, aggressive, oppositional, and easily frustrated. Some evidence indicates that long-term sleep deprivation can even lead to permanent learning disabilities, although this is rare. There should be no need for the problem to get to this stage, however, because sleep deprivation is easily corrected with adequate sleep.

Adolescents

Malls, computers, television, homework, and changing family patterns all contribute to rob adolescents of their nightly sleep, and continued sleep deprivation can lead to tragic consequences. For example, the sudden increase in traffic accidents caused by adolescents and young adults falling asleep at the wheel recently brought national attention to this problem. In 1997, the National Institutes of Health convened a scientific working group to examine the issue of adolescent sleepiness. Much of the research gathered by that group and others was published in 2000 by the National Sleep Foundation (NSF) in a report titled *Adolescent Sleep Needs and Patterns*.

Amount and Patterns of Sleep. The NSF report noted research studies showing the average sleep time for 13-year-olds during the school week was 7 hours, 42 minutes, dropping to just over 7 hours for 19-year-olds. Only 15 percent of adolescents reported sleeping 8.5 hours or more on school nights, and 26 percent reported sleeping 6.5 hours or less each school night.

Weekend sleep schedules were very different from weekday schedules. The adolescents in the studies slept about 1.5 to 2 hours longer on weekends with over 90 percent of them going to bed after 11:00 p.m. Such irregular patterns of weekday to weekend sleep schedules combined with inadequate sleep can shift the adolescent body clock to a later sleep and wake cycle (circadian rhythm) than for the average adult or preadolescent (Wolfson and Carskadon, 1998).

Delayed Sleep Phase Disorder. With their body clocks shifted to a later time for going to sleep (around midnight), adolescents need to sleep until 9:00 a.m. to get their full complement of 9 hours sleep. But on weekdays, they have to wake up around 6:00 a.m. because the school

> *Many adolescents come to school every day with sleep deprivation.*

buses come by at 7:00 a.m. Consequently, many high school students get up after only 6.5 to 7 hours of sleep and with their bodies still loaded with melatonin. Figure 8.2 shows the concentration of melatonin (measured in saliva) in adolescents with a strict 10:00 p.m. sleep and 8:00 a.m. wake cycle, and what this probably would be in adolescents whose sleep-wake cycle has shifted to roughly an hour later (NSF, 2000).

When students arrive at school, they are often drowsy and fall asleep in class at the first opportunity. The mismatch between the shift of adolescents' sleep phase and the time we ask them

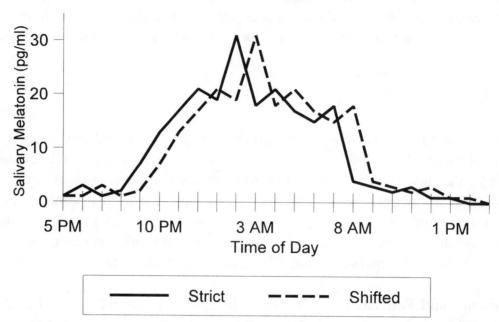

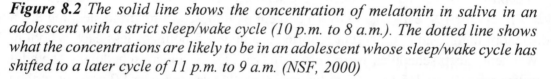

Figure 8.2 *The solid line shows the concentration of melatonin in saliva in an adolescent with a strict sleep/wake cycle (10 p.m. to 8 a.m.). The dotted line shows what the concentrations are likely to be in an adolescent whose sleep/wake cycle has shifted to a later cycle of 11 p.m. to 9 a.m. (NSF, 2000)*

to start high school has led to a chronic condition known as Delayed Sleep Phase Disorder (DSPD). The name is a bit misleading because it implies a permanent systemic or organic condition that can be treated, but not cured. However, DSPD is a temporary condition and can be easily remedied with adequate sleep.

Nonetheless, this disorder can have serious detrimental effects. That is,

♦ Drowsiness and fatigue can lead to accidents, especially motor vehicle collisions.

♦ Sleep loss reduces one's ability to control emotional responses, leading to more arguments, emotional outbursts, and depression.

♦ More high school students with academic problems and with average or lower grades report that they are sleep deprived than do students with better grades.

♦ Sleep deprivation can produce symptoms similar to attention-deficit hyperactivity disorder (ADHD).

♦ Lack of sleep increases the likelihood of the use of stimulants such as caffeine, nicotine, and alcohol.

Sleep Disorders

Several sleep disorders exist that are not the direct result of sleep deprivation, but may cause it. The most common ones are insomnia, sleep apnea, restless legs syndrome, and narcolepsy. These conditions require medical attention and professional intervention.

Insomnia

Most people suffer occasional insomnia, which can be relieved by practicing good sleep habits (see the Strategies to Consider for tips on sleep). Some people have chronic insomnia, which robs them of sleep every night and sets the stage for other medical problems to arise. Chronic insomnia tends to increase with age and may also be a symptom of some underlying medical disorder. For chronic insomnia, researchers are experimenting with light therapy and other ways to alter the body's sleep-wake cycle.

Sleep Apnea

Rarely found in children, this is a condition that interrupts breathing during sleep. It can be caused by the loss of muscle tone with ageing, or by the malfunction of neurons that control breathing during sleep. The individual's effort to inhale causes the windpipe (trachea) to collapse during sleep, reducing the supply of oxygen to the body. When the blood oxygen level falls too low, the brain awakens the individual enough to open the windpipe. As the person falls back asleep, the windpipe closes again. This cycle can be repeated hundreds of times a night, leaving the person feeling groggy and irritable in the morning. Sleep apnea can be treated through weight loss, sleeping on one's side, or surgery.

Restless Legs Syndrome

Another condition of ageing, but also found in young children, restless legs syndrome is a genetic disorder that causes tingling or prickling sensations in the legs and feet and an urge to move them to get relief. This constant leg movement leads to insomnia at night. The disorder is treated with drugs that affect the neurotransmitter dopamine, which suggests that dopamine abnormalities may be the underlying cause of the syndrome.

Narcolepsy

Narcolepsy affects an estimated 250,000 Americans. It is characterized by frequent and overwhelming urges to sleep at various times during the day, even if the person has had a normal night's sleep. The sleep sessions can last from several seconds to 30 minutes. The disorder often begins in adolescence but is difficult to identify and diagnose at that age. It is usually hereditary, but can also result from head injury or neurological disease. Narcolepsy is most often treated with antidepressant and stimulant drugs.

What Is the Future of Research in Sleep Disorders?

This area has been attracting the attention of more researchers, especially as brain scanning technologies are revealing how different brain regions function during sleep. Understanding the factors that affect sleep may lead to therapies to help those with sleep deprivation and sleep disorders.

What Do Educators Need to Consider?

Educators may want to review their schedules and discuss with parents and community groups the merits of a later start time for high school students. Some results of a study of several school districts that made such a change are shown in the Strategies to Consider at the end of this chapter. In the meantime, teachers, school health providers, and parents should be educated about adolescent sleep patterns and needs, becoming alert for signs of sleep deprivation or sleep disorders.

> *Information about sleep should be part of every high school curriculum.*

Students, too, should learn about the physiology and benefits of sleep and the consequences of sleep deprivation. A sleep education unit needs to be considered as part of every high school curriculum. It could be included in biology, health, psychology, and driver education courses, for example.

Impact on Learning

- Students who come to school with Delayed Sleep Phase Disorder (DSPD) typically have a difficult time focusing and concentrating for an extended period of time.

- Sleep deprivation robs the brain of the time it needs to encode information into long-term storage sites (a process that occurs during REM sleep).

- Loss of sleep affects student performance in all areas of school life including athletics, music, and drama.

- Prolonged sleep deprivation interferes with motor coordination, so driving vehicles and operating machinery can be very hazardous.

Strategies to Consider

Starting High Schools Later

One way to address Delayed Sleep Phase Disorder in adolescents is to delay the start times for high schools. This is no easy task, given all the ramifications such a change has for bus schedules, athletic programs, employment of adolescents in the community, family schedules, and safety issues related to daylight and darkness. But some communities have dealt successfully with these ramifications. A recent study of the effects of later start times on these high schools and their students has yielded such positive results that more communities nationwide are considering doing the same. Here is a part of what that study found (Wahlstrom, Wrobel, and Kubow, 1998).

1. What Is the Desirable Start Time for High Schools? The study asked nearly 3,000 high school teachers to suggest the optimal high school start time. Figure 8.3 shows the summary of their responses. Note that nearly 80 percent of the teachers preferred a start time of 8:00 a.m. or later, and 35 percent preferred 8:30 a.m. or later.

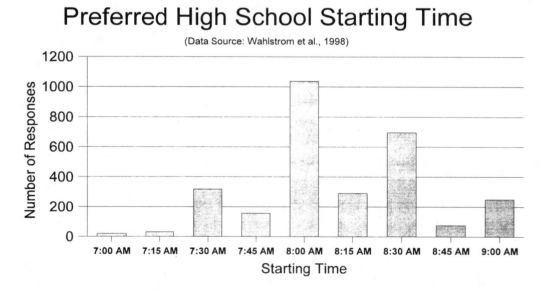

Figure 8.3 *This chart shows the responses of nearly 3,000 secondary teachers who were asked the optimal start time for the first high school class.*

172

Starting High School Later—Continued

2. What Did Teachers Observe? In schools with later start times, 335 teachers were asked whether students seemed more alert and attentive during the first two periods of the day. Figure 8.4 shows the percentage of teachers who agreed or disagreed with this question, or had no opinion. Note that over 57 percent of the teachers agreed or strongly agreed that students were more alert during the early part of the school day.

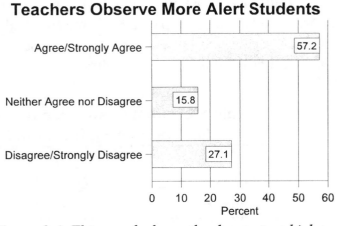

Figure 8.4 *This graph shows the degree to which teachers agreed that students were more alert in the first two class periods. (Wahlstrom et al., 1998)*

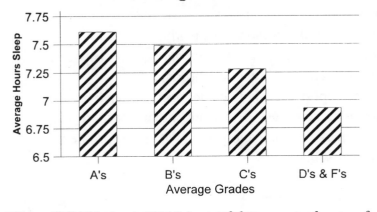

Figure 8.5 *This is a comparison of the average hours of sleep that students had on school nights to their self-reported average grades. (Wahlstrom et al., 1998)*

3. Does Student Performance Improve With More Sleep? The study examined how the amount of sleep that students got on school nights compared to the grades they received. Figure 8.5 compares the amount of average school-night sleep time to the students' self-reported average grades. No causal relationship is implied, here. That is, the researchers cannot say that longer school-night sleep time was the *cause* of the better grades. Nonetheless, this finding has been observed in all of the few studies of later high school start times to date.

– Continued –

Starting High School Later—Continued

4. Parents' Response to Later Start Times. Parents in the Edina, MN, schools were surveyed and asked if they were pleased with the later high school start time. Table 8.2 shows the results of that survey. Over 93 percent of all the parents surveyed said they were pleased with the change in start time (Wahlstrom et al., 1998).

Table 8.2 Parent Responses to "Are You Pleased With the Later High School Start Time?"			
Parents of:	Percent "Yes"	Percent "No"	Percent "Not Sure"
Sophomores	90.6	5.6	3.8
Juniors	94.4	4.5	1.1
Seniors	96.0	4.0	0
Totals	93.1	4.9	2.0

5. Other Considerations. The study also reported the following findings (NSF, 2000):

- Overall student attendance increased and tardiness decreased.
- Some students reported eating breakfast more frequently.
- Teachers noticed better student behavior; the hallways were quieter between periods and there was less misbehavior in the lunchroom.
- Suburban teachers did not report any noticeable decrease in student participation in extracurricular activities. However, urban teachers did notice a decrease in extracurricular participation along with some problems for students who worked after school.

Strategies to Consider

Tips for Teachers on Dealing With Sleep

1. **Learn about sleep.** Get educated about the sleep needs and patterns of children and adolescents. Students with excessive sleepiness during the day may have some other underlying biological disorder that needs attention.

2. **Teach about sleep.** Tell your students (with age-appropriate language) about the importance of sleep. Remind them that deep sleep is necessary for the brain to store the information and skills they are learning into their long-term memory sites.

3. **Keep the lights on.** One effective way to reduce the amount of melatonin in the blood is with bright light. Taking students for a quick walk in the sun will also help. Resist the temptation to turn the lights off when using an overhead projector or television, especially in the early morning. Better to have some glare on the screen and most students awake than to have a beautiful picture and students half asleep.

4. **Help students assess their sleepiness.** High school students are often unaware of how sleepy they are during their day and evening. Ask them to assess their sleepiness (especially during school days) for at least one school week by using a five-point rating scale to record how tired they are at different times (see sample at right). Review the overall class results with them. Explain that recording a 3 or greater when they should be feeling alert is an indication of sleep deprivation.

Rating the Degree of Sleepiness

Rating Scale:
1. Feeling alert and wide awake
2. Functioning okay, but not at peak
3. Somewhat groggy, tough to concentrate
4. Groggy, losing interest, sluggish
5. Fighting sleep, want to lie down

Name of Student:_____ Date:_____

Time of Day	Rating	Time of Day	Rating
8:00 AM		3:00 PM	
9:00 AM		4:00 PM	
10:00 AM		5:00 PM	
11:00 AM		6:00 PM	
12:00 PM		7:00 PM	
1:00 PM		8:00 PM	
2:00 PM		9:00 PM	

– Continued –

Tips for Teachers on Dealing With Sleep—Continued

5. **Talk to parents.** When talking with parents, emphasize the importance of their children getting adequate sleep. Cite any specific evidence you have of sleepiness that you have noticed in their children.

6. **Look for opportunities to accommodate the school to adolescent sleep needs.** Talk with other educators about the appropriateness of a later start time for high school. Incorporate some physical activity into those early morning lessons.

7. **Use more interactive strategies.** Cooperative learning groups, simulations, demonstrations, and role-playing activities are more likely to keep students alert, especially during the early hours.

8. **Get enough sleep.** It is difficult to be alert and to encourage others to get adequate sleep if you yourself are sleep deprived. Getting adequate sleep makes you a good role model for the class and for your own children.

Strategies to Consider

Tips for Parents About Sleep

When talking to parents about sleep, consider sharing some helpful tips (NSF, 2000). Say to parents the following:

- Learn about the sleep needs and patterns of your children at the various stages of their development.

- Consider whether your children should have television sets in their bedrooms. This is seldom a good idea because watching television interferes with reading, homework, and hobbies. Further, it isolates children from the family and may rob them of their sleep.

- Enforce regular sleep schedules for all your children. Adjust the schedules as they grow older. Remember that it is normal for the sleep-wake cycle of adolescents to be different from that of younger children.

- Look for signs of sleep deprivation in your children. They are not always easy to spot but may include irritability during the day, unusual sleepiness at times when they should be alert, sleeping much longer on weekends, and persistent difficulty in waking up in the morning. Don't allow a drowsy teenager to drive to school or anywhere else.

- Talk to your children about their sleep habits. Does after-school employment or extracurricular activities interfere with their sleep? Make adjustments as needed.

- Encourage your children to keep track of their sleep and wake schedule. This information will be helpful in determining whether their sleep schedules need to be revised or can be used by professionals should you seek outside help for your children's sleepiness.

- Be a good role model and practice good sleep habits.

Strategies to Consider

Tips for Teens About Sleep

When talking to teenage students about sleep, consider sharing some of these tips (NSF, 2000). Encourage them to

❏ Get enough sleep. Your brain needs it to store information and your body needs it to repair itself. Even mild sleep deprivation can hurt your academic and athletic performance.

❏ Keep a regular sleep schedule. You need between 8 to 9 hours a night. Plan your homework time and other activities carefully to allow enough time for sleep.

❏ Get some bright light as soon as possible in the morning. Bright light helps to awaken the brain. Avoid bright light in the evening so that the sleep cycle can begin normally.

❏ Get to know your own body clock. Try to get involved in stimulating activities during that groggy period. Avoid driving if you feel sleepy.

❏ Later in the day, stay away from substances that can interfere with your sleep, such as coffee, sodas containing caffeine, and nicotine. Alcohol also disrupts sleep.

❏ Start relaxing about one hour before bedtime. Avoid heavy reading or computer games during this time. Don't fall asleep watching television because the flickering light and sound can inhibit deep sleep, which is important for complete rest.

EMOTIONAL AND BEHAVIORAL DISORDERS

It has been only in recent years that researchers have really begun to recognize the contribution that the emotions make to the development of the human brain and the impact they have on the learning process. Although these contributions are not always considered to be positive, understanding their impact can help parents and educators make appropriate decisions to meet the emotional needs of children and adolescents.

Emotions, Behavior, and Learning

The brain is genetically programmed to gather information and to develop skills that are likely to keep its owner alive. Among other things, human survival depends on the family unit, where emotional bonds increase the chances of producing children and raising them to be productive adults. Consequently, the human brain has learned over thousands of years that survival and emotional messages must have first priority when filtering through all the incoming signals from the body's senses.

The brainstem monitors and regulates survival functions such as body temperature, respiratory rate, and blood pressure (Chapter 1). Emotional messages

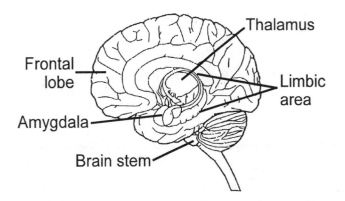

Figure 9.1 Survival functions are controlled from the brainstem. Emotional signals are processed and interpreted by the limbic area and frontal lobe.

are carried through and interpreted in the limbic area, usually with the help of the frontal lobe (Figure 9.1). These survival and emotional messages guide the individual's behavior, including directing its attention to a learning situation. Specifically, emotion drives attention and attention drives learning.

But even more important to understand is that emotional attention comes before cognitive recognition. You see a letter from a former lover in the mail and within a few seconds your palms are sweating, your breathing is labored, and your blood pressure rises—all this before you even know what is written in the letter. Joseph LeDoux (1996) has done extensive research on emotions and, as a result of using brain imaging, concludes that the amygdala is the part of the limbic system responsible for emotional responses, and that it can act without input from the cognitive parts of the brain (usually the frontal lobe in the cerebrum). This is an intriguing finding because it suggests that the brain can respond emotionally to a situation without the benefit of cognitive functions, such as thinking, reasoning, and consciousness. Of course, we have already sensed the truth of this from our past experiences.

Pathways of Emotional Signals

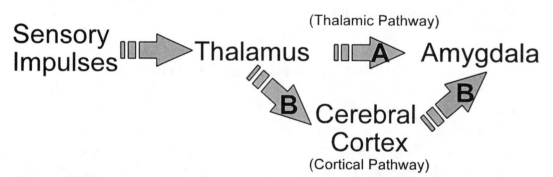

Figure 9.2 *Sensory information travels to the thalamus where it can be routed directly to the amygdala (thalamic pathway, A) or first to the cerebrum and then to the amygdala (cortical pathway, B). (See also Figure 1.2)*

In Chapter 1, we learned that the thalamus receives all incoming sensory impulses (except smell) and directs them to other parts of the brain for further processing. As a result of his research, LeDoux is convinced that incoming sensory information to the thalamus can take two different routes to the amygdala. The quick route (called the thalamic pathway) sends the signals directly from the thalamus to the amygdala (pathway A in Figure 9.2). The second possibility (called the cortical pathway) is for the thalamus to direct the signals first to the cerebral cortex (in the cerebrum) for cognitive processing and then to the amygdala (pathway B).

The time it takes for signals to travel along the two pathways is different. For example, it takes sound signals about 12 milliseconds (a millisecond is 1/1,000th of a second) to travel pathway A and about twice as long to travel pathway B. Which pathway the signals take could mean the difference between life and death. If the sound from a car blasting its horn travels along pathway A, it will probably be fast enough to get you to jump out of the way even though you are not sure what is coming. Only later does your cerebral cortex provide the explanation of what happened. Survival is the first priority, an explanation second.

Disturbances in this dual pathway system can explain some abnormal behaviors. Anxiety disorders, for example, can result whenever a certain action, such as walking into a crowd, is associated with fear. If this activity always takes pathway A, then a phobia develops that cannot be easily moderated through rational discussion. This probably explains why psychotherapy alone is rarely successful in treating phobias and anxiety disorders (Restak, 2000).

Different Brain Areas for Different Emotions

Although the amygdala is the center of emotional response, neuroscientists now believe that different areas of the brain interpret specific emotions. The frontal cortex of the left hemisphere deals with positive emotions; the right frontal cortex is concerned with negative emotions. Damage to the front of the left hemisphere results in feelings of hopelessness and bouts of depression. However, if the front right side is damaged, the individual often expresses inappropriate cheerfulness, even denying the injury.

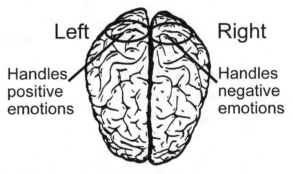

Left — Handles positive emotions

Right — Handles negative emotions

Figure 9.3 The left hemisphere's frontal cortex is concerned with positive emotions. The right hemisphere's frontal cortex deals with negative emotions and nuance.

People who normally have right hemisphere preference (Sousa, 2001) tend to have basically anxious and fearful approaches to life. Those with left hemisphere preference exhibit a more confident approach. The preference is probably caused by a number of factors including genetics, experience, and the way an individual's brain is organized.

The Nature of Anxiety. Anxiety serves a useful purpose in that it signals us that something needs to be corrected in our environment. The anxious feelings you got when seeing the letter from a former lover were soon tempered when cognitive reflection reminded you that a wedding was coming soon, and this was most likely an invitation to it. This return to emotional stability is the result of the interactions between the emotion-generating amygdala and the emotion-inhibiting left frontal cortex. Both the amygdala and left frontal cortex need to be functioning properly for this balance to be maintained and, thus, for good mental health. If either one is malfunctioning, then the person's behavior will be abnormal.

First Survival and Emotions, Then the Textbook

The human brain is programmed to deal first with its owner's survival and emotional needs. Therefore, the brain is unlikely to attend to any other task until it is assured that these needs have been met and that the environment poses no threat. If we transfer this notion to schools, it means that students are not going to care about the curriculum unless they feel physically safe and emotionally secure.

> *Students must feel physically safe and emotionally secure before they can focus on the curriculum.*

Physical Safety. For students to feel physically safe, schools must be free of weapons and violence. A student will have trouble concentrating on the lesson if a nearby student displays a weapon or threatens physical harm. Physical safety also refers to the safe condition of the student's body. Has the student had enough sleep and an adequate breakfast? Rest and fuel are important requirements for attention and learning.

Emotional Security. Emotional security refers to the degree to which a student feels accepted as a valued member of a group. In my opinion, the emotional needs of children can be met in just three places:

- in the home (and those entities to which the family belongs, such as religious or community groups)
- in school, through the formal organization of educators and school groups
- outside the school, from an informal organization of peers

Until recently, the emotional needs of children and adolescents were met at home. The family dined together nightly, spending quality time to strengthen emotional bonds through reassurances, caring, and love. In today's fast-paced lifestyle, many families dine together only once or twice a week. Hectic family schedules mean that parents and children have less time together. When the children *are* at home, they spend more time in their own bedrooms—playing computer games and watching television—than with their parents. A recent survey showed that children 10 to 17 years of age spend an

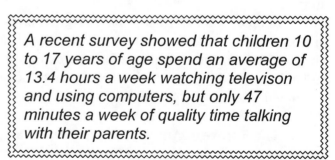

> *A recent survey showed that children 10 to 17 years of age spend an average of 13.4 hours a week watching televison and using computers, but only 47 minutes a week of quality time talking with their parents.*

average of 13.4 hours a week watching televison and using computers, but only 47 minutes a week of quality time talking with their parents. These children are spending about 17 times more time connecting to their outside world than to their inside world.

Because the amount of quality time at home is so small, many students are not getting their emotional needs met. They come to school looking for emotional support from the formal organization through teachers and other professionals in the school environment. Finding emotional support in the primary grades is easier because those teachers are trained to provide it. But it is an entirely different matter in secondary schools. High school teachers are trained to deliver curriculum efficiently and effectively. Few have had training in how to deal with the emotional needs of students, and even fewer ever believed that such training would be necessary. However, more high school teachers are now recognizing that they must meet the emotional needs of their students before they can be successful at presenting the curriculum.

If the students' emotional needs are not met in the home or in school, then some students resort to the third alternative—joining an informal organization of peers, usually called a gang. These are family-like units that have a name, a set of values, and a system of rewards and punishments. Regrettably, their behavior is too often directed toward deviant, rather than socially acceptable, goals.

Emotional and Behavioral Disorders

Because emotions and behavior affect each other and are so closely intertwined, disorders of these areas are usually discussed together. Although a few of these disorders can appear in early adulthood or later, many appear in childhood and adolescence. Some are more common than others, and conditions can range from mild to severe. Often, a person has more than one disorder.

The causes of all the types of disorders can be biological, environmental, or a mixture of both. Biological factors include genetics, chemical imbalances in the body, and damage to the central nervous system, such as a head injury. Environmental causes can include exposure to violence, extreme stress, or the loss of an important person, such as by death or divorce.

A discussion of all the major types of emotional and behavioral disorders that afflict humans is beyond the scope of this book. Rather, the following represents those emotional and behavioral disorders that are most common among children and adolescents and that educators are likely to encounter in almost any school.

Anxiety Disorders

Most people experience feelings of anxiety before an important event, such as a business presentation, big test, or first date. But people with anxiety disorders have anxiety and fears that are chronic and unrelenting, and that can grow progressively worse. Sometimes, their anxieties are so bad that people become housebound.

Anxiety disorders are the most common of childhood disorders, affecting an estimated 8

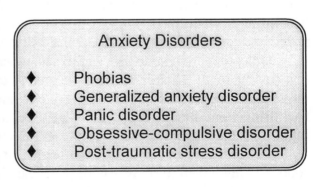

Anxiety Disorders

♦ Phobias
♦ Generalized anxiety disorder
♦ Panic disorder
♦ Obsessive-compulsive disorder
♦ Post-traumatic stress disorder

percent of the child and adolescent population. These young people experience excessive worry, fear, or uneasiness that interferes with daily routines. Anxiety disorders include the following:

▸ **Phobias** – Two major types are social phobia and specific phobia. Children with social phobia have an overwhelming fear of scrutiny, embarrassment, or humiliation when with their peers. Specific phobia is an unrealistic and overwhelming fear of some situation or object that leads to avoiding the situation or object.

▸ **Generalized anxiety disorder** – A pattern of unrealistic and excessive worry not attributable to any recent experience, but disruptive to routine life and events. Those with the disorder almost always anticipate the worst even though there is little reason to expect it. It usually strikes in childhood or adolescence.

▸ **Panic disorder** – Repeated episodes of terrifying attacks of panic that strike without warning. They include physical symptoms such as rapid heartbeat, chest pain, abdominal distress, and dizziness.

▸ **Obsessive-compulsive disorder** – A pattern of repeated thoughts and behaviors (e.g., hand washing or counting) that are impossible to control or stop. Although rare in young children, the occurrence of the disorder increases slightly in adolescents.

▸ **Post-traumatic stress disorder** – A pattern of flashbacks and other symptoms that occurs in children who have experienced a psychologically distressing event (e.g., physical and sexual abuse, being a witness or victim of violence, or exposure to some other traumatic event, such as a hurricane or bombing). Nightmares, numbing of emotions, and feeling angry or irritable are common symptoms.

What Causes Anxiety Disorders? Normal emotional behavior relies on the integrating balance between the emotions initiated by the amygdala and the mediating effect of our thoughts. If either one of these components malfunctions, problems arise. Brain imaging has helped neuroscientists gain a greater understanding of the source of these problems and, thus, the causes of anxiety disorders. For example, if a malfunction causes nonthreatening sensory signals to always take the thalamic pathway (Figure 9.2), panic attacks result because the signals are not benefitting from the mediating effect of cognitive thought. Here is an example: To most of us, the sound of a car backfiring is annoying but we usually would not mistake it for a gunshot. However, to an adolescent brought up in a neighborhood where gunfire has killed a friend or family member, that backfiring could activate a full-fledged stress response. This post-traumatic stress response might send the adolescent diving for cover and in full panic. Apparently, the sounds of the backfiring went directly to the amygdala (thalamic pathway), triggering the panic behavior. No input from the cerebral cortex was present to curtail the post-traumatic response.

For many years, psychiatrists thought that obsessive-compulsive disorder had psychological roots and attempted to treat it with psychoanalysis. Recent brain scans, however, suggest that obsessive-compulsive behavior is the result of hyperactivity in a circuit of the brain that connects the frontal lobe to a part of the limbic area called the caudate nucleus. Activity in this circuit decreases between obsessive-compulsive episodes and after treatment. The disorder responds to a combination of drugs that increases the action of the neurotransmitter serotonin, followed by psychotherapy that addresses the specific nature of the behavior. It is common for anxiety disorder to accompany depression, eating disorders, substance abuse, or another anxiety disorder. These conditions can also coexist with physical disorders.

Depressive Disorders

Children and adolescents with learning disabilities are susceptible to chronic depression. Although much of the scientific research on depression has focused on adults, recent studies have revealed that an unexpectedly large number of today's youth suffer from some type of depressive disorder. A study by the National Institute of Mental Health estimates that about 6 percent of 9- to 17-year-olds have major depression. In addition, the study indicated that the onset of depressive disorders is occurring earlier in life today than ever before (NIMH, 2000). The depressive disorders, including major depressive disorder (unipolar depression) and bipolar disorder (manic-depression), can have far-reaching effects on the functioning and adjustment of young people. Children and adolescents with depressive disorders are at an increased risk for illness and interpersonal and social difficulties. These adolescents also have an increased risk for substance abuse and suicidal behavior.

Unfortunately, depressive disorders in adolescents often go unrecognized because their signs are interpreted as normal mood swings typical of this age group. For example, instead of communicating how bad they feel, they may act out and be irritable toward others, which may be interpreted simply as misbehavior or disobedience. Research has

---

Depressive Disorders

Depression: Symptoms common to all ages
- Persistent sad or irritable mood
- Loss of interest in activities once enjoyed
- Significant change in appetite or body weight
- Difficulty sleeping or sleeping too much
- Psychomotor agitation or retardation
- Loss of energy
- Feelings of worthlessness or inappropriate guilt
- Difficulty concentrating
- Recurrent thoughts of death or suicide

Bipolar Disorder: Symptoms for pre-teens and older
- Severe changes in mood
- Overly-inflated self-esteem
- Increased energy
- Able to go without much sleep
- Talks too fast and too much, cannot be interrupted
- Excessive involvement in risk behaviors

found that parents are even less likely to identify major depression in their adolescents than are the adolescents themselves.

Symptoms. The symptoms of major depressive disorders are common to children, adolescents, and adults. Five or more of these symptoms must persist for an extended period of time before a diagnosis of depression is indicated. Because of the difficulty in diagnosing younger people using just the common symptoms, clinicians often look for other signs that are usually associated with the disorder.

Bipolar disorder, or manic-depression, in children and adolescents is marked by exaggerated mood swings between extreme lows (depression) and highs (excitedness or manic behavior). Periods of quiet may occur in between. The mood swings may recur throughout life.

Causes of Depressive Disorders. Below-normal concentrations of one or more neurotransmitters were often cited as the underlying cause of depression. Support for this notion came from the apparent relief that drugs targeting neurotransmitters gave to depressed patients. Drugs that increased the levels of neurotransmitters (e.g., dopamine, norepinephrine, and serotonin) exerted an antidepressant effect; drugs that depleted their levels made the depression worse.

Neuroscientists today realize that depression is far more complicated than previously thought. It seems that depression can result from the imbalance of any one of many neurotransmitters. Another contributing factor seems to be a problem that causes neurons in the limbic area to overproduce a hormone called corticotropin releasing factor, or CRF. Several studies of patients with chronic depression showed they had about twice the normal level of CRF in their bodies. Apparently, elevated CRF makes one vulnerable to depressive disorders. This finding is leading to the development of drugs that inhibit CRF production in the hope that reducing CRF will reduce the incidence of chronic depression (Restak, 2000).

Depressive Disorders

Signs associated with depressive disorders in children and adolescents

- Frequent, nonspecific complaints of headaches, tiredness, and stomach and muscle aches
- Frequent absences from school or poor performance in school
- Talking about running away from home
- Outbursts of crying, shouting, and complaining
- Being bored
- Lack of interest in playing with friends
- Alcohol or substance abuse
- Social isolation, poor communication
- Fear of death
- Extreme sensitivity to rejection or failure
- Increased hostility and irritability
- Reckless behavior
- Difficulty with relationships

Treatment. Treatment for depressive disorders in children and adolescents often involves short-term psychotherapy, medication, or the combination of both plus targeted interventions involving the home and school environment. Recent research shows that certain types of short-term psychotherapy, particularly cognitive-behavioral therapy (CBT), can help relieve depression in children and adolescents. CBT is based on the premise that people with depression have cognitive distortions in their views of themselves, the world, and the future. CBT, designed to be a time-limited therapy, focuses on changing these distortions. A study supported by the National Institutes of Mental Health that compared different types of psychotherapy for major depression in adolescents found that CBT led to remission in nearly 65 percent of cases, a higher rate than either supportive therapy or family therapy. CBT also resulted in a more rapid treatment response time (NIMH, 2000).

Research clearly demonstrates that antidepressant medications, especially when combined with psychotherapy, can be very effective treatments for depressive disorders in adults. Using medication to treat mental illness in children and adolescents, nevertheless, has caused controversy. Many doctors have been understandably reluctant to treat young people with psychotropic medications because, until fairly recently, little evidence was available about the safety and efficacy of these drugs in youth. In the last few years, however, researchers have been able to conduct studies with children and adolescents showing that the newer antidepressant medications, specifically the selective serotonin reuptake inhibitors (SSRIs), are safe and effective for the short-term treatment of severe and persistent depression in young people.

Treatment of children and adolescents diagnosed with bipolar disorder has been based mainly on experience with adults because so far there is limited data on the safety and effectiveness of mood stabilizing medications in youth. Researchers currently are evaluating both pharmacological and social interventions for bipolar disorder in young people.

Other Emotional and Behavioral Disorders

A number of other emotional and behavioral disorders are found in the school population, such as the following:

Attention-Deficit Hyperactivity Disorder (ADHD). This disorder has received much attention from the media and from researchers. ADHD is discussed more fully in Chapter 3.

Oppositional-Defiant Disorder. All children are occasionally oppositional by arguing, talking back, or defying their parents, teachers and other adults. However, persistent and openly hostile behavior that interferes with a child's daily functioning is called Oppositional-Defiant Disorder. It is characterized by deliberate attempts to annoy others, excessive arguing with adults, frequent temper tantrums, and refusal to comply with adult requests. The cause is unknown, but treatment centers around psychotherapy. If the child does not respond to treatment, the behavior may worsen and become a general conduct disorder.

Conduct Disorder. This disorder usually begins with the appearance of hostile and defiant behavior during the preschool years, known as oppositional-defiant disorder. As the child gets older, conduct disorder may appear which causes children and adolescents to act out their feelings or impulses toward others in destructive ways. Young people with conduct disorder consistently violate the general rules of society and basic rights of others. The offenses they commit get more serious over time and include lying,

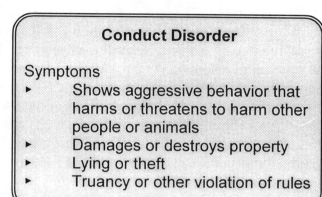

Conduct Disorder

Symptoms
- Shows aggressive behavior that harms or threatens to harm other people or animals
- Damages or destroys property
- Lying or theft
- Truancy or other violation of rules

aggression, theft, truancy, setting fires, and vandalism. However, most young people with conduct disorder do not have lifelong patterns of conduct problems or antisocial behavior.

Conduct Disorder is one of the most difficult behavior disorders to treat. Even so, progress can be made with family therapy, parent training, and the use of community support services. A recent study of children and adolescents with conduct disorder showed that their aggressive behavior also responded to treatment with lithium carbonate. Further studies are planned because although lithium may be safe for short-term treatment, there is concern over its adverse side effects if used for extended periods (Malone, Delaney, Luebbert, Cater, and Campbell, 2000).

Eating Disorders. Anorexia nervosa (the compulsive need to continually lose weight) and bulimia nervosa (the compulsion to eat large amounts of food and to take subsequent radical measures to eliminate it) can be life threatening disorders. No generally accepted view of the causes of these disorders exists at present, although most experts believe the problem to be psychologically based.

Adolescents displaying the symptoms of these disorders need immediate medical attention. Various forms of treatment are available, such as psychotherapy (individual, group, or family), counseling, self-help groups, and medication.

Autism. Autism is a spectrum disorder that usually appears before the child's third birthday. Children with autism have difficulty communicating with others and display inappropriate and repeated behaviors over long periods of time. Autism is discussed more fully in Chapter 10.

Impact on Learning

■   All students need to be in schools where the learning environment is physically safe and emotionally secure before they can focus on the curriculum.

■   With appropriately trained teachers, students with emotional and behavioral problems sometimes can have their needs met in the context of what they are learning in the classroom.

■   Teachers can take *ad hoc* opportunities in class to teach students how to handle their emotions, to delay gratification, to control impulses, and to conduct themselves in personal relationships.

■   Any positive emotional experience—such as praise and other positive reinforcement techniques—will enhance learning.

Strategies to Consider

Establishing a Positive Emotional Climate in the Classroom

All students—especially those with emotional and behavioral disorders—need to be in an emotionally secure setting before they can be expected to give attention to curriculum. The classroom climate is set by the teachers and the school climate is set by the administration. Teachers and administrators need to recognize that many more students than ever come to school wanting to get at least some of their emotional needs met. Working together, faculty and staff should take **purposeful** steps to ensure that a positive emotional climate is established and maintained in the school and in all classrooms. Some ways to set a positive emotional climate are as follows:

❑   **Use humor, but not sarcasm.** Humor is a very effective device for getting attention and for establishing a warm climate. Laughter is common to us all and it helps diverse people bond and feel good about being with each other. Sarcasm, on the other hand, is destructive. It hurts, no matter how familiar a teacher is with students. Occasionally, a teacher has said, "Oh, he knows I was only kidding." In fact, we don't know that, and we need to wonder whether the student's sly grin means the brain is laughing or plotting revenge. Besides, there is so much good humor available that there should be no need for sarcasm.

❑   **Insist on respect among students.** Not only is it important for teachers to respect students, and vice versa, but teachers must also ensure that students show respect for each other. This includes
  ▶   listening to each other's class contributions (as opposed to just waiting for their turn to speak),
  ▶   respecting different and opposing opinions,
  ▶   acknowledging other students' comments,
  ▶   complimenting and helping each other when appropriate,
  ▶   asking others for their opinions, and
  ▶   refraining from sarcasm.

Establishing a Positive Emotional Climate—Continued

❏ **Have just a few rules that all teachers enforce.** Students with emotional problems are likely to get upset when they believe that they are not being treated fairly. Studies on school discipline show that schools with few discipline problems tend to be those with just a few rules (five to seven) that all teachers enforce uniformly. Keep in mind that secondary students usually see six to eight teachers during the school day. Perhaps one teacher allows gum chewing, but it drives the next period's teacher to distraction. An absent-minded, gum-chewing student going from the first to the second teacher's class may be headed for trouble.

❏ **Get training in how to handle emotional situations.** Most secondary teachers were not trained to deal with the emotional scenarios that appear in today's classrooms, mainly because emotional needs of adolescents are expected to be addressed in the family. But the reality is that more students are turning to the school setting for emotional fulfillment, and teachers must be trained to cope effectively with this situation.

❏ **Look for opportunities to teach students how to handle their emotions.** With training, teachers can use classroom and school opportunities to teach students how to handle their emotions. Look for ways to help them delay gratification, control impulses, express their feelings, and conduct themselves in their in-school relationships.

❏ **Use genuine praise.** Students with emotional problems often have low self-esteem. Genuinely praising their efforts can go a long way in helping them improve their self-image. Use "you" statements rather than "I" statements. For example, "You should be proud of the work you accomplished" is more effective for building self-esteem than, "I am pleased with what you accomplished."

Strategies to Consider

Interventions for Students With Behavioral Problems

Research on programs designed to help students with behavioral problems covers a wide variety of students, situations, and settings. As a result, there is a broad range of possible approaches that teachers and schools can take to make a difference in students' behavior. Here are some suggestions from that research.

♦ **Identifying the cause of the misbehavior.** Problem behavior is obvious, but the reasons for it might not be. Schools need to investigate **why** the student is exhibiting undesirable behavior. As more is known about the cause, appropriate interventions can be identified and implemented.

♦ **Selecting classroom management and teaching strategies.** Walker, Colvin, and Ramsey (1995) note that blaming, punishing, and threatening students works only in the short term. They found that effective teachers rely instead, on proactive strategies, such as reinforcing social behavior and teaching social problem solving. For difficult students, they use point or token systems, time-out, contingent reinforcement, and response cost.

♦ **Adapting curriculum and instruction.** Disruptive behavior is sometimes the result of inappropriate curriculum and ineffective teaching. When investigating the cause of student misbehavior, check whether curricular and instruction modifications have been made to accommodate these students (Deschenes, Ebeling, and Sprague, 1994).

♦ **Teaching social problem solving.** Effective programs for preventing discipline problems include the direct teaching of social problem solving. Although the interventions vary, they usually teach thinking skills that students can use to avoid and resolve interpersonal conflicts, resist peer pressure, and cope with their emotions and stress. The most effective programs also include a broad range of social competency skills taught over a long period of time.

Interventions for Students With Behavior Problems—Continued

♦ **Schoolwide and districtwide programs.** School and district policies should make clear that appropriate behavior is a precondition to learning. Rules of behavior should be clear and communicated to staff, parents, and students. It is important that they be consistently enforced so students perceive the system as fair. The staff should also be trained to teach alternatives to vandalism and disruptive behavior.

♦ **Parental involvement.** Effective programs to control behavior almost always have a parental component. Kazdin (1994) found that parental management training and family therapy are two promising approaches for controlling student behavior. Parental management training teaches techniques such as strategic use of time-out, rewards, praise, and contingency contracting. Parents have ongoing opportunities to discuss, practice, and review these techniques. Family therapy is designed to empower parents with the skills and resources to solve their own family problems. Although parental management training and family therapy are very effective approaches, less intensive parental training should suffice for most children and adolescents.

♦ **Some cautions.** A study by Gottfredson (1997) examined various approaches to dealing with disruptive students. She found that some programs are not effective in controlling disruptive and antisocial behavior in the long run. These ineffective programs included individual counseling, peer counseling and peer-led information groups, and programs designed to arouse students' fears and appeal to their sense of right and wrong. Schools considering these types of programs may wish to rethink their decision or do further investigation before investing their resources.

Strategies to Consider

Reducing the Risk of Antisocial Behavior

Behavior is the result of the interaction of environmental influences and genetic predispositions. Schools can do nothing to alter the genetic coding. But recent research seems to indicate that genes affecting personality traits are either activated or repressed by the individual's environment. Consequently, if schools undertake comprehensive efforts to provide supportive structures and reduce risk factors, then fewer children may fall victim to emotional and behavioral problems that can seriously interfere with their schooling and life. These efforts that will encourage prevention of problem behaviors fall into the broad areas of school organization and effectiveness, student achievement and early intervention, parent and community involvement, and professional development for staff (Appalachia Educational Laboratory, 1996).

School Organization and Effectiveness	The school should ▸ Have high expectations for learning and behavior for all students and help all children achieve them ▸ Clearly communicate expectations for learning and behavior to all students ▸ Include staff, students, parents, and community members in the decision-making process ▸ Promote student engagement and attachment ▸ Have a consistent system of reinforcement and recognition to shape student behavior ▸ Provide alternatives to suspension and expulsion ▸ Conduct risk assessment as part of safe schools improvement plans
Student Achievement and Early Intervention	The school should ▸ Intervene early to identify and assist students who fail to meet expectations for learning and behavior ▸ Evaluate students' social, emotional, and adaptive functions, as well as cognitive function ▸ Include special education students in regular classrooms ▸ Not disproportionately discipline students with disabilities

Reducing the Risk of Antisocial Behavior—Continued

Parent and Community Involvement

The school should

▸ Work with parents and community groups to educate and care for children

▸ Involve parents and community groups in developing the safe schools improvement plan

▸ Provide information to parents about how to help their children learn and behave appropriately in school

▸ Collaborate with other agencies to meet family and community needs

Professional Development for Staff

The school should

▸ Train teachers to use a variety of instructional and classroom management strategies to prevent academic failure and problem behavior for all students

▸ Encourage preservice programs in teacher-training institutions to provide this training

▸ Encourage state departments of education to include this training in their inservice programs

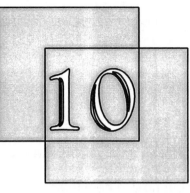

AUTISM

In previous chapters we have discovered how the brain acquires language, learns to read and write, calculates, and generates the emotions to interact and communicate with other human beings. Different neural networks must work in harmony to carry out these activities successfully. When several networks malfunction early in a child's life, developmental disorders appear. Describing and categorizing these disorders are not easy. Nonetheless, the Diagnostic and Statistical Manual of Mental Disorders (DSM-IV) calls this category Pervasive Developmental Disorder, which includes five disorders: Autistic Disorder, Asperger's Disorder, Rett's Disorder, Childhood Disintegrative Disorder, and Pervasive Developmental Disorder Not Otherwise Specified.

In Autistic Disorder (or autism), neurological problems develop that make it difficult for a person to communicate and form relationships with others. It is a spectrum disorder that runs the gamut from mild to severe. Some people with autism are relatively high functioning (called high-functioning autism), while others are mentally retarded or have serious language delays.

> *Autism affects one person in 500, and four out of five of those affected are males. The prevalence of autism has probably been underestimated in the past.*

Autism affects about one person in 500, and four out of five of those affected are males. Although it may appear that the incidence of autism is increasing in American children, the medical community believes it is more likely that the prevalence of autism has been underestimated in the past.

The symptoms of autism usually appear before the age of three. Children with autism do not interact and may avoid eye contact. They may resist attention and affection, and they rarely seem upset when a parent leaves or show pleasure when the parent returns. Understanding the cues of others—such as a smile, wink, or grimace—is difficult for them as well. Some children with autism also tend to be physically aggressive at times, particularly when they are in a strange or overwhelming environment. At times they will break things, attack others, or harm themselves.

Areas Affected by Autism

Autism can cause language difficulties, repetitive and obsessive behaviors, sensory overload, and problems with memory and recall (NIMH, 1997).

Language difficulties. About one-half of the children diagnosed with autism remain mute throughout their lives. Others will only parrot what they hear (a condition known as *echolalia*). Those who do speak tend to confuse pronouns like "I," "my," and "you," and may use the same phrase, such as "milk and cookies," in many different situations.

It is very difficult to understand the body language of people with autism. Most of us smile when we talk or shrug our shoulders when we cannot answer a question. But the facial expressions and movements of children with autism rarely match what they are saying. In addition, their tone of voice does not usually reflect their feelings. Without meaningful gestures or the language to ask for things, these children are at a loss to communicate their needs. Consequently, they may simply scream or grab what they want.

Repetitive and obsessive behaviors. Most children with autism appear physically normal and have good muscle control. But some exhibit repetitive actions, such as flicking their fingers, rocking back and forth, or running from room to room tuning lights on and off. Others demand consistency in their environment and develop fixations with certain objects, such as eating the same foods at the same time and sitting in the same place every day. Does this repetitive-obsessive behavior have the same underlying neurological cause as obsessive-compulsive disorder? It is possible but not likely.

> *Children with autism demand consistency in order to bring stability to a world of sensory confusion.*

Researchers seem to favor the explanation that the demand for consistency is an attempt to bring stability in a world of sensory confusion and to block out painful stimuli.

Sensory symptoms. Many children with autism are highly attuned to the input from their senses but have difficulty sorting the input into a coherent whole. As a result, their sensory world can be confusing and lead to overwhelming sensitivity. For example, the feel of their clothes can be very disturbing. Some children will cover their ears and shout at a ringing telephone or vacuum cleaner. For some, the senses are scrambled in that they experience certain sounds as color, make audible sounds when someone touches their skin, or gag when feeling a texture.

Memory and recall. A few studies have looked at how well children with autism learn information, encode it accurately, and retrieve it correctly. This ability is known as "recall readiness." The results showed that most children with autism had greater difficulty in recall readiness compared to those without autism (Farrant, Blades, and Boucher, 1999). The study did not include any of the rare population of "savants" who can remember enormous amounts of information.

Diagnosis

To date, there are no medical tests that reliably detect autism. No two children display the disorder in exactly the same way. Further, some children can exhibit autistic-like symptoms that may indicate other disorders and not autism. These possibilities also need to be investigated.

Specialists use a variety of methods to identify the disorder. They evaluate language and social behavior, talk with parents about the child's developmental milestones, and may test for certain genetic and neurological problems. They may consider other conditions that exhibit the same behaviors and similar symptoms to autism, such as Rett's Disorder or Asperger's syndrome. Rett's Disorder is a progressive brain disease that affects only girls and can lead to loss of language and social skills. Asperger's syndrome is explained later in this chapter.

The diagnosis of autism will be made only if there is clear evidence of

- ▸ poor or limited social relationships
- ▸ underdeveloped communication skills
- ▸ repetitive behaviors, interests, and activities.

The diagnostic criteria also require that these symptoms appear by the age of 3 years. Children with fewer or milder symptoms are often diagnosed as having Pervasive Developmental Disorder.

What Causes Autism?

No one knows for sure, but it is not the result of poor parenting. Researchers in the past 15 years have made great strides in understanding the impaired abilities of people with autism and have used this understanding to develop theories about its cause. One of the prevailing theories is that people with autism fail to construe the mental states of others—a deficit in what has been called the "theory of mind." This theory refers to the everyday ability to infer what others are thinking or believing in order to explain and predict their behavior. That is, children with autism have difficulty viewing situations from another person's perspective. This may explain why they have such difficulty with simple behaviors such as attending to a situation and playing games with others.

Another notion is that autism is caused by deficits in the frontal lobe's ability to carry out its executive functions, such as controlling behavior, especially in new circumstances. The deficit reflects frontal lobe abnormalities and may explain the repetitive and obsessive behavior in autism (Russell, 1998).

More recent studies of brain structures in people with autism have led neuroscientists to look for a biological basis. Reviewing first the inheritance factor, examinations of siblings of people with autism have shown a 3 to 8 percent chance of the sibling being diagnosed with the same disorder. Although this is greater than the 0.2 percent chance (1 in 500) in the general population, it is far less than the 50 percent chance that would indicate a single dominant gene or the 25 percent chance of a single recessive gene. When an identical twin has autism, the chances of the other twin (who has the identical genes) being diagnosed with the disorder is only 60 percent. These data favor the conclusion that autism is the result of the variance of several genes contributing to the outcome, and that this situation may be modified by environmental factors. The search for the cause of autism is complicated because researchers do not know how the various factors combine to make some people display the disorder while others escape it (Rodier, 2000).

> **Theory of Mind**
>
> In one of the first studies to focus on this notion, researchers quizzed children on the following scenario: Sally puts a marble into a covered basket and leaves the room. While Sally is out, her friend Anne moves the marble from the basket to a nearby covered box. When asked where Sally would later look for the marble, children without autism said she would look in the basket because that is where she *thinks* it is. By contrast, the children with autism (including some quite bright adolescents) said that Sally will look in the box, where the ball really is. This failure to interpret Sally's belief has been taken as evidence of impaired theory of mind in autism (Baron-Cohen, Tager-Flusberg, and Cohen, 1993).

Although deficits in language, planning, and social cues are associated with the frontal lobe, other symptoms, such as lack of facial expression, hypersensitivity to sound and touch, and sleep disturbances, are more closely associated with the cerebellum and the brain stem (see Chapter 1). One consistent finding is that people with autism tend to have a proportionally smaller cerebellum than normal. A recent study found that certain parts of the brain stem were also smaller or missing in a brain with autism, a condition that probably originated between the 20th and 24th day after conception as a result of coding by a variant gene known as HOXA1. Researchers have identified at least three genes that could be responsible for autism and they are searching for more.

It is possible, so the theory goes, that the causes of this baffling disorder may lie in changes in the brain stem during early embryonic developments as a result of malfunctioning genes (Rodier, 2000). The theory is further supported by a study showing that blood samples taken at birth from children who eventually developed autism had high levels of four proteins involved in

Vaccines and Autism

Newspapers and television have reported an alleged connection between the MMR (measles/mumps/rubella) vaccination and autism. The report was based on a study of 12 patients in England that suggested the MMR vaccine may have caused bowel problems leading to decreased absorption of essential nutrients, triggering autistic behavior.

The results of that study have not been supported by subsequent tests. Further, the current theories of the causes of autism rule out vaccinations as a potential cause. More information is available at the Center for Disease Control and Prevention website: www.cdc.gov.

brain development. The finding suggests that some abnormal processes were already underway at birth (NAAR, 2000).

Tracking down all of the genes associated with autism will not be easy, and it is possible that the genetic variants will not explain all the causes of the disorder. The genetic component may just represent a predisposition to the disorder that is triggered by some other nongenetic factor. But every risk factor that is identified takes away some of the mystery and, in time, may help alleviate the suffering caused by this disorder.

Treatment. At present, there is no cure for autism, nor do children outgrow it. Nonetheless, more than ever before, people with autism can be helped. A combination of early intervention, special education support, and medication is helping children and adolescents with autism lead more normal lives. Medications can alleviate some of the symptoms and therapy can help a child to learn, communicate, and interact with others in productive ways.

Unusual Abilities

About 10 percent of people with autism display remarkable abilities and skills. At a time when other children are drawing lines or scribbling, some children with autism can draw detailed, realistic pictures with proper dimensional perspective. Some begin to read before they speak or play musical instruments without being taught. Others can memorize enormous amounts of information, such as pages from a phone book, many years of sport scores, or entire television shows. Such abilities are known as *savant skills*, and the extreme forms are rare.

> *About 10 percent of people with autism display remarkable abilities and skills.*

Researchers have been trying to explain why certain people with autism possess savant skills. The current theory is that one characteristic of autism may provide both advantages and disadvantages. This characteristic is called *central convergence* and refers to the ability of the brain to process incoming information in its context, that is, to put parts together into a meaningful whole. Because this ability is weak in people with autism, it may explain why they focus on details

200

and parts at the expense of global meaning. It may also explain why they have difficulties in social situations and why their piecemeal processing of faces could hamper their recognition of emotions in others (Happé, 1997).

The notion that children with autism show weak central convergence has been supported by a growing number of studies. For example, several studies have shown that children with autism are less likely to be tricked by optical illusions and are better at finding objects imbedded in pictures than children without autism. This superior ability may be due to disembedding skills in which they can perceive parts of the object independent of the surrounding context (Figure 10.1).

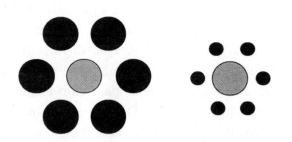

Figure 10.1 The presence of the outside circles causes most people to believe that the inner circle on the right is larger than the inner circle on the left (The inner circles are the same size). People with autism perceive these figures in a less unified way and are less likely to succumb to the illusion.

People with autism do appear to integrate the properties of a single object (e.g., its color and shape), and to process the meaning of individual words. The difficulty seems to be in connecting the objects and words to form larger contexts and a convergent whole.

Central convergence, then, may explain some of the assets, as well as deficits, of people with autism. Studies show that children with autism are better at learning the names of musical notes and at retaining absolute pitch later. They also do better at drawings that have details and lines of perspective. Both of these findings can be explained by a mental bias toward processing and remembering detail. A question currently under investigation is whether central convergence is an aspect of autism that is transmitted genetically (Happé, 1997).

Asperger's Syndrome

Identified in 1944 by Austrian physician Hans Asperger, this syndrome is a developmental disorder with many of the same symptoms of autism. It is usually referred to as a mild form of autism because people with Asperger's syndrome generally have higher mental functioning than those with typical autism. Like autism, Asperger's syndrome is a lifelong condition. However, the DSM-IV classifies Asperger's as a separate disorder and controversy exists as to whether Asperger's is a distinct syndrome or a form of autism. Some professionals believe that the definition of autism should include Asperger's because no biological tests have been yet identified for either disorder.

How do Asperger's and autism differ? Although many of the symptoms of the two disorders are similar, there are important differences. Because of these differences, some argue that Asperger's should carry a distinct diagnosis, which paves the way for more appropriate education and treatment. Both Asperger's and autism are classified as Pervasive Developmental Disorders, which means impairments exist in social interaction, communication, and the range of interests and activities. Differences in the two conditions are found primarily in the *degree* of impairment. For example, although an individual with autism may experience a delay in speech, an individual with Asperger's does not possess a clinically significant delay in language. However, an individual with Asperger's may have difficulty understanding abstract forms of spoken language, such as humor or irony (APA, 2000).

Cognitive ability is another distinction between the two disorders made in the DSM-IV. Persons with autism experience mental retardation, but the criteria for Asperger's state that the individual cannot possess a clinically significant cognitive delay. Of course, some people with autism do not have mental retardation, but a person with Asperger's must possess an average to above average intelligence (APA, 2000).

Professionals working with these disorders add that, compared to people with autism, those with Asperger's syndrome have a need for high stimulation, have an overdeveloped use of imagination, tend to be more social, have fewer language deficits, and are more willful in their behavior. As a result of these differences, young children with Asperger's syndrome often go undiagnosed through their early elementary years because their strengths mask their deficits.

What Is the Future of Research on Autism?

Research continues to look for genetic variants associated with autism in the hope that this may provide a more accurate diagnostic tool for the future, at least in terms of estimating the chances that the children of siblings of a person with autism may inherit the disorder. Attention is also being directed to the role that neurotransmitters, especially serotonin, play in negating the disruptive behavior associated with the disorder. The effectiveness of selective serotonin reuptake

> **A Word About Secretin**
>
> In 1997, television and newspaper stories publicized the claims of several families that injections of the human hormone secretin had caused noticeable improvement in the behavior of their children who had been diagnosed with autism. To date, research has not been able to affirm that secretin has any therapeutic benefit for the treatment of autism, although the clinical trials continue. One major study found no benefit from a single secretin injection (Sandler, Sutton, DeWeese, Girardi, Sheppard, and Bodfish, 1999).

inhibitors (SSRIs) in improving some of the behaviors in autism may also lead to new insights into biochemical mechanisms (Piven, 1997).

Although preliminary results are inconclusive, toxic substances ingested by the mother during pregnancy as well as drugs used to induce labor continue to be investigated as possible causes of autism. Brain imaging studies are revealing variations in the brains of children with autism that may lead to the discovery of underlying physiological mechanisms of the disorder. Of particular interest is the observation that people with autism often have enlarged brains. Other studies are examining whether the normal process of synaptic pruning and programmed cell death (apoptosis) in early childhood proceeds normally in children with autism. Failure of either of these processes could lead to an enlarged brain. As researchers learn more about the development of the human brain, they will be better able to unlock the genetic, biochemical, psychological, and physiological mysteries of autism.

> *Brain imaging is revealing variations in the brains of children with autism that may lead to the discovery of underlying physiological mechanisms of the disorder.*

What Do Educators Need to Consider?

Autism is a neurological disorder that affects children's overall ability to communicate and interact socially. Their behavior may be difficult to control at times. Teachers need to be adequately trained to use interventions that will preserve a positive educational climate in the classroom for these students and their peers.

Adolescents diagnosed with autism have to bear both the burden of coping with the teenage years as well as the recognition that they are different from their peers. They typically lack friends and neither date nor plan for the future. Awareness of this often drives them to learn new and unacceptable behaviors. Success in school for students with autism should be measured not so much by whether they pass algebra, but by whether they acquire the knowledge and skills that will make them more self-sufficient as adults.

Impact on Learning

Much of what we have gleaned about how people with autism learn comes not just from professional observation but also from those with autism who have written about their world (Grandin, 1996). Children diagnosed with autism may display

- Behavioral issues that often detract from learning

- A learning style biased toward piecemeal processing

- A reluctance to communicate making it difficult to assess what they have learned

- A savant skill that can be tapped

- Ability to think more in pictures than in words

- A difficulty with long sentences or strings of verbal information

- Attention to only one sensory channel at a time

- A difficulty with generalizing.

Strategies to Consider

Enhancing Learning in Students With Autism

Children and adolescents diagnosed with autism will have an Individualized Educational Program (IEP) developed for them when enrolled in public schools. The plan serves as an agreement between the school and the family about the student's educational goals.

The items listed here are for consideration by any educator responsible for helping these students successfully cope with their situation and become self-sufficient adults (Quill, 1995).

♦ **Different learning style.** Students with autism learn differently in that they have difficulty understanding the perceptions of others, experience sensory overload, and use intellect instead of emotion to guide their social interactions.

♦ **Need for structure.** These students need structure. Their activities should
  ▸ organize their materials,
  ▸ give clear instructions,
  ▸ provide stability,
  ▸ establish patterns,
  ▸ provide consistency and predictability, and
  ▸ increase independence.

♦ **Social interaction.** These students need to learn ways to interact socially with their peers and adults. When teaching them about social interaction, use
  ▸ a predictable sequence of interactions (no surprises),
  ▸ a planned set of conversational scripts,
  ▸ lots of repetition,
  ▸ messages linked to what the student is doing,
  ▸ speech and visual cues simultaneously, and
  ▸ messages mixed with ongoing activities.

Strategies to Consider

Helping Students With Asperger's Syndrome

Children and adolescents diagnosed with Asperger's syndrome usually have average or above average cognitive abilities. They tend to have excellent rote memory skills and often exhibit a precocious vocabulary. However, they have problems with abstract thinking. They frequently do not understand the logic of classroom instruction and discussion and are easily distracted. Educational structure and classroom management strategies become important. Here are a few points to consider that could help students diagnosed with Asperger's syndrome to succeed in the classroom.

✓ **Educational Structure and Classroom Management.**
- Provide a predictable environment and routine and prepare students for any upcoming changes
- Ensure that each student is seated in a position of least distraction and close to the teacher or other source of information to which the student must respond
- Be consistent and do not ask for an option if there is none
- Do not do for the students what they can do for themselves
- Give clear, precise, concrete instructions, and don't assume that mere repetition means that the student has understood
- Find ways to tie new situations to old ones that students have experienced
- State expectations clearly and allow each student time to process the information
- Concentrate on changing unacceptable behaviors and do not worry about those which are simply odd
- Break tasks up into manageable segments and plan a completion schedule with the student
- Do not rely on emotional appeals by assuming students want to please you

Helping Students With Asperger's Syndrome—Continued

✓ **Instructional Approaches.**

- ▸ Support verbal information with visual aids
- ▸ Model the action you want students to use, and maintain the behavior with visual cues
- ▸ Use cooperative learning groups, but teach appropriate social responses to use in this activity
- ▸ Minimize assigned written work because these students do not understand the logic of repeating activities
- ▸ Assign enrichment activities related to the students' interests, as they will be more satisfied and productive gathering facts about a subject they like
- ▸ Avoid abstract language (e.g., metaphors and irony), and fully explain any constructions that you do use

✓ **Support and Discipline Strategies.**

- ▸ Have a strategy ready in case the students cannot cope due to overstimulation or confusion
- ▸ Have a time-out area for discipline when needed, and make sure the time-out is not more appealing than the curricular activity
- ▸ Explicitly teach the rules of social conduct
- ▸ Inform parents on a regular basis of the students' successes and failures and ask for parental advice when appropriate
- ▸ Give students some space and avoid cornering or trapping them
- ▸ Use an unemotional tone of voice when telling them what they need to do, and give sincere praise when they do it correctly
- ▸ Try not to confuse lack of tact with rudeness
- ▸ Protect them from teasing and bullying
- ▸ Teach them how to meet someone, how to recognize when someone will not talk to them, and how to tell when someone is teasing them

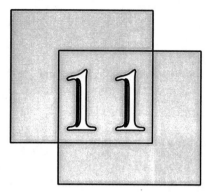

PUTTING IT ALL TOGETHER

The preceding chapters have described some of the recent research on the human brain that may shed light on problems affecting learning. Some of the problems may result from genetic mutations, fetal brain injury during gestation, or environmental impact. Whatever the cause, teachers represent the essential link between the students with learning problems and the strategies and services selected to help them.

> *Students with learning problems **can** learn when teachers find the appropriate ways to teach these students.*

It is important to remember that students with learning problems *can* learn when teachers spend the time and use their expertise to find the appropriate ways to teach these students. To that end, here are some suggestions to consider that can be adapted to most grade levels.

1. **Learn about learning.** Educators in all areas need to update their knowledge base about what neuroscience is revealing about how the brain learns. These discoveries and insights can help explain problems and improve classroom skills. Teachers should draw on the knowledge of special educators and researchers to address specific problems.

2. **Look for the warning signs.** Very often, the regular classroom teacher is the first to recognize a potential learning problem. Although many students encounter learning problems at one time or another, these problems are usually temporary and quickly overcome. For others, the problems persist

and result in a lag in academic achievement compared to their learning potential. These students need help.

3. **Assess the situation.** The question now is whether the learning problem can be addressed in the regular classroom. Asking students to take an inventory similar to the one below will help you and them learn from their perceptions of how well they perform certain tasks. Working with a student on the comments section can provide useful insights on instructional approaches to consider.

Assessment Inventory			
Area	**Strengths**	**Challenges**	**Comments**
Attention			
Speaking			
Reading			
Writing			
Calculating			
Memory			

4. **Look for abilities, not just disabilities.** Sometimes we get so concerned about the students' problems that we miss the opportunity to capitalize on their strengths. Many studies indicate that using an individual's strengths to mitigate areas of weakness often results in improved performance and a well-needed boost to that person's self-esteem.

5. **Design a learning profile for each student with learning problems.** For students with learning problems, keep a simple record of their
   ▸ reasoning ability,
   ▸ learning style,
   ▸ classroom participation,
   ▸ comprehension,
   ▸ work level, and
   ▸ progress.
Design the profile to spot trends in each area. Use this information to build on students' existing strengths and identify areas needing improvement.

6. **Use technology.** Computers and other forms of advanced technology are useful tools for helping students with learning problems. Word processing programs with voice recognition are just one example of hardware and software components that can capitalize on students strengths and minimize their weaknesses.

7. **Modify the learning environment.** Just a few changes in the learning environment can sometimes make a significant difference in student achievement. Consider which students might benefit if you
   ▸ Seat student in an areas free of distractions.
   ▸ Consider using study carrels.
   ▸ Keep the student's work area free of unnecessary materials.
   ▸ Use a checklist to help get the student organized.
   ▸ Stand near the student when giving directions.
   ▸ Provide organizational strategies such as charts and timelines.
   ▸ Assist in organizing the student's notebook.
   ▸ Use materials that address the students' learning styles.
   ▸ Provide opportunities for movement.

8. **Modify instructional strategies.** Consider modifying instructional strategies to meet the various learning styles and abilities of students with learning problems. Here are some strategies to consider:
   ▸ Allow students to audiotape lectures.
   ▸ Break assignment into shorter tasks.
   ▸ Adjust the reading level of the classroom material.
   ▸ Teach the concrete before the abstract.
   ▸ Relate the new learning to students' experiences.
   ▸ Reduce the number of concepts presented at one time.
   ▸ Give an overview of the lesson before beginning.
   ▸ Check the student's comprehension of the language used for instruction.
   ▸ Monitor the rate at which you present material.
   ▸ Require verbal responses from the student to check for comprehension.
   ▸ Provide clear and concise directions for homework assignments.
   ▸ Allow typewritten or word processed assignments.
   ▸ Consider the oral administration of tests and open book tests.
   ▸ Provide practice test questions for study.

210

- ▶ Allow use of dictionary or calculator during test.
- ▶ Provide extra time to finish a written test.

9. **Modify the curriculum materials.** Modifications to curriculum materials will vary depending on the nature of the student's learning problem. For those with **spoken language** difficulties, you can

- ▶ Paraphrase complex information.
- ▶ Slow the rate of presentation.
- ▶ Provide written directions to supplement verbal directions.
- ▶ Keep sentence structures simple.
- ▶ Avoid the use of abstract language such as puns, idioms, and metaphors.
- ▶ Get the student's attention before expressing key points.
- ▶ Use visual aids such as charts and graphs.
- ▶ Call student by name before asking questions.

For those with **written language** difficulties,

- ▶ Allow student to use cursive or manuscript writing.
- ▶ Permit student to type, record, or give oral answers instead of writing.
- ▶ Provide copies of class notes.
- ▶ Avoid the pressure of speed and accuracy.
- ▶ Reduce the amount of copying from the textbook or board.
- ▶ Establish realistic standards for neatness.
- ▶ Accept key word responses instead of complete sentences.

For those with **organizational problems**,

- ▶ Establish clear rules and consistently enforce them.
- ▶ Provide an established daily routine.
- ▶ Consider making contracts with students and use rewards when the contract is completed.
- ▶ Ensure that due dates are clearly understood.
- ▶ Provide a specific place for turning in assignments.

10. **Get the reluctant starter going.** Some students have difficulty getting started and need the teacher's guidance to move forward. For them,

- ▶ Give a personal cue to begin work.
- ▶ Check progress often, especially after the first few minutes of work.

> ▸ Provide immediate feedback and reinforcers.
> ▸ Divide work into smaller units.
> ▸ Suggest time periods for each task.
> ▸ Ensure that the student understands the instructions.
> ▸ Present the assignment in sequential steps.
> ▸ Provide a checklist for multitask assignments.

11. **Maintain attention.** Because some students with learning problems can be easily distracted, look for ways to maintain attention during the lesson.
> ▸ Seat the students close to you.
> ▸ Provide praise for correct answers.
> ▸ Relate new learning to students' experiences.
> ▸ Give an advance warning when a transition is going to occur.
> ▸ Use physical proximity and appropriate touch to help student refocus.

12. **Use group instruction and peers.** Although some students with learning problems do not always work well in groups, persistence and guidance can often result in a productive experience.
> ▸ Assign a peer tutor to record material dictated by the student.
> ▸ Use cooperative learning strategies when appropriate.
> ▸ Assign a peer helper to read important directions and information to the student and to check for understanding.

13. **Adjust time demands.** Meeting timelines and deadlines is not always easy for some students with learning problems. Some get involved in minute details, while others dart from one idea to another and lose track of time.
> ▸ Increase time allowed for the completion of tests or assignments.
> ▸ Reduce the amount of work or length of tests.
> ▸ Introduce short breaks or change of tasks.
> ▸ Follow a specific routine and be consistent.
> ▸ Alternate active and quiet tasks.
> ▸ Help students prioritize the steps needed to complete an assignment.
> ▸ Set time limits for completing specific tasks.

14. **Deal with inappropriate behavior.** Inappropriate behavior is not acceptable. But keep in mind that the misbehavior may not have been intentional.
> ▸ Provide clear and concise classroom expectations and consequences

- ► Enforce rules consistently.
- ► Avoid confrontational techniques; they often escalate the situation.
- ► Provide the student with alternatives.
- ► Avoid power struggles.
- ► Designate a cooling-off location in the classroom.
- ► Ignore attention-getting behavior for a short time (extinction).
- ► Assign activities which require some movement.
- ► Deal with the behavior and avoid criticizing the student.
- ► Speak privately to the student about inappropriate behavior.
- ► Check for levels of tolerance and be aware of signs of frustration.

15. **Modify homework assignments.** Homework can be a valuable learning tool for students with learning problems if it is relevant and not excessive.
- ► Consider allowing student to work on homework in school.
- ► Give frequent reminders about due dates.
- ► Give short assignments.
- ► Allow for extra credit assignments.
- ► Develop an award system for in-school work and homework completed.

16. **Communicate with parents.** Frequent communication with parents is important so that you are all working together to assist the student in meeting expectations.
- ► Develop a daily and weekly journal and share it with the parents.
- ► Schedule periodic parent-teacher meetings.
- ► Provide parents and students with a duplicate set of textbooks that they can use at home during the school year.
- ► Provide weekly progress reports to parents.
- ► Mail the parents a schedule of class and homework assignments.

Not all of these recommendations apply to every student, and individual strategies should be developed to address the needs of individual students with learning problems. Implementing accommodations such as those listed here can improve the academic achievement of students with learning disabilities. In mainstreamed classrooms, take care to balance these accommodations so as not to appear unfair to the students who are not in need of these strategies.

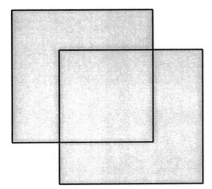

GLOSSARY

Alphabetic principle. The notion that written words are composed of letters of the alphabet that intentionally and systematically represent segments of spoken words.

Amygdala. The almond-shaped structure in the brain's limbic system that encodes emotional messages to long-term storage.

Aphasia. The loss of language function.

Apoptosis. The genetically programmed process in which unneeded or unhealthy brain cells are destroyed.

Attention deficit hyperactivity disorder (ADHD). A syndrome that interferes with an individual's capacity to regulate activity level, inhibit behavior, and attend to tasks in developmentally appropriate ways.

Autism. A spectrum disorder that affects an individual's ability to communicate, form relationships with others, and relate appropriately to the environment.

Brain stem. One of the major parts of the brain, it receives sensory input and monitors vital functions such as heartbeat, body temperature, and digestion.

Broca's area. A region in the left frontal lobe of the brain believed responsible for generating the vocabulary and syntax of an individual's native language.

Cerebellum. One of the major parts of the brain, it coordinates muscle movement.

Cerebrum. The largest of the major parts of the brain, it controls sensory interpretation, thinking, and memory.

Circadian rhythm. The daily cycle of numerous body functions, such as breathing and body temperature.

Computerized tomography (CT, formerly CAT) scanner. An instrument that uses X-rays and computer processing to produce a detailed cross-section of brain structure.

Corpus callosum. The bridge of nerve fibers that connects the left and right cerebral hemispheres and allows communication between them.

Cortex. The thin but tough layer of cells covering the cerebrum that contains all the neurons used for cognitive and motor processing.

Delayed sleep phase disorder. A chronic condition caused mainly by a shift in an adolescent's sleep cycle that results in difficulty falling asleep at night and waking up in the morning.

Dendrite. The branched extension from the cell body of a neuron that receives impulses from nearby neurons through synaptic contacts.

Dopamine. A neurotransmitter believed to control mood, behavior, and muscle coordination.

Dyscalculia. A condition that causes persistent problems with processing numerical calculations.

Dysgraphia. A spectrum disorder characterized by difficulty in mastering the sequence of movements necessary to write letters and numbers.

Dyslexia. A learning disorder characterized by problems in expressing or receiving oral or written language.

Frontal lobe. The front part of the brain that monitors higher-order thinking, directs problem solving, and regulates the excesses of the emotional (limbic) system.

Functional magnetic resonance imaging (fMRI). An instrument that measures blood flow to the brain to record areas of high and low neuronal activity.

Glial cells. Special "glue" cells in the brain that surround each neuron providing support, protection, and nourishment.

Gray matter. The thin but tough covering of the brain's cerebrum also known as the cerebral cortex.

Hippocampus. A brain structure that compares new learning to past learning and encodes information from working memory to long-term storage.

Limbic system. The structures at the base of the cerebrum that control emotions.

Magnetic resonance imaging (MRI). An instrument that uses radio waves to disturb the alignment of the body's atoms in a magnetic field to produce computer-processed, high-contrast images of internal structures.

Melatonin. A hormone that helps regulate the body's sleep-wake cycle.

Mnemonic. A word or phrase used as a device for remembering unrelated information, patterns, or rules.

Motor cortex. The narrow band across the top of the brain from ear to ear that controls movement.

Myelin. A fatty substance that surrounds and insulates a neuron's axon.

Neuron. The basic cell making up the brain and nervous system, consisting of a globular cell body, a long fiber called an axon which transmits impulses, and many shorter fibers called dendrites which receive them.

Neurotransmitter. One of nearly 100 chemicals stored in axon sacs that transmit impulses from neuron to neuron across the synaptic gap.

Orthography. The written system for a language.

Phonemes. The minimal units of sound in a language that combine to make syllables.

Phonemic awareness. The ability to deal explicitly and segmentally with sound units smaller than the syllable (i.e., the phoneme).

Phonological alexia. The inability to retain words in memory long enough to establish meaning.

Phonological awareness. The ability to recognize the production and interpretation of the sound patterns (rather than the meaning) of language.

Positron emission tomography (PET) scanner. An instrument that traces the metabolism of radioactively tagged sugar in brain tissue producing a color image of cell activity.

Prosody. The rhythm, cadence, accent patterns, and pitch of a language.

Rehearsal. The reprocessing of information in working memory.

Retention. The preservation of a learning in long-term storage in such a way that it can be identified and recalled quickly and accurately.

Reticular activating system (RAS). The dense formation of neurons in the brain stem that controls major body functions and maintains the brain's alertness.

Suprachiasmatic nucleus. A pair of small clusters of neurons within the immediate vicinity of the optic nerve that regulate the body's circadian sleep-wake cycle.

Synapse. The microscopic gap between the axon of one neuron and the dendrite of another.

Thalamus. A part of the limbic system that receives all incoming sensory information, except smell, and shunts it to other areas of the cortex for additional processing.

Transfer. The influence that past learning has on new learning, and the degree to which the new learning will be useful in the learner's future.

Visual magnocellular-deficit. A disorder of the visual processing system that leads to poor detection of visual motion, causing letters to bunch up or overlap during reading.

Wernicke's area. A section in the left temporal lobe of the brain believed responsible for generating sense and meaning in an individual's native language.

White matter. The support tissue that lies beneath the cerebrum's gray matter (cortex).

Windows of opportunity. Important periods in which the young brain responds to certain types of input to create or consolidate neural networks.

Working memory. The temporary memory wherein information is processed consciously.

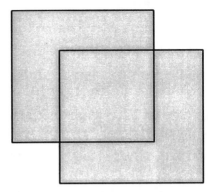

REFERENCES

American Psychiatric Association (APA). (2000). *Diagnostic and Statistical Manual of Mental Disorders*, Fourth Edition, Text Revision (DSM-IV). Washington, DC: American Psychiatric Publishing Group.

Appalachia Educational Laboratory. (1996). *Preventing antisocial behavior in disabled and at-risk students*. Charleston, WV: Author.

Barkley, R.A. (1998, September). Attention-deficit hyperactivity disorder. *Scientific American*, 66-71.

Barkley, R.A. (1998). *Attention-deficit hyperactivity disorder: A handbook for diagnosis and treatment*. New York: Guilford Press.

Baron-Cohen, S., Tager-Flusberg, H, and Cohen, D. J. (Eds.). (1993). *Understanding other minds: Perspectives from autism*. New York: Oxford University Press.

Baroody, A. J. (1999). The development of basic counting, number, and arithmetic knowledge among children classified as mentally handicapped. In L. M. Glidden (Ed.), *International review of research in mental retardation* (Vol. 22, pp. 51-103). New York: Academic Press.

Baum, S. (1994). Meeting the needs of gifted/learning disabled students. *The Journal of Secondary Gifted Education, 5*, 6-16.

Baynes, K., Eliassen, J. C., Lutsep, H. L., and Gazzaniga, M. S. (1998, May 8). Modular organization of cognitive systems masked by interhemispheric integration. *Science, 280*, 902-905.

Beatty, J. (2001). *The human brain: Essentials of behavioral neuroscience*. Thousand Oaks, CA: Sage Publications.

Borkowski, J. G., Estrada, M., Milstead, M., and Hale, C. (1989). General problem-solving skills: Relations between metacognition and strategic processing. *Learning Disabilities Quarterly, 12*, 57-70.

Brody, L. E., and Mills, C. J. (1997, May/June). Gifted children with learning disabilities: A review of the issues. *Journal of Learning Disabilities, 30*, 282-286.

Buckner, R. L., Kelley, W. M., & Petersen, S. E. (1999, April). Frontal cortex contributions to human memory formation. *Nature Neuroscience, 2*, 311–314.

Byrne, B. (1991). Experimental analysis of the child's discovery of the alphabetic principle. In L. Riehen and C. Perfetti (Eds.), *Learning to read: Basic research and its implications* (pp. 75-84). Hillsdale, NJ: Erlbaum.

Chard, D.J., and Dickson, S.V. (1999, May). Phonological awareness: Instructional and assessment guidelines. *Intervention in School and Clinic, 34*, 261-270.

Chard, D.J., and Osborn, J. (1998). *Suggestions for examining phonics and decoding instruction in supplementary reading programs.* Austin, TX: Texas Education Agency.

Cheour, M., Ceponiene, R., Lehtokoski, A., Luuk, A., Allik, J., Alho, K., and Näätänen, R. (1998, September). Development of language-specific phoneme representations in the infant brain. *Nature Neuroscience, 1*, 351-353.

Clements, D. H. (2000, Summer). Translating lessons from research into mathematics classrooms: Mathematics and special needs students. *International Dyslexia Association: Perspectives, 26*, 31-33.

Cole, P.G., and Mengler, E.D. (1994). Phonemic processing of children with language deficits: Which tasks best discriminate children with learning disabilities from average readers? *Reading Psychology, 15*, 223-243.

Coles, G. (2000). *Misreading reading: The bad science that hurts children.* Portsmouth, NH: Heinemann.

Dale, P. S., Simonoff, E., Bishop, D.V.M., Eley, T. C., Oliver, B., Price, T. S., Purcell, S., Stevenson, J., and Plomin, R. (1998, August). Genetic influence on language delay in two-year-old children. *Nature Neuroscience, 1*, 324–328.

DeGrandpre, R.J. and Hinshaw, S.P. (2000, Summer). ADHD: Serious psychiatric problem or all-American copout? *Cerebrum: The Dana Forum on Brain Science,* 12-38.

Deschenes, C., Ebeling, D. G., and Sprague, J. (1994). *Adapting curriculum and instruction in inclusive classrooms: A teacher's desk reference.* Bloomington, IN: Institute for the Study of Developmental Disabilities.

Deshler, D.D., Ellis, E.S., and Lenz, B.K. (1996). *Teaching adolescents with learning disabilities: Strategies and methods.* Denver, CO: Love Publishing.

Deshler, D.D., Shumaker, J.B., Alley, G.R., Clark, F.L., and Warner, M.M. (1981). Paraphrasing strategy. University of Kansas, Institute for Research in Learning Disabilities. Washington, DC: Bureau of Education for the Handicapped.

Deuel, R. K. (1994). Developmental dysgraphia and motor skill disorders. *Journal of Child Neurology, 10*, 6-8.

Diamond, M., and Hopson, J. (1998). *Magic trees of the mind: How to nurture your child's intelligence, creativity, and healthy emotions from birth through adolescence.* New York: Dutton.

Dinklage, K. T. (1971). Inability to learn a foreign language. In G. Blaine, and C. MacArthur (Eds.), *Emotional problems of the student.* New York: Appleton-Century-Crofts.

Edelen-Smith, P.J. (1998). How now brown cow: Phoneme awareness activities for collaborative classrooms. *Intervention in School and Clinic, 33*, 103-111.

Elkonin, D.B. (1973). In J. Downing (Ed.), *Comparative reading: Cross-national studies of behavior and processes in reading and writing* (pp. 551-559). New York: Macmillan.

Ellis, E.S., Deshler, D.D., Lenz, B.K., Schumaker, J.B., and Clark, F.L. (1991). An instructional model for teaching learning strategies. *Focus on Exceptional Children, 23*, 1-24.

Fagerheim, T., Raeymaekers, P., Tønnessen, F.E., Pedersen, M., Tranebjaerg, L., and Lubs, H.A. (1999, September). A new gene (DYX3) for dyslexia is located on chromosome 2. *Journal of Medical Genetics, 36*, 664-669.

Farrant, A., Blades, M., and Boucher, J. (1999, October). Recall readiness in children with autism. *Journal of Autism Developmental Disorders, 29,* 359-366.

Fellows, M., Koblitz, A. H., and Koblitz, N. (1994). Cultural aspects of mathematics education reform. *Notices of the American Mathematical Society, 41*, 5-9.

Foorman, B.R., Francis, D.J., Fletcher, J.M., Schatschneider, C., and Mehta, P. (1998). The role of instruction in learning to read: Preventing reading failure in at-risk children. *Journal of Educational Psychology, 90*, 1-15.

Fowler, M. (1994, October). Attention-deficit/hyperactivity disorder. *National Information Center for Children and Youth with Disabilities Briefing Paper*, 1-16.

Fulk, B. (2000, January). Twenty ways to make instruction more memorable. *Intervention in School and Clinic, 35*, 183-184.

Ganschow, L., and Sparks, R. (1995). Effects of direct instruction in Spanish phonology on native language skills and foreign language aptitude of at-risk foreign language learners. *Journal of Learning Disabilities, 28*, 107-120.

Geary, D. C. (2000, Summer). Mathematical disorders: An overview for educators. *International Dyslexia Association: Perspectives, 26*, 6-9.

Gersten, R., and Baker, S. (1999). *Teaching expressive writing to students with learning disabilities: A meta-analysis.* Eugene, OR: University of Oregon.

Gersten, R., Baker, S., and Edwards, L. (1999, December). Teaching expressive writing to students with learning disabilities. *ERIC/OSEP Digest, E590.*

Goswami, U. (1994). Phonological skills, analogies, and reading development. *Reading Behaviour*, 32-37.

Gottfredson, D. (1997). School-based crime prevention. In L. W. Sherman et al. (Eds.), *Preventing crime: What works, what doesn't, what's promising: A report to the United States Congress.* Washington, DC: U.S. Department of Justice, Office of Justice Programs.

Graham, S. (1990). The role of production factors in learning disabled students' compositions. *Journal of Educational Psychology, 80,* 356-361.

Grandin, T. (1996). *Thinking in pictures: And other reports from my life with autism.* New York: Vintage Books.

Happé, F. G. E. (1997). Central coherence and the theory of mind in autism: Reading homographs in context. *British Journal of Developmental Psychology, 15,* 1-12.

Idol, L. (1987). Group story mapping: A comprehension strategy for both skilled and unskilled readers. *Journal of Learning Disabilities, 20,* 196-205.

Johnson, D.W., and Johnson, R.T. (1989). Cooperative learning: What special educators need to know. *The Pointer, 33,* 5-10.

Johnson, S. (1999, May). *Strangers in our homes: TV and our children's minds.* Paper presented at the Waldorf School, San Francisco.

Jones, S. (2000). Accommodations and modifications for students with handwriting problems and/or dysgraphia. *LDOnline* [Online]. Available at http://www.ldonline. org/ld_indepth/writing/dysgraphia.

Kazdin, A. (1994). Interventions for aggressive and antisocial children. In L. D. Eron, J. H. Gentry, and P. Schlegel (Eds.), *Reason to hope: A psychosocial perspective on violence and youth* (pp. 341-382). Washington, DC: American Psychological Association.

Klingner, J.K., Vaughn, S., and Schumm, J.S. (1998). Collaborative strategic reading during social studies in heterogeneous fourth grade classrooms. *Elementary School Journal, 99,* 3-22.

Learning Disabilities Association of America (LDA). (2000). Speech and language milestones chart. *LDOnline* [Online]. Available at http://www.ldonline.org/ ld_indepth/speech-language/lda_milestones.html.

LeDoux, J. (1996). *The emotional brain: The mysterious underpinnings of emotional life.* New York: Simon and Schuster.

Lenhoff, H. M., Wang, P. P., Greenberg, F., and Bellugi, U. (1997, December). Williams syndrome and the brain. *Scientific American, 280*, 68-73.

Lenz, B. K., Ellis, E. S., and Scanlon, D. (1996). *Teaching learning strategies to adolescents and adults with learning disabilities*. Austin, TX: PRO-ED.

Leonard, L. B. (1998). *Children with specific language impairment*. Cambridge, MA: MIT Press.

Malone, R. P., Delaney, M. A., Luebbert, J. F., Cater, J., and Campbell, M. (2000, July). A double-blind placebo-controlled study of lithium in hospitalized aggressive children and adolescents with conduct disorder. *Archives of General Psychiatry, 7*, 649-654.

Marolda, M. R., and Davidson, P. S. (1994). Assessing mathematical abilities and learning approaches, in *Windows of opportunity*. Reston, VA: National Council of Teachers of Mathematics.

Mazzocco, M. M. (1998, August). A process approach to describing mathematical difficulties in girls with Turner syndrome. *Pediatrics, 102*, 492-496.

McCarthy, R. A., and Warrington, E. K. (1990). *Cognitive neuropsychology: A clinical introduction*. San Diego: Academic Press.

Merzenich, M.M., Jenkins, W.M., Johnston, P., Schreiner, C., Miller, S.L., and Tallal, P. (1996, January 5). Temporal processing deficits of language-learning impaired children ameliorated by training. *Science, 271*, 77-81.

Moats, L.C. (2000, October). *Whole language lives on: The illusion of "balanced" reading instruction*. Washington, DC: Thomas B. Fordham Foundation.

Montgomery, J. W. (2000, April). Verbal working memory and sentence comprehension in children with specific language impairment. *Journal of Speech, Language, and Hearing Research, 43*, 293-308.

National Alliance for Autism Research (NAAR) (2000, Summer). Autism in the blood: Can proteins in a newborn's blood predict autism, or lead us to new therapeutic opportunities? *Naarative, 6*, 1, 18-23.

National Center for Education Statistics. (1996). Pursuing excellence: Initial findings from the Third International Mathematics and Science Study, NCES 97-198. Washington, DC: Author.

National Information Center for Children and Youth with Disabilities (NICHCY). (1997, August). Interventions for students with learning disabilities. *NICHCY News Digest, 25*, 2-12.

National Institute of Mental Health (NIMH). (1995). *Learning disabilities*. Bethesda, MD: Author.

National Institute of Mental Health (NIMH). (1997). *Autism*. Bethesda, MD: Author.

National Institute of Mental Health (NIMH). (2000, August). *Depression in children and adolescents: A fact sheet for physicians.* Bethesda, MD: Author.

National Institute of Neurological Disorders and Stroke (NINDS). (2000, June). *Brain basics: Understanding sleep.* Bethesda, MD: Author.

National Institute on Deafness and Other Communication Disorders (NIDCD). (2000, April). *Speech and language: Developmental milestones.* Bethesda, MD: Author.

National Sleep Foundation (NSF). (2000). *Adolescent sleep needs and patterns.* Washington, DC: Author.

Patterson, K., and Lambon Ralph, M.A. (1999). Selective disorders of reading? *Current Opinion in Neurobiology, 9,* 235-239.

Piven, J. (1997). The biological basis of autism. *Current Opinion in Neurobiology, 7,* 708-712.

Posner, M.I., and Raichle, M.E. (1994). *Images of mind.* New York: Scientific American Library.

Pressley, M., Symons, S., Snyder, B. L., and Cariglia-Bull, T. (1989). Strategy instruction research comes of age. *Learning Disabilities Quarterly, 12,* 16-30.

Quill, K. (1995). *Teaching children with autism: Strategies to enhance communication and socialization.* Albany, NY: Delmar Publishing.

Raborn, D. T. (1995, Summer). Mathematics for students with learning disabilities from language-minority backgrounds: Recommendations for teaching. *New York State Association for Bilingual Education Journal, 10,* 25-33.

Restak, R. (2000). *Mysteries of the mind.* Washington, DC: National Geographic Society.

Richards, R. G. (1998). *The writing dilemma: Understanding dysgraphia.* Riverside, CA: RET Center Press.

Rief, S.F. (1998). *The ADD/ADHD Checklist: An Easy Reference for Parents and Teachers.* New York: Prentice Hall.

Rodier, P. (2000, February). The early origins of autism. *Scientific American, 282,* 56-63.

Rueckert, L., Lange, N., Partiot, A., Appollonio, I., Litvan, I., LeBihan, D., and Grafman, J. (1996, April). Visualizing cortical activation during mental calculation with functional MRI. *Neuroimage, 3,* 97-103.

Rumsey, J.M., Horwitz, B., Donohue, B.C., Nace, K.L., Maisog, J.M., and Andreason, P. (1999, November). A functional lesion in developmental dyslexia: Left angular gyral blood flow predicts severity. *Brain and Language, 70,* 187-204.

Russell, J. (Ed.). (1998). *Autism as an executive disorder.* New York: Oxford University Press.

Sandler, A. D., Sutton, K. A., DeWeese, J., Girardi, M. A., Sheppard, V., and Bodfish, J. W. (1999, December). Lack of benefit of a single dose of synthetic human secretin in the treatment of autism and pervasive developmental disorder. *New England Journal of Medicine, 341*, 1801-1806.

Schacter, D. (1996). *Searching for memory: The brain, mind, and the past.* New York: Basic Books.

Shankweiler, D., Crain, S., Katz, L., Fowler, A.E., Liberman, A.E., Brady, S.A., Thornton, R., Lunquist, E., Dreyer, L., Fletcher, J.M., Steubing, K.K., Shaywitz, S.E., and Shaywitz, B.A. (1995). Cognitive profiles of reading-disabled children: Comparison of language skills in phonology, morphology, and syntax. *Psychological Science, 6*, 149-156.

Shannon, T.R., and Polloway, E.A. (1993). Promoting error monitoring in middle school students with LD. *Intervention in School and Clinic, 28*, 160-164.

Sharma, M. (1989). *How children learn mathematics: Professor Mahesh Sharma, in an interview with Bill Domoney.* London: Oxford Polytechnic, School of Education, Education Methods Unit. Videocassette.

Shaywitz, S.E. (1996, November). Dyslexia. *Scientific American*, 98-104.

Shaywitz, S.E., Shaywitz, B.A., Pugh, K.R., Fulbright, R.K., Constable, R.T., Mencl, W.E., Shankweiler, D.P., Liberman, A.M., Skudlarski, P., Fletcher, J.M., Katz, L., Marchione, K.E., Lacadie, C., Gatenby, C., and Gore, J.C. (1998, March 3). Functional disruption in the organization of the brain for reading in dyslexia. *Neurobiology, 5*, 2636–2641.

Snow, C. E., Burns, M. S., and Griffin, P. (Eds.). (1998). *Preventing reading difficulties in young children.* Washington, DC: National Academy Press.

Sousa, D. A. (2001). *How the Brain Learns*, (2nd ed.). Thousand Oaks, CA: Corwin Press.

Sousa, D. A. (1997). Sensory preferences of New Jersey students, grades 3 to 12. Unpublished data collected by graduate students at Seton Hall University, 1994-1997.

Sowell, E. R., Thompson, P. M., Holmes, C. J., Jernigan, T. L., and Toga, A. W. (1999). In-vivo evidence for post-adolescent brain maturation in frontal and striatal regions. *Nature: Neuroscience, 2*, 859–861.

Sparks, R., and Ganschow, L. (1993). Searching for the cognitive locus of foreign language learning difficulties: Linking first and second language learning. *Modern Language Journal, 77*, 289-302.

Stein, J., Richardson, A., and Fowler, M. (2000). Monocular occlusion can improve binocular control and reading in dyslexics. *Brain, 123*, 164-170.

Stein, J., Talcott, J., and Walsh, V. (2000). Controversy about the visual magnocellular deficit in developmental dyslexics. *Trends in Cognitive Sciences, 4*, 209-211.

Stein, M., Dixon, R. C., and Isaacson, S. (1994). Effective writing instruction for diverse learners. *School Psychology Review, 23*, 392-405.

Sturomski, N. (1997, July). Teaching students with learning disabilities to use learning strategies. *NICHCY News Digest, 25*, 2-12.

Suresh, P. A., and Sebastian, S. (2000). Developmental Gerstmann's syndrome: A distinct clinical entity of leaning disabilities. *Pediatric Neurology, 22*, 267-278.

Swanson, J., Castellanos, F. X., Murias, M., LaHoste, G., and Kennedy, J. (1998). Cognitive neuroscience of attention deficit hyperactivity disorder and hyperkinetic disorder. *Current Opinion in Neurobiology, 8*, 263-271.

Swanson, L. J. (1995, July). *Learning styles: A review of the literature.* ERIC Document No. ED 387 067.

Tallal, P., Miller, S. L., Bedi, G., Byma, G., Wang, X., Nagarajan, S., Schreiner, C., Jenkins, W. M., and Merzenich, M. M. (1996, January 5). Fast-element enhanced speech improves language comprehension in language-learning impaired children. *Science, 271*, 81-84.

Tomblin, J. B., and Buckwalter, P. (1998). The heritability of poor language achievement among twins. *Journal of Speech, Language, and Hearing Research, 41*, 188-199.

United States Department of Education (USDE). (1998, January 9). *The state of mathematics education: Building a strong foundation for the 21st century.* [Online]. Available at http://www.ed/gov/inits.html#2. Washington, DC: U. S. Government Printing Office.

United States Department of Education (USDE). (1999, August). *Annual report to Congress on the implementation of the Individuals with Disabilities Education Act.* Washington, DC: U.S. Government Printing Office.

United States Department of Education (USDE). (2000). *The condition of education 1999.* Washington, DC: U.S. Government Printing Office.

Van Petten, C., and Bloom, P. (1999, February). Speech boundaries, syntax, and the brain. *Nature Neuroscience, 2*, 103-104.

Viadero, D. (2001, January). Soft science. *Teacher Magazine, 12.*

Wagner, A. D., Schacter, D. L., Rotte, M., Koutstaal, W., Maril, A., Dale, A. M., Rosen, B. R., & Buckner, R. L. (1998, August 21). Building memories: Remembering and forgetting of verbal experiences as predicted by brain activity. *Science, 281*, 1188–1191.

Wahlstrom, K., Wrobel, G., and Kubow, P. (1998). *Minneapolis Public Schools Start Time Study.* Center for Applied Research and Educational Improvement, University of Minnesota.

Walker, H. M., Colvin, G., and Ramsey, E. (1995). *Antisocial behavior in school: Strategies and best practices.* Pacific Grove, CA: Brooks/Cole.

Weismer, S. E., Evans, J., and Hesketh, L. J. (1999, October). An examination of verbal working memory capacity in children with specific language impairment. *Journal of Speech, Language, and Hearing Research, 42*, 1249-1260.

Williams, D., Stott, C. M., Goodyer, I. M., and Sahakian, B. J. (2000, June). Specific language impairment with or without hyperactivity: Neuropsychological evidence for frontostriatal dysfunction. *Developmental Medical Child Neurology, 42*, 368-375.

Wing, A. M. (2000). Mechanisms of motor equivalence in handwriting. *Current Biology, 10*, R245-R248.

Wolfson, A. R., and Carskadon, M. A. (1998). Sleep schedules and daytime functioning in adolescents. *Child Development, 69*, 875-887.

Wong, B. Y. L., and Jones, W. (1982). Increasing metacomprehension in learning disabled and normally achieving students through self-questioning training. *Learning Disability Quarterly, 5*, 409-414.

Wood, D., Rosenburg, M., and Carran, D. (1993). The effects of tape-recorded self-instruction cues on the mathematics performance of students with learning disabilities. *Journal of Learning Disabilities, 26*, 250-258, 269.

Wood, K. D., and Jones, J. (1998, Fall). Flexible grouping and group retellings include struggling learners in classroom communities. *Preventing School Failure, 43*, 37-38.

Wright, B. A., Bowen, R. W., and Zecker, S. G. (2000). Nonlinguistic perceptual deficits associated with reading and language disorders. *Current Opinion in Neurobiology, 10*, 482-486.

Zametkin, A., Mordahl, T. E., Gross, M., King, A. C., Semple, W. E., Rumsey, J., Hamburger, S., and Cohen, R. M. (1990). Cerebral glucose metabolism in adults with hyperactivity of childhood onset. *New England Journal of Medicine, 2*, 1361-1366.

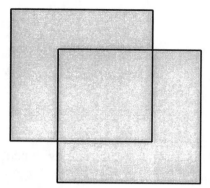

RESOURCES

TEXTS

Cavey, D.W. (2000). *Dysgraphia: Why Johnny can't write.* Austin, TX: Pro-Ed.

Diamond, M., and Hopson, J. (1998). *Magic trees of the mind: How to nurture your child's intelligence, creativity, and healthy emotions from birth through adolescence.* New York: Dutton.

Grandin, T. (1996). *Thinking in pictures: And other reports from my life with autism.* New York: Vintage Books.

Fowler, M. (1999). *Maybe you know my kid: A parent's guide to identifying, understanding, and helping your child with ADHD* (3rd ed.). New York: Birch Lane Press.

Nadeau, K. (1998). *Help4ADD@high school.* New York: Advantage Press.

Quill, K. (1995). *Teaching children with autism: Strategies to enhance communication and socialization.* Albany, NY: Delmar Publishing.

Richards, R. G. (1998). *The writing dilemma: Understanding dysgraphia.* Riverside, CA: RET Center Press.

Rief, S. F. (1998). *The ADD/ADHD Checklist: An Easy Reference for Parents and Teachers.* New York: Prentice Hall.

Silver, L. (1998). *The misunderstood child: Understanding and coping with your child's learning disabilities* (3rd ed.). New York: Time Books.

Sousa, D. A. (2001). *How the brain learns* (2nd ed.). Thousand Oaks, CA: Corwin Press.

ORGANIZATIONS

American Speech-Language Hearing Association (ASHA)
10801 Rockville Pike
Rockville, MD 20852
(800) 638-8255
E-mail: webmaster@asha.org   Web: www.asha.org

Asperger Syndrome Coalition of the U.S.
P.O. Box 49267
Jacksonville Beach, FL 32240
E-mail: info@asc-us.org   Web: www.asperger.org

Autism Society of America, Inc.
7910 Woodmont Avenue
Suite 650
Bethesda, MD 20814
(800) 3-AUTISM
Web: www.autism-society.org

Children and Adults with Attention Deficit Hyperactivity Disorder (CH.A.D.D.)
8181 Professional Place, Suite 201
Landover, MD 20785
(800) 233-4050
E-mail: national@chadd.org Web: www.chadd.org

Council for Exceptional Children
1920 Association Drive
Reston, VA 20191-1589
(800) 641-7824
Web: www.cec.sped.org

Council for Learning Disabilities (CLD)
P.O. Box 40303
Overland Park, KS 66204
Web: www.cldinternational.org

International Dyslexia Association
Chester Building, Suite 382
8600 LaSalle Road
Baltimore, MD 21286-2044
(800) 222-3123
E-mail: info@interdys.org   Web: www.interdys.org

International Reading Association (IRA)
800 Barkdale Road
P.O. Box 8139
Newark, DE 19714-8139
(800) 336-READ
Web: www.reading.org

Learning Disabilities Association of America (LDA)
4156 Liberty Road
Pittsburgh, PA 15234
(888) 300-6710
E-mail: ldanatl@usaor.net   Web: www.ldanatl.org

National Alliance for Autism Research
414 Wall Street, Research Park
Princeton, NJ 08540
(888) 777-NAAR
E-mail: naar@naar.org   Web: www.naar.org

National Attention Deficit Disorder Association
P.O. Box 1303
Northbrook, IL 60065-1303
E-mail: mail@add.org   Web: www.add.org

National Center for Learning Disabilities
381 Park Avenue, Suite 1401
New York, NY 10016
(888) 575-7373
Web: www.ncld.org

National Sleep Foundation
1522 K Street, NW
Suite 500
Washington, DC 20005
Web: www.sleepfoundation.org

National Information Center for Children and Youth with Disabilities (NICHCY)
P.O. Box 1492
Washington, DC 20013-1492
(800) 695-0285
E-mail: nichcy@aed.org   Web: www.nichcy.org

National Institute on Deafness and Other Communication Disorders
31 Center Drive, MSC 2320
Bethesda, MD 20892-2320
(800) 241-1044
Web: www.nidcd.nih.gov

National Institute of Mental Health
6001 Executive Boulevard, Room 8184, MSC 9663
Bethesda, MD 20892-9663
(301) 443-4513
E-mail: nimhinfo@nih.gov   Web: www.nimh.nih.gov

U.S. Department of Education
600 Maryland Avenue SW
Washington, DC 20202
(800) USA-LEARN (872-5327)
Web: www.ed.gov

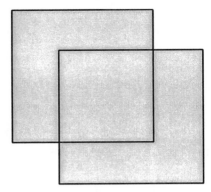

INDEX

Page numbers in **boldface** are **Strategies to Consider**.

Brain-Compatible Learning from David A. Sousa

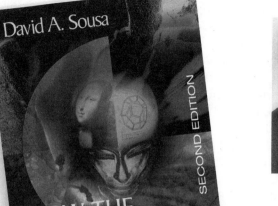

How the Brain Learns, Second Edition

David Sousa's practical and powerful best seller enters the 21st century with a valuable new edition, incorporating the previously published main text, the companion learning manual, and the latest discoveries in neuroscience and learning. All the newest information and insights are here, including an updated Information Processing Model, a whole new chapter on the implications of arts in learning, and an expanded list of primary sources.

Brain-Based Learning
The Video Program for *How the Brain Learns*

Join David Sousa for a dynamic 40-minute presentation in which he brings the concept of *How the Brains Learns* to life and gives specific examples of how brain-based learning can be put to use in your classroom. Charts, diagrams, and David Sousa's own clear and engaging style make this unique video a valuable tool for self-learning and an essential part of a larger professional development program for teachers and administrators alike.

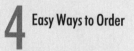

Order Form

Ship to

Name _____ Title _____
Institution _____
Address _____ No. _____
City _____ State _____ Zip + 4 _____
Country _____ Telephone _____

(Required for credit card and institutional purchases)

Fax: _____ E-mail: _____

(Actual Purchase Order must accompany order)

Bill to (if different) _____ P.O. # _____
Name _____
Institution _____
Address _____ No. _____
City _____ State _____ Zip + 4 _____
Country _____ Telephone _____

Method of Payment

☐ VISA   ☐ MasterCard   ☐ DISCOVER   ☐ AMERICAN EXPRESS

Check # _____
Account # _____ Exp. Date _____
Signature _____

Qty.	Book #	Title	Price
	0-7619-7765-1	**How the Brain Learns, Second Edition**	**$39.95**
	0-7619-7522-5	**Brain-Based Learning Video**	**$99.95**
	0-7619-7851-8	**How the Special Needs Brain Learns**	**$34.95**

(Attach a sheet of paper for ordering any other Corwin books.)

In CA and NY, add appl. Sales Tax	
In IL, add 6¼% Sales Tax	
In MA, add 5% Sales Tax	
In Canada, add 7% GST*	
Subtotal	
Shipping and Handling*	
Amount Due	